2004 01 28

Dying and Death
in Canada

Herbert C. Northcott is a professor of sociology at the University of Alberta. His teaching and research focus on the sociology of aging and the sociology of health and illness. His previous publications include *Aging in Alberta: Rhetoric and Reality* (second edition 1999), *Changing Residence: The Geographic Mobility of Elderly Canadians* (1988) and *Under Pressure: A Study of Job Stress* (with G. Lowe, 1986).

Donna M. Wilson is an associate professor of nursing at the University of Alberta. Her teaching and research focus on end-of-life care, health services utilization, and health policy. Of note, her publications include a book on the Canadian Health Care System, research articles on the use of tube feeding and other forms of life support, and research articles on location of death and myths about extensive use of health services by terminally ill and dying persons.

Dying and Death in Canada

Herbert C. Northcott
Donna M. Wilson

Garamond Press

This book is dedicated to my students, both undergraduate and graduate, who have taught me as much as I have taught them. – HN

I would like to dedicate this book to those dear friends and family who, through their life and through their dying and death, helped bring special meaning and purpose to life. I would also like to thank my family and acknowledge my nursing career for providing me with the opportunities to see dying and death for what it is— a fundamentally important challenge and thus opportunity for growth. – DW

Printed and bound in Canada

A publication of Garamond Press,
63 Mahogany Court,
Aurora, Ontario L4G 6M8

Editor: Barbara Tessman
Publisher: Peter R. Saunders
Typesetting and Layout: Gerda Rowlands
Cover Illustration © Peter Griffith

Canadian Cataloguing in Publication Data

Northcott, Herbert C., 1947
    Dying and death in Canada

Includes bibliographical references and index.
ISBN 1-55193-023-4

    1. Death–Canada. 2. Death–Social aspects—Canada. 3. Death–Psychological aspects. I. Wilson, Donna M. (Donna Marie), 1955-
II. Title.

BF789.D4N67 2001   C81316   C2001-902114-3

Garamond Press gratefully acknowledges the support of the Department of Canadian Heritage, Government of Canada, for its publishing program, and of the Canadian Studies Bureau of the same Department for support of this specific publication.

Contents

Acknowledgments

Wendy Maurier and Michael Stingl reviewed the entire manuscript, Kathryn Wilkins reviewed chapters 3 and 4, and Christy Nickerson reviewed chapters 4 through 6. All of these reviewers provided helpful suggestions. Chapters 1 through 3 benefited from excellent statistical data analysis and research assistance provided by Corrine Truman. Data access and analysis for chapters 1 to 3 were made possible by a National Health and Research Development Program operational research grant (#6609-2096-96) and the University of Alberta which provided a Social Science Research grant and an EFF Support for the Advancement of Scholarship grant. Chapters 4 through 6 benefited from library research conducted by Christy Nickerson. Chapters 5 and 6 include personal accounts concerning dying and death provided by persons who must remain anonymous. We are very grateful to these anonymous contributors for sharing their stories. Finally, the authors are grateful to Barbara Tessman for her excellent editorial work, and to our publisher, Peter Saunders of Garamond Press, for his support of this project.

Preface

Until the 1960s, death, like sexuality, was present but rarely discussed. While dying and death have long been a focus of attention in religion, philosophy, popular culture, and the arts, it has nevertheless been argued that dying and death are among the last taboos to be explored by twentieth-century social science. Since the 1960s, this taboo has been breached and the social science discourse on dying and death in North America has begun to develop (Aiken, 1991: ix, 21, 24; see also Lucas, 1968: 15).

This book is about dying and death in Canada. Dying is a process; death is an event (Aiken, 1991: 3). For the dying person, the process of dying culminates in the event of death. For that reason, throughout this book the term dying typically precedes the term death and discussions of dying typically precede discussions of death. This is in contrast to the more common usage which curiously focuses first on death and adds dying almost as an afterthought.

This book focuses on Canada and on Canadian work in the area of dying and death. The material is meant to serve as a supplement to larger texts such as Kastenbaum (1998) or DeSpelder and Strickland (1999) written outside of Canada but often used in this country. Although this book is written primarily for students who wish to learn about dying and death and for practitioners who work with the dying and the bereaved, it can also be used by the dying and the bereaved themselves, and by the general public in Canada.

Dying and death in a society reflect the material and social conditions of that society. For example, dying and death come frequently and early in life in a society where there is widespread poverty, austere living conditions, inadequate nutrition, unclean water, inadequate sewage and garbage disposal, war and civil unrest, and underdeveloped medical technology and health care delivery systems. In contrast, dying and death typically come late in life in a more "developed" society such as Canada at the beginning of the twenty-first century. The point is, how we live influences how and at what age we die.

The society and culture in which we live influences what we think and do about dying and death. Dying is both a personal experience and a social role given shape and meaning by social practices and cultural definitions (Lucas, 1968). Death itself is both a personal event and an event with social significance. The same is true for the bereaved who lose a loved one to death. The bereaved grieve and mourn in both personal and social terms and the meaning assigned to dying and death is both personally and socially constructed.

This book is divided into three parts. Part I explores the causes of dying and death in Canada both historically and at present. Part II examines the societal and cultural responses to dying and death. Part III discusses dying and death from the personal points of view of the dying and the bereaved.

Part I contains two chapters. Chapter 1 examines the history of dying and death in Canada, focusing in particular on factors affecting changes in death and dying among different groups at different times. Chapter 2 examines dying and death in Canada at the beginning of the twenty-first century by focusing on the trends in and causes of dying and death.

Dying and death are given meaning both individually and collectively. Part II discusses the collective constructions of—that is, the social and cultural response to—dying and death in Canada. The social and cultural context is important because it, in part, shapes the meaning that an individual assigns to the experience of dying and death. Chapter 3 discusses dying and death from the point of view of Canadian social institutions such as family, religion, health care, and the legal system. Chapter 4 discusses the cultural constructions of the meaning of dying and death and the social rituals that attend death and help to give it a collectively shared meaning.

Part III discusses individual constructions of the meaning of dying and death. Chapter 5 examines individual perspectives on dying and death from the point of view of the person who is dying while Chapter 6 discusses dying and death from the point of view of persons who are associated with the dying and the dead as surviving family members and/or caregivers.

Part I

The Demography and Epidemiology of Dying and Death

Chapter 1

The History of Dying and Death in Canada

Death is inevitable. All people die, and their dying follows a course that can range in length from only a few minutes to many years. The typical course of dying, the causes and timing of death, and the social response to death tend to vary from one society to another and from one historical time to another. Perhaps the greatest challenge in writing about death historically is finding sufficient meaningful information on deaths in the past. Until recently, and despite such early efforts as a 1678 Quebec law mandating the keeping of vital statistics (Harding le Riche, 1979), information on dying and death in Canada has been limited. Information on any given death, and the dying process that led to it, has often been restricted to a single line on a church's burial roster or a hospital's daily record of admissions and discharges (Fair, 1994). Even today, information on dying and death continues to be sparse and incomplete, despite more routine and consistent data collection procedures.

Although death is becoming less of a taboo subject, most people today do not dwell on their own death because death has largely become a circumstance of old age (Nault and Wilkins, 1995; Sebag-Lanoe et al., 1998). As such, dying and death can be dismissed by most people as topics for which little re-search and information is needed. Yet, death used to be a common life event, and high death rates in Canada until the second half of the twentieth century meant bereavement was experienced much more frequently than it is today. Following the Second World War, advances in health care and in the health care delivery system brought about radical changes in the circumstances of dying and death. As a result, most Canadians began to expect to live a long life.

At the same time that death was becoming increasingly associated with old age, it also became increasingly associated with the hospital. That is, death was moved from the home, family, and community into the hospital, where the process of dying was largely removed from public scrutiny and consciousness (Wilson et al., 1998). It is not surprising, then, that dying and death became neglected topics.

This chapter examines the history of dying and death in Canada. It begins with dying and death among the Aboriginal people of Canada in the pre-contact era and then reviews the situation in colonial Canada before progressing to the twentieth century. Trends in life expectancy, historical changes in the causes of death, and historical contexts relevant to dying and death in Canada are presented.

DYING AND DEATH AMONG ABORIGINAL PEOPLE IN CANADA IN THE PRE-CONTACT ERA

Prior to the arrival of European explorers and settlers, dozens of Aboriginal nations lived across Canada, from the Arctic to the Great Lakes, from the East Coast to the West, each nation with its unique lifestyle and culture. Centuries after contact between Norse settlers and the Native peoples of Newfoundland, Jacques Cartier landed on the Gaspé Peninsula and claimed the land for France in 1534 (Morton, 1997); more than half a century later, the first French settlement was founded in Acadia (Nova Scotia and New Brunswick). Given the sheer size of the land, and the limited number of Europeans who first settled it, many Native groups were not greatly influenced by the Europeans until decades or even centuries after these events. Indeed, almost 250 years after Cartier's landing, fur traders in western Canada remarked on meeting Native groups who had never before encountered a white man (Bryce, 1902).

In the pre-contact era, shamans and other Native healers[1] in Canada provided health care to their people. Since "medicine to the Indians was not only physical but spiritual" (Stone, 1962: 6), Native healers were adept at gathering and using medicines and at employing a "supernatural article or agency which may be of aid in curing disease" (Stone, 1962: 5). Native peoples in those days were aware of and used the medicinal properties of roots, leaves, herbs, barks, and other naturally occurring substances.[2]

Although death frequently came early in life for Natives in the pre-contact era, not all deaths were premature; an unknown proportion of Native people reached advanced age. Stone (1962) indicated that, as a consequence of clean environments, natural foods, ongoing physical labour, and other positive life-style factors, a "considerable" number of Native persons reached old age in pre-colonial North America. Longevity was also possible after the arrival of Europeans. For instance, an Indian woman who died in 1800 at a Hudson's Bay fort in Manitoba was said to have been "upwards of one hundred years old" (Brown, 1980: 68). In 1884, three Native men on a western Canadian re-serve were said to be in their mid-nineties (Carter, 1973). Despite instances of advanced ages, existence could be precarious for Aboriginal groups. Food sup-plies often were limited (Stone, 1962). Starvation would especially have threat-ened seniors and children. Abandonment of seniors may have also been prac-tised to some degree (Burch, 1988; de Beauvoir, 1973; Brown, 1980; Dickason, 1984) and may have occurred when a person began to require care or assistance in activities of daily living, could no longer perform a necessary function within the community, or developed a serious health problem.

It is unlikely that older indigenous persons were free of disabling arthritis, limitations in eyesight, and any number of other disorders that commonly af-fect senior citizens today. Stone (1962) reported that Native people tended to develop rheumatism and arthritis as a result of injury, repetitive physical la-bour, and bouts of scurvy. They also developed eye infections as a result of smoke irritation from cooking and heating fires; colds, pleurisy, and pneumo-nia; and gastro-intestinal problems due to bouts of starvation alternating with times of plenty (Stone, 1962). These conditions would have contributed indi-rectly or directly to death. For example, if older Native persons had limitations such as reduced eyesight, arthritis, loss of teeth, or dementia, then their ability to procure, prepare, and eat food would have been considerably impaired. Their ability to migrate with a nomadic tribe would have also been compro-mised. The seriousness of this issue is illustrated by a report that Indians were relieved to leave their weak, elderly, or disabled dependants at a fur trading fort instead of leaving them behind in the wilderness to fend for themselves until death (Brown, 1980). Dickason (1984) also reported that infants, as well as weak and elderly Native people were left at early hospitals to be cared for.

Life expectancy[3] among Native peoples would have been considerably lower than is currently the case for all Canadians. On the eve of the arrival of the Europeans, Native life expectancy would likely have been only thirty to forty years, as it was in Europe at the time. It is not surprising then that Corlett (1935) reported that cancer seldom afflicted Aboriginal peoples in North America; cancer is most often seen among older persons (Gaudette et al., 1998). Moreover, Native groups may not have been exposed to many of the environmental and lifestyle factors that are associated with cancer today.

Although there may have been some gender differences in life expectancy among Aboriginal groups, the majority of deaths for both sexes would have occurred prior to old age. Death from injury sustained in the course of hunting or war-related activities would have been common, with younger men and boys most prone to such injuries. Men were also sometimes tortured to death following capture by an enemy group (Dickason, 1984), although it is not known how often death occurred under such circumstances. By contrast, captured women and children were typically not tortured or killed in intertribal conflict. Instead, they were usually kept to perform various functions within the adopting tribe.

Women may also have been more vulnerable than men during times of food shortages. Hunters, who were primarily if not solely male, may have survived when those dependent on them for sustenance did not. Hunters had more immediate access to food sources than did women or children; moreover, hunters may have been given preferential access to food when it was in short supply. According to Bryce (1902: 103), one fur trader was told by a Native chief that, on fur-trade expeditions, women "are maintained at a trifling expense, for as they always stand cook, the very licking of their fingers in scarce times is sufficient for their subsistence."

Children, too, would have been vulnerable in times of shortages. Children, then, as now, are particularly susceptible to insults to their health. Starvation has a more serious impact on younger children in comparison to older children and adults, either through loss of life or permanent damage to growing organs, muscles, and bones. Infanticide was practised by some Native groups in response to unwanted children and multiple births, and "in defence against privation and hunger" (Brown, 1980: 150). There is no evidence to suggest that male children were favoured during times of food shortages, or that female children were deliberately euthanized. Generally, children of both sexes were highly valued, considered necessary to ensure the continuance of the groups and to provide assistance to their elders (Morton, 1997). Nonetheless, it is likely that Native children had a high death rate.

As a consequence of a much higher death rate than today and the greater visibility of dying and dead people in smaller, more intimate communities, dying and death would have been a common life event for Native peoples. There is no evidence that dying people or dead bodies were shunned. Other evidence suggests an acceptance of, if not reverence for, the dead. For instance, Dickason (1984: 115) indicated that "burial customs formed the most distinctive aspect of Huron culture." Whenever a village moved, the bones of deceased persons were exhumed, cleaned, wrapped, and reburied in a common grave during a ten-day ceremony. An ossuary (a burial site for the bones of the dead) could hold between eight hundred and four thousand skeletons (Carter, 1973).

Carter (1973), who studied burial customs of Indians in Canada, indicated that many tribes regularly revisited their dead every eight to twelve years in a "Feast of the Dead." He relates an eyewitness account of a Native woman caressing her children's and father's bones. This revisiting was made possible by careful storage of the body, which was prepared so that the bones, and at times skin or hair, would be preserved. It was apparently common for the deceased to be bound tightly together by straps so that the knees were touching the chest, although at times the body was wrapped in a prone position. Women prepared the bodies for burial, and in some cases performed the burial unaided by men (Carter, 1973).

Aboriginal burial customs varied across Canada and included cremation (partial or full body), mummification (a few mummies consisting of skin wrapped around bones after the flesh was removed have been found on the West Coast), grave burials, surface burials (using stones, furs, and/or wood to cover the body), tree or scaffold burials, water burials (the body might be sent downstream in a canoe), urn burials of cremated remains or bones, and ossuarial (group) burials (Carter, 1973). According to Carter, (1973), the most common burial involved a round grave dug approximately five feet deep with the tightly bound body placed to rest sitting on the heels and facing east. Bark and furs were used to keep the earth from touching the body, and various articles, such as clothing, were placed next to the body. Loud wailing and other displays of grief continued for approximately ten days after the rapid burial (within one day of death) had taken place. Mourning continued for one year, during which time remarriages did not occur, in part, perhaps, because isolation of the bereaved was common.

Dying persons frequently participated in preparing for their own death by praying, calling together their family, and making other preparations. If a Native healer were not able to heal a person, then the healer's role was to call upon the spirits to help the dying person and to assist the soul in its journey into the afterlife (Carter, 1973).

It is likely that, in the past, dying was considered a normal life event among Native peoples. The folklore surrounding elderly, disabled, or starving Inuit, and their apparent willingness to sacrifice their own life for the good of the family or community, is but one example (Burch, 1988). Indeed, at times death may have been welcomed if it occurred during a battle to defend territory or kinfolk, during a hunt to test manhood, or as an end to suffering (Carter, 1973; Heagerty, 1928). Folklore about Native souls revisiting earth provides another example of how death was perceived (Burch, 1988). If indigenous peoples considered death to be a part of the natural cycle of life, just as the seasons ebb and flow, then it may not have been as unexpected or as unacceptable as it is to most Canadians today. Morton (1997) makes the point that Native North Americans saw themselves as one with nature, not masters of nature. While death would have precipitated grief and mourning, it nevertheless, could have been perceived as more of a practical issue: an unfortunate loss of hunters, gatherers, or defenders would threaten the lives and well-being of others in a community, and the loss of women and children would threaten the continuity of the community.

In summary, for Aboriginal people in Canada during the pre-contact era, death often came early in life. Nevertheless, some individuals survived to old age. In contrast to persons dying at an early age, elderly persons were more likely to die from chronic ailments or frailty. Dying and death were familiar in early Aboriginal societies because death was a common, expected, accepted, and visible occurrence.

DYING AND DEATH IN CANADA FOLLOWING THE ARRIVAL OF THE EUROPEANS

Impact on Aboriginal Peoples In general, associations between Natives and newcomers initially followed a pattern of sporadic contact, later followed by more sustained relations between Aboriginal people and European explorers, fur traders, missionaries, farmers, and settlers. Permanent Native camps tended to be established close to missions and fur trading posts. Both the missions and the trading posts had an enormous impact not only on Native ways of life, but also ways of dying and death.

It is estimated that, in the 1500s, the Native population of Canada numbered between 200,000 and 500,000, the majority living in central and eastern Canada (McNaught, 1970; Morton, 1977). By 1861, however, there were only slightly more than 23,000 Native people living in central and eastern Canada (Morton, 1997). What had happened to so drastically reduce the Native population?

The most significant factor was disease. Contact with European fur traders and missionaries meant exposure to infectious pathogens to which Native peoples had little or no natural resistance. Because the first European settlements were in eastern and central Canada, a rise in the death rate for Native peoples started in these areas and then spread to the north and west. Trading posts that opened across the northwest following the formation of the Hudson's Bay Company in 1670 served to widen contact between Europeans and Native groups (Morton, 1997; Wilson, 1983).

Reductions in Native populations were dramatic. Morton, (1997) reports that one half of the Huron, who lived near the Great Lakes, died of contagious illnesses within the first five years of contact with Europeans. By 1650, the Huron had ceased to exist as a nation, victims of disease and starvation; by 1680, their rivals, the Iroquois, were also reeling from the effects of European diseases (Heagerty, 1928). Smallpox was the deadliest of the epidemics. The first such epidemic likely occurred in 1627, and recurrences afflicted both Aboriginal peoples and Europeans until well after the cowpox inoculation was developed in 1806 (Heagerty, 1928). According to Bryce (1902: 98), smallpox completely blotted out several bands of Indians: "Of one tribe of four hundred lodges, only 10 persons remained; the poor survivors, in seeking succour from other bands, carried the disease with them."

Recurring epidemics radiated outward as European explorers and traders fanned across the country. In the nineteenth century, many of the Aboriginal peoples living on the Prairies succumbed to infectious diseases (Statistics Canada, 1998). In the North, the first epidemic of measles did not reach the Inuit until 1952, at which time it brought death to seven out of every hundred cases (Coleman, 1985).

Traditional Native methods of healing were all but useless in the face of these epidemics. The poor outcome of Native health care for treating the new infections is thought to have been a powerful factor in Native adoption of European health care measures, although these were no more effective against the raging epidemics (Dickason, 1984; Heagerty, 1940; Stone, 1962). An alternative explanation for the adoption of European medicine by the First Nations peoples is that many Native healers died of infection, perhaps in greater numbers than the general Native population, due to their more frequent exposure to the infectious agents. Their store of knowledge, which had been gained through trial and error over the centuries (Erichsen-Brown, 1979), would have been decimated.

In the days before public health, immunization, and antibiotics, contagious diseases also took the lives of many Europeans as well. Ewart's (1983) study of the daily records of York Factory, a Hudson's Bay Company fur trading post in northern Manitoba, reveals a continuously high death rate from infections among the European inhabitants—but higher still among their Native contacts. Not surprisingly, cemeteries typically grew quite large around fur trade forts (Brown, 1980).

Unquestionably, infectious disease imported by Europeans was the most important factor in the considerable reduction in life expectancy among Native populations after the sixteenth century. Yet this was not the only cause of death that could be traced to the Europeans' arrival. Territorial disputes also resulted in Native deaths. Outright wars and ongoing skirmishes between Native and European factions, and among Native groups, continued throughout the colonial period (Morton, 1997). Much of the conflict concerned trade with the French and English or land claims.

Finally, the displacement of Aboriginal peoples from their traditional lands by European settlement and the reduction of food sources as a result of the growing European presence in Canada were two other reasons for the decline and, in some cases, the total destruction of Native populations. The last surviving Beothuk, a nation native to Newfoundland, died in 1829. Although the direct cause of death of the last Beothuk was tuberculosis, the disappearance of the nation as a whole "was at least partly owing to their loss of access to the coast and its food resources" (Dickason, 1984: 100), as the Beothuk were effectively barred from sea access by the presence of European fishers and, later, settlers. On the Prairies, the destruction of the buffalo herds by overhunting throughout the nineteenth century had a major impact on local Aboriginals and Métis, depriving them of their primary source of food and trade goods (Wilson, 1983).

Thus, the impact of the Europeans on the Aboriginal peoples of Canada was devastating. Infectious diseases previously unknown to First Nations increased death rates and decimated whole populations. Armed conflict and the gradual destruction of Native economies and ways of life further contributed to high rates of death.

Largely as a result of inadequate provisions, misadventure, and infectious diseases, early European settlers in Canada had a very high rate of death (Morton, 1997). The incidence of death would have been much higher if Native people had not provided direct assistance in the form of food and shared knowledge about survival in the new land (Morton, 1997). For example, over the winter of 1535-6 local Native people showed Cartier how to brew white spruce and hemlock bark to treat scurvy (Roland, 1985; Stone, 1962). Prior to this intervention, Cartier had resorted to prayer when European medicines failed to prevent death from this disease (Jack, 1981). The Natives who demonstrated this rapid and effective cure to Cartier were annihilated by disease soon after. It would be another three hundred years before Europeans began to use a vitamin C food supplement to prevent scurvy (Stone, 1962); thus, the disease remained a major cause of death in Canada until the nineteenth century (Heagerty, 1928).

Europeans in Canada Prior to the Twentieth Century

The adoption of the Aboriginal treatment for scurvy seems to have been something of an exception. Although folklore hints at the adoption of some Aboriginal medicines by the early Europeans in North America (Dickason, 1984), it is not evident that there was much transfer of health care knowledge from Natives to non-Natives. In general, Europeans neither understood nor valued Native peoples' health care knowledge (Erichsen-Brown, 1979); Stone, 1962). This is unfortunate, as some Native health care practices were more effective than European ones (Heagerty, 1928).

The harsh climate, tough pioneer existence, low standard of living, and unsanitary habits of settlers contributed to many early deaths in the colonies. Between one-quarter and one-third of all Europeans who immigrated to Canada before 1891 died of infectious diseases (Marsh, 1985). Virtually every ship that arrived from Europe brought a new wave of infection. The death rate on these transatlantic voyages was high; one in three travellers became ill and one in seven died (Heagerty, 1928). To try to protect the inhabitants of the colonies from imported diseases, a quarantine was established in 1720. Later in that century, legislation was passed to authorize quarantine hospitals and screening centres in strategic parts of the country (Amyot, 1967). After immigrant-bearing ships introduced cholera to British North America in 1832, a permanent quarantine station was set up on Grosse Île near Quebec City in an ultimately unsuccessful attempt to stop its spread (Heagerty, 1940).

The death rate from infections was high. Although the existence and significance of germs began to be understood as a result of the development of the microscope by Zacharias Janssen in 1590 and its perfection in the mid-1600s by Antony van Leeuwenoek, it was not until much later that information about germ transmission and avoidance (asepsis) was applied in society. Although surgeons in Canada were first introduced to the principles of asepsis in the 1890s, the medical profession showed considerable resistance to the introduction of aseptic technique (Roland, 1985). At the time of the First World War, some Canadian physicians were still performing surgery with their bare hands (Agnew, 1974).

Inadequate health care was another major contributor to the low life expectancy and high death rate in colonial Canada. From the 1500s through the 1800s, health care was often more of a liability than an asset in preserving life (Coleman, 1985; Dickason, 1984). Although Europeans possessed only rudimentary knowledge of the human body and health care, they were interventionist in their approach to treatment (Bettmann, 1956). This could be a deadly combination. European health care had been based on reducing imbalances in the four humours (blood, phlegm, bile, and lymph) of the body, and treatment usually consisted of blood letting, enemas to induce the passage of stool, and emetics to induce vomiting[4] (Lessard, 1991). Throughout the colonial period in Canada, bleeding was a common treatment for a range of ills. Through this or a variety of other questionable health care practices, a well-intentioned healer could spread an infectious agent from one person to another, or from one site of the body to another site (Heagerty, 1928; 1940).

Most people could not afford either the expense of a hospital stay or the services of the very small number of doctors in colonial Canada. Given the primitive state of medical care, this was not entirely to their disadvantage. It is not surprising that the few hospitals that existed were considered places of death (Heagerty, 1940; Stone, 1962).[5]

Reducing suffering during the dying process does not appear to have been a common focus of care by European healers in early Canada. For many centuries, healers across Europe are thought to have shunned dying people because the death of patients would negatively affect their reputations (Veatch, 1989). Palliative care knowledge and skills consequently remained undeveloped. Trade with the Far East did bring opium to Europe in the mid to late 1600s, and the substance is thought to have been one of the few early analgesics used in Europe (Bettmann, 1956). It is not clear how available opium actually was, particularly for use by the vast majority of people. Alcohol was a common analgesic. Healers in colonial Canada were thus unlikely to have either the tools or the expertise to effectively reduce unpleasant symptoms during the dying process. Religious doctrine may also have served to restrict efforts to relieve suffering. Until the eighteenth century, Europeans commonly thought illnesses were a punishment or warning from God and that suffering was to be accepted (Lessard, 1991).[6]

Other factors are also certain to have had an impact on dying and death in early Canada. One was the gender imbalance in the colonies. Almost all of the early explorers and settlers were men, as were the Scottish fur traders arriving to work in Hudson's Bay Company posts (Brown, 1980). These young men had a high risk of death through misadventure and starvation during explorations to map the land and gather furs. Because their travels took them away from the major centres, where hospitals and other health care would most likely be available, it is not known how much assistance was provided to these men when they were dying. In any case, male gender roles emphasized stoicism. This quality may have been enhanced through contact with First Nations cultures, which tended to consider pain and suffering an intrinsic aspect of living, and which valued courage in the face of such challenges.

The demographic make-up of colonial Canada changed slowly. Precarious European settlements dominated by single men became home to an increasing number of women and men with families. French settlement schemes brought a number of unmarried women to New France to promote the development of new families. Traders in the Northwest had children with Native women and their Métis descendants. By the early nineteenth century, waves of British immigrants, many of them families with children, arrived in the British North American colonies. The increasing presence of European women in Canada brought new patterns of dying and death. For example, maternal and child deaths began to occur frequently and served to further reduce the life expectancy of Europeans in Canada.

As the number of European immigrants increased, the cultural values they brought with them began to change the meaning attached to life and death.

Christian religious views of life and death were in sharp contrast to the values common among First Nations (Dickason, 1984). For Aboriginal peoples, death was more likely to be a natural or unavoidable part of life, explained by Native cosmology and given meaning by Native spirituality. Death began to take on a new significance when viewed in the context of everlasting suffering in hell or eternal reward in heaven. Similarly, new meanings of dying and death were introduced, such as death being a punishment for sin, and suffering during dying being a means of securing a place in heaven (Lessard, 1991).

In addition to their religious values, the new immigrants brought with them the contemporary European emphasis on the individual (Morton, 1997). In traditional Native communities, the loss of an individual, while a serious occurrence, could be somewhat compensated for within the larger group. The individualism and self-reliance of pioneer life meant that death took on a different value, becoming more personally significant. Moreover, in practical terms, the death of either wife or husband in an isolated pioneer family could be disastrous for the survivors.

And death did come. The life of pioneer families was extremely difficult. Morton's (1997) account of early life is particularly revealing: "For pioneers in a harsh and unfamiliar land, survival was a preoccupation, to be achieved only through relentless, back-breaking work.... Pioneers were described as being reduced to an unsmiling grimness by loneliness and labour. Women faced the terror of childbirth without even a neighbour to help. A single careless blow with an axe could cripple a man or leave him to die in the stench and agony of gangrene" (39).

Life in colonial Canada could be difficult and dangerous, and the state did little to make it safer. It was not until the late nineteenth century that public health measures were introduced by various levels of government, reflecting the public health movement that originated in England earlier in the century (Baumgart, 1992; Langham and Flagel, 1991; Leftwich, 1993). Long before medical care was effective at saving lives, public health was rapidly extending life expectancy in Canada (Baumgart, 1992). Public health significantly reduced maternal and child death rates. Enhanced cleanliness, including sewage management, more effective quarantines, and better quality water and food reduced people's contact with infectious agents and raised the level of health among Canadians. Public health measures significantly reduced many common infectious diseases including measles, cholera, scarlet fever, influenza, diphtheria, tetanus, tuberculosis, and typhoid. These illnesses typically had claimed the lives of younger persons, particularly children. By the turn of the century, campaigns for clean water and pasteurised milk were beginning to reduce the high death rates among children from gastro-intestinal diseases, particularly among the urban poor.

In summary, prior to the twentieth century, the Europeans in Canada had a relatively low life expectancy, and many died from infectious diseases. Health care tended to be ineffective and public health practices tended to be inadequate, although they were beginning to change. Death came frequently, often claiming young people. Little could be done for the dying. Although health care was practised in various forms in early Canada by both Native healers and European doctors and other practitioners (Heagerty, 1940), its success in preventing death was limited. Prior to the emergence of modern health care measures, death for both Native and non-Native people was a common outcome of severe illness or injury. The dying process was typically shorter than it is today because a severe illness or injury without specific and effective care often leads quickly to death.

Dying and Death in Twentieth-Century Canada

Up until the twentieth century, there had been no dramatic gains in life expectancy in Canada. From the early 1900s on, gradual changes served to reduce the death rate and enhance the prospect of long life. These changes were mainly due to improvements in the standard of living and changes brought about by a concerted public health movement. These improvements benefited some Canadians more than others. Native Canadians, for example, suffered from a lower standard of living than their European counterparts (Corlett, 1935; Wilson, 1983), increasing the incidence of health problems among Native groups and leading to a high death rate and low life expectancy. Chief George Baker recounted how, when he was a child in the early 1900s, every member of a poor Native family he knew died of smallpox, and how during the epidemic no doctor came to the reservation (Wilson, 1983). By the 1970s, when health care advances had significantly reduced the incidence of death from acute conditions among the general population, pronounced differences continued to exist between Native and non-Native people in terms of health status, life expectancy, and rates of illnesses and injuries causing sickness and death (Statistics Canada, 1998).

Modern health care treatments provided in hospitals by doctors and nurses, and the 1957 federal Hospital Insurance and Diagnostic Services Act, which initiated an equitable national health care system to serve all Canadians, are commonly believed to be the most important factors explaining the dramatic increase in life expectancy in Canada in the twentieth century (Langham and Flagel, 1991; Leftwich, 1993). However, most of the reductions in the death rate and the resulting increases in life expectancy occurred prior to the development of the Canadian health care system and the availability of the surgical and medical treatments that now extend the lives of sick individuals. In 1770, the death rate in Canada was 37 per 1,000 persons, but the rate increased to more than 50 per 1,000 during epidemics (Heagerty, 1940). By 1926, the death rate had decreased to 13.5 deaths per 1,000 and by 1939 it had dropped even further to 10.4 (Heagerty, 1940). Today the death rate is between 6 and 7 deaths per 1,000 (Statistics Canada, 1998). Although there was a substantial decline in Canadian mortality rates between 1931 and 1981 (Blishen, 1991), much of this decline occurred prior to the 1950s. It is attributable largely to the public health movement's impact on life expectancy through disease prevention.[7]

Public health measures had the effect of reducing the incidence and severity of most types of illnesses, infections, and other types of health problems.[8] Millar (1995) credits public health for improvements in longevity and increases in life expectancy, citing "public health programs in the areas of infectious disease control, maternal and child health, chronic disease prevention, environmental health, nutrition education, and injury prevention" (25). As we have seen, public health measures at the beginning of the twentieth century included sewage management, milk pasteurization, and the sanitation of drinking water (McGinnis, 1985). Other public health initiatives included the promotion of cleanliness in the home and community and the enactment of legislation to ensure the safety of food, drugs, and health products. In general, the public health movement led to increased community and personal standards for cleanliness and health.

In addition to continuing efforts to improve sanitation, hygiene, and food safety, public health efforts after the First World War began to include immunization programs. Immunizations create resistance to infectious pathogens. In the past, resistance usually developed through surviving a bout of illness, but, of course, many did not survive serious illnesses such as smallpox and diphtheria. Mass immunizations were able to greatly reduce the death rate from infectious diseases (Harding le Riche, 1979). For instance, diphtheria was one of the leading causes of childhood death until its vaccine became available in 1930. Now few, if any, deaths occur from diphtheria in Canada. Mass immunizations for diphtheria, as well as smallpox, whooping cough, and tetanus, were administered in Canada in the 1940s (Grant, 1946). Some vaccines were developed even more recently, such as those to prevent poliomyelitis, which were developed in the 1950s.

It is important to note that epidemics continued during and after what could be considered the heyday of public health—that is, the period preceding the introduction and subsequent widespread use of antibiotics in the 1940s. The influenza epidemic of 1918–20, the polio epidemic of the 1950s, and other less well-known episodes claimed tens of thousands of lives in Canada. Indeed, the influenza epidemic following the First World War killed between 50,000 and 70,000 Canadians (Buckley, 1988; MacDougall, 1994). The federal Department of Health was established in 1919 as a direct result of this epidemic (McGinnis, 1985). One reason why this epidemic was studied, reported, and acted upon was the fear that it induced. Death from this strain of influenza was particularly gruesome—the individual tended to drown slowly from fluid buildup in the lungs. It also tended to strike young adults, who were considered to be in the prime of life.

Changes in the historical rate of death from tuberculosis (TB) present a more positive assessment of the impact of public health measures across Canada. The incidence of tuberculosis, which had become the most common cause of death in Canada during the late 1800s, had been very much reduced by the 1920s through public health measures. This abatement occurred fully twenty years before antibiotics began to be used widely to treat infections, including those arising from the TB bacillus (Zilm and Warbinek, 1995).

As early as the 1930s, immunization and other public health measures had reduced infectious diseases as the leading cause of death in Canada. Throughout the remainder of the century, the cause of death shifted from infectious disease to chronic disease—that is, to illnesses that are progressive and usually have long-term and increasingly debilitating effects.

Health care did not become increasingly important for effecting cures until after the Second World War. For instance, although Canadians Frederick Banting and C.H. Best developed insulin in the 1920s, its successful use in conjunction with a dietary and exercise regimen for the treatment of diabetes was not perfected until after the 1940s (Winterfeldt, 1991). Antibiotics such as penicillin and the sulfonamides were also not in wide use until after the Second World War. Furthermore, even though the X-ray machine and laboratory testing of blood and other bodily fluids were developed around the beginning of the twentieth century, these advancements in diagnostic capacity did not immediately lead to improvements in health. Most parts of Canada had neither a reliable laboratory nor an X-ray machine until after the 1940s, when the federal government began to directly fund hospital construction and modernization (Agnew, 1974). Major surgery such as heart surgery, vascular surgery, and kidney transplants did not begin in Canada until the 1960s (Audette, 1964; Hayter, 1968). Intensive care units and coronary care units, along with the technologies common to them, also did not become available until after 1960. The modern method of closed-chest cardiopulmonary resuscitation (CPR) was developed in 1960 (Kouwenhoven et al., 1960), with death quickly becoming a much less certain outcome of cardiac arrest. Tremendous breakthroughs in knowledge and the subsequent progress in diagnostic capacity and in surgical or medical procedures for treating illnesses have had a marked effect on society. Faith in health care increased, justified to a degree, as the efficacy of health care grew quickly and substantially.

These and other new developments seemed to overshadow the successes of public health measures. In comparison to public health programs, which promoted health and sought to prevent the development of illnesses that would cause disability and death, modern health care appeared to be a more immediate and dramatic way of saving lives. An illness care perspective quickly began to prevail in the Canadian health system (Ajemian, 1992), with efforts focused on treating illnesses and preventing death rather than preventing illnesses or providing palliative care to the terminally ill.

This shift from prevention to treatment was reinforced by the increasing role of hospitals, which do not exist to prevent illnesses so much as to diagnose and treat illnesses (Ajemian, 1992). Until the 1940s, health promotion and health care were most often carried out in homes by family members and visiting nurses or physicians. Thereafter, health care began to shift increasingly to hospitals (Bradley, 1958; McPherson, 1996; Wilinsky, 1943).

As we have seen, in colonial Canada, because of the ineffectiveness of their health care, hospitals had been thought of as places of death and were often shunned. Throughout the twentieth century, however, as the number of hospitals grew, the care of dying persons began to shift to these institutions (Wilson et al., 1998). In 1930, 40 per cent of deaths in Alberta occurred in the ninety hospitals operating at that time (archived Vital Statistics data for Alberta beginning with the year 1930). By 1953, four years before hospital care was guaranteed to Canadians by law, half of all deaths in Canada took place in hospitals. In 1994, over three-quarters of all deaths in Canada were recorded as occurring in hospitals (Wilson et al., 1998).

Not only was the location of death changing, so were its causes. The shift from acute to chronic illnesses has had a remarkable, although largely untold, effect on society. As a consequence of this shift, Canadians have tended to lose their fear of sudden, premature death. For instance, pneumonia used to be feared as an illness that could bring a relatively quick death at any age. It could strike any person, and without good nursing care, or even despite good nursing care, death frequently occurred. After antibiotics began to be used, pneumonia became almost unheard of as a cause of death.

The shift from acute to chronic illnesses also impacted nursing. Although well-meaning people have nursed the sick and dying for centuries, the 1890 to 1940 era is significant in that many nursing schools opened across Canada to ensure enough well-educated nurses for public demand (McPherson, 1996). Most schools then were hospital based, with student nurses a source of reliable, high quality, as well as cheap labour (McPherson, 1996). Upon graduation, nurses normally provided private care in the home (McPherson, 1996). Often, they cared for the chronically ill and dying (Ostic, 1940; What is the VON? 1943). By 1943, however, only 2,000 of all 16,000 registered nurses in Canada were working in private practice (Canadian Nurses Association, 1966). Dire working conditions and unemployment or underemployment had forced private duty nurses to seek more secure and familiar work in hospitals (McPherson, 1996). Almost every town and city across Canada had a hospital by the 1920s (Agnew, 1974). Ongoing demand for skilled nursing care, in hospitals predominantly, and the need to keep pace with rapid hospital-based care developments continued to impact nursing into the 21st century.

It is important to note that nursing the sick and dying became less significant in the excitement generated by medical developments during the latter half of the twentieth century (Langham and Flagel, 1991; Leftwich, 1993). Furthermore, with medicine tending to focus on preserving life, it is not surprising that there was little progress in palliative care. Palliative care—the art and science of caring for and comforting dying persons—was not formally emphasized in Canada until 1975, when a Montreal hospital opened an in-patient unit dedicated to the non-curative care of dying persons (Ajemian, 1990).

Although dying and death were frequent topics in the health literature until the 1940s, there is little mention of either in the health literature from 1950 to 1990, nor is there much discussion about providing supportive care to dying persons. One issue that did generate concern during these years was aging. Starting in the mid-1940s, numerous reports highlighted the growing number of older persons in Canada and the need to provide appropriate care for this distinct population (Canadian Nurses Association, 1964; Hall, 1947; Miller, 1960).[9]

Most illnesses acquired as a consequence, in part, of aging, such as heart and lung diseases, are progressively debilitating in nature and therefore not amenable to a complete cure. For example, atherosclerosis—that is, hardening of the arteries—develops over a period of many years and is not fully dissipated by life-saving surgery, which opens (sometimes temporarily) a few blocked arteries. Although surgery and other medical treatments have proven to be very successful for saving lives, these treatments have also extended the length of terminal illnesses and the final dying process (Millar and Hill, 1995). In the twentieth century, death shifted from being an inevitable and generally quick outcome to a much less certain outcome of diagnostic testing and therapeutic treatment. In short, death was often delayed through health care, even though the underlying disease remained.

In the mid-1970s, there was a concerted attempt to reduce the incidence and impact of unhealthy lifestyles, in which chronic and unrelieved stress, inactivity, obesity, unhealthy dietary habits, and the use of tobacco products or excessive alcohol intake lead to serious health problems (Lalonde, 1978). This health promotion movement has helped reduce the incidence of death from acquired illnesses and from accidents.[10] For instance, seat belt legislation in the 1970s and 1980s greatly reduced the incidence of accidental vehicular deaths (Hauser, 1974; MacKillop, 1978). More recently, the environmental movement is drawing attention to the unhealthy consequences of pollution and mismanagement of the environment in which we live.

Public perceptions of health care are beginning to change. For example, the aging of the Canadian population is becoming more evident, as are limitations in medical treatment (Millar and Hill, 1995). For all our progress, human beings have not escaped death. At the beginning of the twenty-first century, the optimism generated by the wonder of modern scientific health care has begun to dissipate. Canadians have once again become more conscious of the inevitability of dying and death.

Summary

In summary, for Aboriginal peoples in Canada before the arrival of the Europeans, death was common, visible, familiar, and often came early in life. Life expectancy was modest, although some reached advanced old age. Death followed a similar pattern for the Europeans who came to Canada from 1500 to 1900. However, the consequences of the European presence were disastrous for Aboriginal peoples, who were decimated by epidemics and by the destruction of their economies and ways of life. By the end of the nineteenth century, the public health movement and increasing standards of living were slowly benefiting the European immigrants. As a consequence, death rates declined and life expectancy increased.

In the twentieth century, the public health movement continued to produce significant gains in health status. The development of modern medicine and the public health care system led to further gains. Indeed, the successes of modern medicine eclipsed the public health movement in public consciousness. In the twentieth century, the causes of death shifted from infectious diseases to chronic diseases. The timing of death shifted increasingly to later life. The care of the dying was transferred from family members to health care professionals, and dying and death was moved from the home and community to the hospital. Death, which had been common and familiar, became unfamiliar, remote, invisible, and expected only in old age.

Notes

1. There is some conjecture over how much training these Native healers had. It is possible that the training of medicine men and women was lifelong (Barbeau, 1958; Ericksen-Brown, 1979; Stone, 1962), and that healers shared information among themselves. Dellenbaugh (1906), however, indicated that the Iroquois healers had no specialized training and that their effectiveness, in his opinion, was based largely on theatrics. If this is true, the placebo effect could have brought about the same positive outcomes as it does today. The placebo effect refers to the psychological impact of care. Assistance in the form of personal attention, a "sugar" pill, or sham surgery can be beneficial to people if they believe they are being helped.

2. A considerable number of illnesses were treated by these substances, many of which had to be harvested at select times of the year and during certain times of the day (Erichsen-Brown, 1979). Various forms of first aid were also provided, and it is thought that most Native people also possessed this knowledge (Stone, 1962). Wounds, fractures, and dislocations of limbs were common, and Native treatment for them, such as suturing, keeping wounds clean, reducing dislocations, splinting fractures, and physiotherapy, were later observed by the Europeans to be very effective (Stone, 1962). Sweat lodges were also commonly used; the use of heat would have been very helpful for arthritic and other skeletal-muscular conditions (Erichsen-Brown, 1979; Heagerty, 1928; Stone, 1962); they were far less successful in the treatment of infectious diseases like smallpox. There is little evidence of the successful practice of surgical procedures for extending life (Stone, 1962). Furthermore, the efficacy of many of the Native medicines is largely unknown (Erichsen-Brown, 1979). Few records of the health care practices of Native people were made by the Europeans, despite some medicines being taken from the New World to the Old following contact between the two continents (Bettman, 1956; Coleman, 1985; Erichsen-Brown, 1979). Tobacco, for instance, was widely used in Europe to treat asthma, cancer, and headaches after trade was established with the New World (Bettman, 1956). Sassafras was also taken to Europe in great quantities in the early 1600s to combat syphilis (Erichsen-Brown, 1979), which was prevalent in Europe in the 1500s and 1600s (Bettman, 1956; Coleman, 1985).

3. The term life expectancy indicates the average age at the time of death for persons who are born in the same year. As an average, it means that a number of persons would live much longer than the group's life expectancy, and a number of others would live much shorter lives.

4. Bloodletting through direct blood-vessel laceration, cupping (creating a vacuum next to the skin to remove blood and other fluids), scarification (scratching the skin), and the application of leeches did not begin to be

considered harmful until 1628 (Coleman, 1985). Until that time, bleeding was widely used in cases of illness; it is thought to have been in common use from as early as 1000 AD (Bettmann, 1956). The treatment for new arrivals to Canada suffering from typhus, for instance, was to bleed them at the temple (Heagerty, 1940). Other stock remedies in the way of herbs, bark, or plants were in use by physicians and non-physicians (Bettmann, 1956). Despite having few effective drug therapies and minimal infection control, the many European wars had provided much opportunity for surgeons to advance, by trial and error, their orthopedic and surgical techniques for repairing broken bones and injured bodies (Bettmann, 1956). Surgery was commonly being done to attempt reconstruction or save lives, although cautery was almost always used with devastating effect to seal a wound and stop bleeding (Bettmann, 1956). Cautery was accomplished by pouring boiling fluids into a wound or by applying hot irons (Bettmann, 1956).

5. Some communities by the mid-1600s had hospitals and health insurance plans started by individuals or community groups to provide citizen access to health care (Baumgart, 1992; Heagerty, 1940). Dickason (1984) reported that the early Jesuit missionaries developed hospitals for Native people in the early 1600s as a direct strategy for converting them to Christianity. These early hospitals were thought of as death houses by the Natives, though, because death usually occurred there (Dickason, 1984; Heagerty, 1940). Later, hospitals enjoyed a much better reputation (Lessard, 1991). Hospitals were usually initiated by a religious group. Nurses were commonly from religious orders, such as the Grey Nuns (Kerr, 1991). Although some nurses may have been educated in Europe, it was not until 1890 that nursing truly began in Canada as a result of rigorous training programs based on the model of Florence Nightingale (McPherson, 1996). The non-profit, secular Victorian Order of Nurses was also not formed by an act of Parliament until 1895; these nurses mainly provided home care, but also ran some hospitals (McPherson, 1996).

6. There are additional reasons why unpleasant symptoms during a dying process were unlikely to be successfully eased in early Canada. Effective medications to relieve symptoms were fewer than they are today and, even if they were available in Europe, they were less available in the New World. General anaesthesia through the use of ether or chloroform did not become available until 1846 or 1847 (Heagerty, 1940; Roland, 1985). Until then amputations and other procedures depended largely upon strong physical restraints of the patient and the speed of the surgeon (Heagerty, 1940). One surgeon's technique was noted: "from the point of the knife entering, until the leg was on the floor, was one minute and forty-two seconds. The vessels were tied and the wound dressed in three minutes" (Heagerty, 1940: 104). The acceptance and widespread use of general anaesthesia soon after its discovery is thought to have spurred attention to, and then developments in, pain management (Roland, 1985). Trained health care personnel were also few in number, and persons with little or no preparation, such as the clergy, filled in when needed (Lessard, 1991). It was not until 1824 that the first Canadian medical educa-

tion program was initiated in Montreal to increase the supply of physicians (Roland, 1985).

Trading of medicines between Europeans and native North Americans began during the 1400s. Erichsen-Brown (1979) reported that Native people knew how to make and use solutions which had analgesic (pain killing) and antibiotic properties. They also knew how to make and use poison, how to abort fetuses through ingested prepared medicines, and how to brew solutions for committing suicide (Erichsen-Brown, 1979). Aboriginal peoples may have considered pain and suffering to be an inseparable aspect of living and so developed few measures beyond stoicism and extreme physical endurance to counter it (Corlett, 1935; Dickason, 1984); nor is it evident that Europeans had successfully addressed pain management. The net result is that dying Natives and non-Natives in early Canada would have suffered when dying, particularly if dying was difficult or protracted.

7. The economic boom following the Second World War likely also did much to boost life expectancy in Canada. Malnutrition had been the primary reason why 25 to 50 per cent of the young men reporting for duty in both the First and Second World Wars were found unsuitable for active duty (National Nutrition, 1943; Ostry, 1994; Pett, 1943). Maternal deaths at that time were often linked to poverty and to overwork (Buckley, 1988).

8. Public health measures tend to be credited only with reducing the incidence of mortality from infectious diseases (Baumgart, 1992). However, preventing infectious diseases also greatly reduces the incidence of secondary illnesses and other complications arising from infectious illnesses. Measles, for example can result in deafness from ear infections, reduced mental functioning if encephalitis occurs, and birth defects or spontaneous abortion if the infection occurs in pregnant women. Mumps can cause pancreatitis, meningitis, and, if it occurs in boys past the onset of puberty, it can result in infertility. Poliomyelitis often causes paralysis. Chicken pox is well known for laying the foundation for painful shingles later in life.

9. Many of the health problems of aging were thought to be related to chronic, non-curative conditions such as arthritis, partial or full blindness, and osteoporosis, which caused suffering but did not directly cause death. Since aging cannot be arrested, the need for restorative and rehabilitative health care, occupational therapy, early medical intervention when treatable illnesses occur, and health promotion to prevent illnesses, gradually became apparent beginning in the mid-twentieth century.

10. There have been changes over time in the relative mix of death from injuries, accidents, and suicides (Nault, 1997; Statistics Canada, 1998). Suicides, for example, have become more common in younger persons (Statistics Canada, 1998).

Chapter 2
Dying and Death in Canada Today

This chapter examines contemporary patterns of dying and death in Canada. It explores who experiences what terminal illnesses, when, and under what circumstances. Circumstances include the length and course of the dying process, and the timing and location of death. The chapter begins with a discussion of the current causes of death and then examines death by age, sex, and other variables.

CAUSES OF DYING AND DEATH

Figure 1 shows that the most common cause of death among Canadians in 1996 was circulatory disease, which accounted for close to 40 per cent of all deaths that year. Cancer was the second leading cause, accounting for over one-quarter of all deaths. Other less common causes of death in 1996 were: respiratory diseases (9 per cent of all deaths), of which pneumonia and chronic obstructive pulmonary disorders were the most common; accidents, injuries, and suicides (about 6 per cent of all deaths); infectious or parasitic diseases (less than 2 per cent of all deaths), of which AIDS was the most common; and nervous system or sense organ disorders (less than 1 per cent of all deaths), of which Alzheimer's disease and Parkinson's disease were the most common.

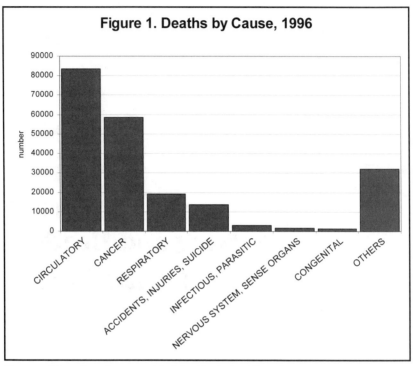

Figure 1. Deaths by Cause, 1996

Source: Mortality data provided by Statistics Canada

Although circulatory disease appears to be the most common cause of death in Canada (Johansen et al., 1998b), some argue that cancer deaths have actually become more prevalent (Belliveau and Gaudette, 1995; Stokes and Lindsay, 1996). This argument is supported by an understanding of how circulatory diseases are reported. Deaths from diseases of the heart and diseases involving blood vessels in other locations of the body (such as the brain) are usually combined into one category for reporting purposes. Circulatory disease is therefore a broad disease classification. If 1996 deaths from diseases of the heart were reported separately from those of blood vessel (vascular) diseases, then heart diseases caused 57,355 deaths and blood vessel diseases (of which stroke is the most common) caused 26,070 deaths. Cancer, with 58,641 deaths, could thus be considered the most common cause of death in Canada (Wilson et al., 1998).

Determining the primary cause of death is an inexact science. It is often not possible to determine with complete accuracy why a person died. For instance, a person may have had cancer slowed by ongoing treatment. If this person died suddenly from a heart attack, stroke, complication of cancer or cancer treatment, or another condition, what should be listed as the primary cause of death?

Selecting the primary cause of death is important. The reported incidence of a disorder, particularly if it causes premature disability and death, is a significant indicator of the level of effort and resources that will be devoted to combat it. It is said that more money has been devoted to researching the treatment of heart disease, which is perceived to be Canada's number one health issue, than has been committed to all other illnesses combined. Tremendous advancements in emergency and post-emergency cardiac care have resulted from this massive, targeted effort. These advancements have helped reduce deaths from heart disease (American Heart Association, 1994; Levy, 1981; Stern, 1979). Furthermore, in some one hundred instances each year in Canada, hearts are transplanted when they cannot be repaired—another indication of the success of the concerted effort to eliminate death from heart disease. Nevertheless, the motivational slogan "cancer can be beaten," and cancer's rising predominance in causing death may indicate that more effort is being expended to battle cancer (Scott, 1992a).

Heart attack is one of the most common lethal heart diseases, along with cardiac arrhythmia (altered heart functioning due to an irregular heart beat) (American Heart Association, 1994). Most deaths from heart diseases occur in mid to late life. Heart diseases are most often acquired after birth, and the disease is typically progressive and chronic in nature. This is not to say that heart diseases are untreatable; rather, most cannot be entirely eliminated or reversed once they have become symptomatic (Federal, Provincial and Territorial Advisory Committee, 1996). Furthermore, the risk factors for acquiring heart disease (such as smoking, inactivity, and a high fat diet) are most often associated with long-standing personal habits and lifestyle choices (American Heart Association, 1994; Statistics Canada, 1999).

Like heart disease, cancer tends to be diagnosed in later life. Recent data shows that 72 per cent of all new cases of cancer were diagnosed in persons aged sixty or older (Gaudette et al., 1998). There are many different sites of cancer, but lung cancer is by far the most common lethal cancer, followed by cancer of the breast, colon, and pancreas (Wilson et al., 1998). All other cancers are much less common causes of death (each accounts for 5 per cent or less of all cancer deaths). Although cancer can cause death quickly, it is more typically a chronic illness as its cause, impact, progression, and treatment are all usually long term (Belliveau and Gaudette, 1995; Federal, Provincial and Territorial Advisory Committee, 1996).

The process of dying, including the symptoms of illness and the speed at which death occurs, varies in relation to the disease or diseases present. A terminal illness may progress rapidly to death or may be evident for weeks, months, or even years. Dying processes are influenced by the age, will, and strength of the dying individual (Chochinov et al., 1999) as well as by the treatments used to combat the disease or manage symptoms arising from the disease.

Heart diseases are associated with variable dying processes. A person who experiences a heart attack or arrhythmia, for instance, may die immediately, with little or no warning. It is also possible that this person may be resuscitated one or more times. If resuscitated quickly and without incident, the individual may experience few lasting effects. On the other hand, the survivor may remain critically ill, needing a ventilator to assist breathing and sustain life. During this illness episode, the person may or may not be conscious. Numerous medications may also be needed to sustain life, along with other treatments and technologies available in an intensive care or coronary care unit in the hospital. Complete recovery or partial recovery may result from treatment, but death may still occur in one or more days. Death is almost inevitable if a critical mass of heart tissue has been irrevocably damaged (and no heart transplant occurs), or if the brain and other organs have been severely damaged by a lack of oxygen resulting from restricted or interrupted blood flow.

Another example of the variation in cardiac dying processes is presented by a heart disease that is simply called heart failure, or congestive heart failure. Approximately 5 per cent of all deaths from heart disease are reported as having occurred from heart failure (Wilson et al., 1998), yet most people who survive a heart attack will develop heart failure. Persons with heart failure usually live for at least five years with a progressively weaker heart. Sudden death often comes as a result of a fatal disturbance in the heart rhythm (American Heart Association, 1994). The dying process can also be much more gradual. Signs of heart failure are present whenever the heart is not strong enough to pump blood throughout the body. These signs result from an insufficient amount of blood being pumped from the heart, along with a congestion of blood in the lungs, liver, and other parts of the body. Weakness and shortness of breath typically occur, and worsen over time. Acute air hunger can result, with restlessness and agitation when near death. Persons suffering from heart failure may or may not be conscious during the end-stage dying process. The physical and mental states of these people, as well as the length of the dying process, are often dependent upon the treatments employed. Oxygen is commonly used during acute episodes of heart failure to reduce the work of breathing and raise the oxygen level within the bloodstream, thereby improving the condition of the heart and other bodily tissues. If the heart continues to fail, however, and oxygen continues to be used, then the dying process tends to be lengthened.

The dying process is also quite variable in cancer deaths, although sudden death from cancer is rare. Although death may occur relatively quickly, it normally does not come for a few months, if not years, after a diagnosis of cancer has been made. Johansen et al. (1994) found frequent hospitalizations followed a diagnosis of cancer; indeed, the highest hospital readmission rates were among persons diagnosed with cancer. The 1994/95 National Population Health Survey (NPHS) also established a strong relationship between hospitalization and cancer. "Nearly four out of every ten persons who reported they had cancer had spent at least one night in hospital during the 12 months before the NPHS" (Wilkins and Park, 1997: 30). The cancer disease trajectory is thus marked by frequent separations from home and loved ones.

Symptoms during the dying process depend a great deal on the location and extent of the cancer. Symptoms are often associated with the specific afflicted organ and with the bodily processes that are affected by the cancerous growths. Common symptoms include pain, fatigue, weakness, nausea and vomiting, anorexia (loss of appetite), weight loss, and breathing problems (Curtis et al., 1991; Donnelly et al., 1995; Ventafridda et al., 1990). Cancer symptoms have been found to progressively worsen as death nears (Curtis et al., 1991; Ventafridda et al., 1990). Many of these symptoms, however, could be due in part to the treatments used to arrest the cancer. Chemotherapy, surgery, and radiation are common cancer treatments. These may be undertaken early in the course of an illness, or later, even when it is evident that the end-stage dying process has begun. In some cases, treatment is aimed at reducing the size of a tumour to lessen the symptoms that result from the blocked flow of blood or other normal fluids in the body or from pressure on surrounding tissues and nerves. One of the chief side effects of chemotherapy is nausea and vomiting; a common problem following surgery is pain. Furthermore, analgesics, which combat pain, can cause constipation and other side effects (Bruera et al.,

1994). In short, symptoms arising from treatment can be mistaken for symptoms of the disease.

The most common causes of death vary by age group (Wilkins, 1996). The Statistics Canada mortality data from 1996 show that congenital disorders are the most common cause of death for infants under the age of one (Wilson et al., 1998). Accidents, injuries, and suicides become the most common cause of death in persons one to thirty-nine years of age, although congenital disorders, nervous system or sense organ diseases, and infections are also significant causes of death. In persons aged forty to forty-nine, injuries, accidents, and suicide become the second most common cause of death, with cancer becoming the most common cause. From age fifty to seventy-nine, cancer remains the most common cause of death, followed by heart diseases and respiratory diseases. Heart diseases are the most common cause of death after the age of eighty. Among those in the eighty to eighty-nine age group, cancer is the second most common disorder causing death, followed by vascular (blood vessel) problems. Although heart diseases remain the most common cause of death among people over ninety, vascular and respiratory diseases surpass cancer in terms of fatalities in this age group. It is also notable that this oldest group of individuals has a higher incidence of "unclassified" disorders causing death than any other age group.

Focusing on the main causes of death tends to overshadow life-threatening disorders that are not common causes of death at any age. Two such diseases are diabetes and chronic non-infectious liver failure. Recent technological advances that allow direct blood-sugar testing have almost eliminated death from diabetic coma and insulin reaction. Nevertheless, diabetes, no matter how well controlled, is still considered a major contributor to high blood pressure, heart disease, stroke, kidney failure, and a number of other illnesses. These illnesses are eventually more problematic and life threatening than the original disease. Chronic non-infectious liver failure, resulting most often from excessive alcohol intake, is another illness that has become a rare cause of death in Canada. Alcoholism usually leads to a number of other serious diseases, such as heart disease, bleeding oesophageal or stomach ulcers, stomach cancer, and pancreatitis. Although excessive alcohol intake and chronic liver failure can be fatal, it is more likely that these secondary diseases will end life.

It is important to recognize that most deaths today do not result from a single cause. Instead, the majority of deaths result from a combination of the effects of aging, the accumulated impact of various health insults throughout the years, and the direct and indirect effects of a number of illnesses and health limitations (Wilkins and Park, 1997). As such, listing a medical diagnosis as the primary cause of death on a death certificate does not provide much insight into the real causes of death, nor does it indicate much about the dying process.

Most illnesses, particularly chronic progressive diseases, do not result in death immediately after diagnosis. Instead, a period of decline or improvement in health often follows. The trajectory of life during this period is dependent upon many factors, one of which is the availability and use of effective health care treatments. Most diseases, once correctly diagnosed, can be managed or stabilized through surgery or medication, exercise, change of living habits, and/or change of diet. It is not surprising, then, that some experts are now estimating that terminal illnesses—that is, those which will eventually cause death—can last as long as fifteen years (Allard et al., 1995; Eastaugh, 1996; Kurti and O'Dowd, 1995). Whereas a quick death may have occurred in the past, a much longer end-of-life period is now possible. During a long terminal illness, a person may consider him or herself to be dying; other persons, including the health care providers, may consider the individual to be dying. Yet, the person's health may be stable or only slowly declining during this terminal phase of life. The terms "holding their own" or "losing ground" are often used in response to queries about the health of terminally ill persons. In contrast, the end-stage or active dying process—when death becomes immediate and inevitable—typically proceeds more quickly and with more certainty, occurring within minutes or over a few days.

Although definitions are still evolving, death is commonly considered the end of mental (brain) and physical (cardio-respiratory) functioning and the relatively quick culmination of the end-stage dying process (Wilson, 1997). For example, a massive head injury or stroke can result in almost instantaneous death. A heart attack that stops the heart from beating can similarly cause death in as little as four to ten minutes. In general, a more typical death takes place over one to three days, with unconsciousness and irregular, laboured breathing signalling an irreversible decline prior to the cessation of cardiac, respiratory, and brain functioning (Kerr and Kurtz, 1999; Wilson, 1997).

As we saw in chapter 1, deaths usually take place in hospital where oxygen, intravenous fluids, and other life-saving and life-prolonging technologies are readily available for use. In a western Canadian study of deaths in long-term and acute-care hospitals, 97 per cent of patients died with at least one continuous life-saving technology in use (Wilson, 1997). These same technologies can be transported to the home and to other sites, allowing the final dying process to be extended in any setting.

Most final dying processes are recognized as such by close family members or friends, who see a critical change in the condition of the terminally ill person (Kerr and Kurtz, 1999). Nurses and other health care workers are also likely to recognize impending death (Rutman, 1992). Unconsciousness is likely the most commonly recognized signal of impending death, but losing strength and becoming bedridden, or developing a lack of interest in food or refusing food and fluids may also indicate that death is approaching (Allard et al., 1995). Although some attempts to estimate prognosis and life expectancy among terminally ill persons have been made, they have met with little success (Christakis et al., 1998; den Daas, 1995).[1] Wilson's (1989) research found that dying is largely an unscheduled matter, with families hoping that death is neither too abrupt nor dying too prolonged.

As mentioned previously, there is often considerable uncertainty about the main cause of death. Autopsies are not always done to verify cause of death; generally, they are carried out only if foul play is suspected or if a patient dies in hospital soon after a surgical or diagnostic procedure. Given that heart disease has been the leading cause of death in Canada, it is often assigned by "default" when there is uncertainty about the cause of death (D'Amico et al., 1999; Lloyd-Jones et al., 1998; Iribarren et al., 1998; Myers and Farquhar, 1998). We know that death is often the outcome of many concurrent illnesses. Thus, the practice of recording a single primary illness as the main cause of death means that some illnesses, most often heart diseases, appear to be more prevalent and more serious than they really are, while other diseases do not appear to be as significant as they really are. The consequence of this is serious. If the default method of assigning the cause of death is not considered when population mortality data are examined, then faulty health care and social sector planning follow.

It is also important to recognize that chronic health conditions may exist for years prior to death. Most adult Canadians report having at least one chronic health condition, although they are more common in older persons (Wilkins and Park, 1996). The most common health problems self-reported by seniors include arthritis or rheumatism, high blood pressure, and cataracts (Statistics Canada, 1997). The incidence of health problems tends to vary among non-institutionalized seniors, home-care recipients, and institutionalized seniors. In response to questions in the 1994–95 National Population

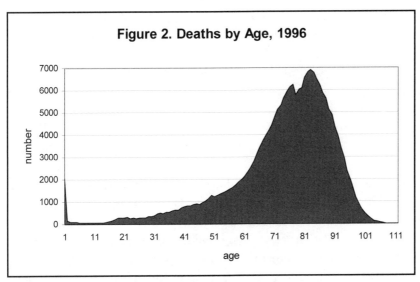

Figure 2. Deaths by Age, 1996

Source: Mortality data provided by Statistics Canada

Health Survey, 73 per cent of non-institutionalized seniors reported "relatively good" health, yet "81 per cent reported that they had at least one chronic health problem that had been diagnosed by a health professional, and 39 per cent said their activity was somewhat restricted by their condition" (Lindsay, 1999: 25). In contrast, one-half of the home-care recipients reported only fair or poor health (Wilkins and Park, 1998). Recipients of government-sponsored home care typically were of advanced age, female, had two or more health conditions (commonly cancer or stroke), had been hospitalized for eight or more days during the past year, and/or lived alone (Wilkins and Park, 1998). The prevalence of health problems in institutionalized seniors was higher than among other seniors, with 58 per cent rating their health as only fair or poor (Tully and Mohl, 1995); one-quarter reported suffering from the effects of a stroke, and half from bowel or bladder incontinence. Reports of arthritis, Alzheimer's disease, and heart disease were also common among institutionalized seniors. Moreover, virtually all reported at least one chronic health condition, 80 per cent reported activity limitations, and 72 per cent reported needing assistance with personal care (Lindsay, 1999).

Chronic health conditions can indirectly influence dying and death. For instance, arthritis and many of the other health limitations that older people experience serve to impede mobility. A number of problems can result from limited mobility: it can reduce not only physical activity and exercise tolerance, but also the ability to obtain and prepare food and to engage in social activities. Although all of these can have serious health consequences, in the end, heart disease will be the most likely primary cause of death to be listed on death certificates, particularly if the deceased is obese or hardening of the arteries is suspected. This situation raises the proverbial "chicken or egg" argument of what came first. Yet, death certificates and other health records generally emphasize what came last and fail to recognize the other factors that contribute to death.

Hospital utilization is at times used to describe the prevalence and seriousness of health problems among seniors.[2] Stokes and Lindsay (1996) analysed national hospital data for 1982–93 and found heart disease was responsible for the highest hospitalization rates among seniors, followed by strokes, chronic respiratory diseases, falls, pneumonia, hernia, prostate cancer, lung cancer, intestinal diseases, gallbladder diseases, bladder and kidney cancers, diabetes mellitus, kidney diseases, and colorectal cancers.[3]

AGE   As figure 2 illustrates, the majority of deaths in Canada occur in old age. More specifically, in 1996, 75 per cent of the people who died were sixty-five years of age or older, 12 per cent were ninety or older, and fewer than 2 per cent were eighteen years of age or younger. As was shown in chapter 1, childhood deaths have become increasingly uncommon since the mid-1900s. If a young person dies, it is usually unexpected and tragic. In contrast, the death of an old person, particularly someone very old, is much more common and more likely to be expected and accepted (Charlton and Dovey, 1995; Davies and Steele, 1996). Furthermore, older individuals experience life-threatening illnesses that middle aged or younger persons typically do not have (Desmeules et al., 1993; Rosenberg and Moore, 1997; Stokes and Lindsay, 1996).

In 1996, the average age at death was 72.3 years, but of the approximately 213,000 Canadians who died that year,[4] 1,390 were one hundred years of age or older (Wilson et al., 1998). These individuals overcame many barriers to a long life. Ongoing public health improvements, social and economic progress, and advances in health care are likely to continue to reduce barriers to a long life. Barring a world war, global economic collapse, or the emergence of new and untreatable illnesses, it is highly likely that more and more Canadians will reach an advanced old age.

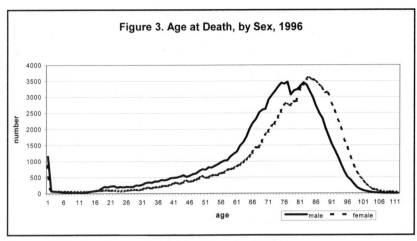

Figure 3. Age at Death, by Sex, 1996

Source: Mortality Date provided by Statistics Canada

Population aging has led to some interesting conjectures on maximum life expectancy. Some experts believe there is a biological limit to life—that is, humans have a fixed life-span (of perhaps 120 years) beyond which life cannot be extended (Fries, 1980). Human life expectancy increased in the twentieth century (Simmons-Tropea and Osborn, 1987), meaning that a much higher proportion of persons are living to old age. This trend may become even more pronounced as the baby-boom generation ages. This large cohort will begin reaching retirement age in 2011 and will contribute significantly to the pattern of deaths in Canada well into the twenty-first century. The baby-boom generation has benefited much from social and health care advances, and so their deaths are expected to further emphasize the trend towards death in old age.

Senescence is the term used to refer to "wearing out" of body parts as a result of aging. With more and more people reaching old age, senescence is becoming a major factor in both the quality and quantity of life (Beckingham, 1993). Senescence tends to be overlooked, though, as a "cause" of death or even as a cause of the many health limitations that can lead to death. For instance, even when a death occurs in a centenarian, a disease or condition is always registered on the death certificate as a cause of death. Chappell (1992) has labelled this phenomenon the "medicalization" of death. She considers dying to be a normal physiological event at the end of a long life (see also Fries, 1980). As we have seen, the practice of labelling every death as an outcome of a potentially treatable disease or condition is problematic. If it appears that people are dying from unsuccessfully treated illnesses, then it is much more likely that health care efforts will focus on finding cures than on finding ways to make dying people more comfortable. This issue is increasingly a concern now that many people are living into their eighties.

At about age eighty-five, considerable physical frailty or senescence often becomes evident (Black et al., 1995; Hertzman and Hays, 1985; Rosenberg and Moore, 1997; Lindsay, 1999). For this reason, persons over the age of eighty-five are often referred to as the "old-old" or the "frail-elderly." This population group is the fastest-growing segment of the Canadian population. In 1996, about 36,000 people, or about 10 percent of all seniors, were eighty-five years of age or older. By 2011, that number is expected to almost double to 70,310 or 14 per cent (Statistics Canada, 1999).

While Canadians in general are living longer than earlier generations, women are living considerably longer than men (see figure 3). In 1996, almost 82 per cent of women, compared to 71 per cent of men died at age sixty-five or older (Wilson et al., 1998). The longevity of females compared to males is further accentuated by an analysis of deaths in the old-old age category. Nearly twice as many women as men were age eighty-five or older at the time of their death (a third of all female deaths compared to a sixth of all male deaths). The difference between males and females is even greater among those who die at age one hundred years or older. Nearly five times more women than men lived to be one hundred years of age or older. It is worth noting that old age is not incompatible with maleness. The oldest person who died in Canada in 1996 was a man of 111 years (Wilson et al., 1998).

In Canada death has been somewhat arbitrarily defined as "premature" if it occurs before the age of seventy-five (Statistics Canada, 1991). That age is also used to calculate potential years of life lost (PYLL), an estimation of the years a person might have lived had premature death not intervened. Cancer deaths result in the highest PYLL (Canadian Council, 1999). Although the concept of a premature death can help distinguish early from late death, using age seventy-five as a marker disregards gender differences. It may be more appropriate, for example, to consider a male death premature if it takes place before the age of sixty-nine, and a female death premature if it takes place before the age of seventy-five. Although this may seem an unimportant distinction, treatment decisions are frequently based on age. If a person is considered to be dying prematurely, then aggressive cure-oriented treatment is more likely to occur (Ajemian, 1992).

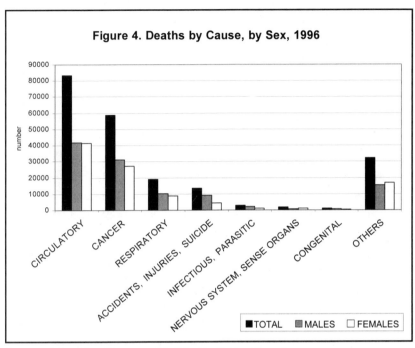

Figure 4. Deaths by Cause, by Sex, 1996

Source: Mortality Date provided by Statistics Canada

Using age seventy-five as a benchmark also disregards more individualized health factors. For instance, many of the infants who died in 1996 were born with serious congenital deformities that were not compatible with life outside the womb. Some people are also born with less serious but still life-threatening conditions, such as cystic fibrosis. Health care has done much to improve and extend life for persons with cystic fibrosis, but few if any such people can expect to reach age seventy-five. In the 1940s, most individuals with cystic fibrosis died in infancy. By the 1970s, the majority of people with cystic fibrosis could expect to live into their twenties. Even today, death from cystic fibrosis usually occurs by age forty (Corey and Farewell, 1996); therefore, death from cystic fibrosis at age forty is not premature.

Another example of the importance of individual factors in aging relates to acquired variations in health among individuals. Some individuals experience negative health consequences from smoking or other risky behaviours, while others have more positive health consequences from regular exercise and other health-promoting behaviours. Such individual behaviours, along with the environment in which a person lives, do much to influence health, and in turn, life expectancy. These individual differences in health are not acknowledged when age seventy-five is used to differentiate premature from non-premature death (Wolfson, 1996).

In summary, most deaths occur in old age. Deaths in childhood and even in middle age have become increasingly uncommon and are often unexpected. Indeed, deaths occurring before old age have been characterized as premature. In contrast, death is more expected in old age.

SEX There are a number of ways in which sex influences dying and death. Statistics Canada mortality data identified more male deaths each year than female deaths. In 1996, there were 111,597 male deaths (52.4 per cent of all deaths) and 101,574 female deaths (47.6 per cent of all deaths) (Wilson et al., 1998). Furthermore, as indicated in the previous section, males tend to die at an earlier age than females. In 1996, the average age of the females who died was 75.7 years while average age for the males who died was 69.3 years (a sex differential of 6.4 years on average). This sex difference in life expectancy has been evident for some time (Millar, 1995); consequently, life expectancy is calculated by Statistics Canada separately for males and females. According to Statistics Canada (1998), the life expectancy for girl babies born in 1995 is eighty-one years and for boy babies it is seventy-five years. The sex differential in life expectancy has been larger in the past. In 1981, it was 7.2 years (Millar, 1995). In recent years, the gap has begun to decrease.[6]

There is ongoing speculation over why women tend to live longer than men (Millar, 1995). The 1996 Statistics Canada mortality data revealed that more male babies than female babies under the age of one year died (1,159 compared to 897). This sex difference continued throughout childhood. Of the children aged one to eighteen who died during 1996, 1,159 were boys and 719 girls. This difference continued throughout adulthood (see figure 3), except that in the old-old age group, the number of female deaths exceeded the number of male deaths because women outnumber men in the oldest years due to their higher rate of survival.

Many analysts believe that the current sex differential in life expectancy will continue to narrow and may be eliminated over time (Millar, 1995; Nault, 1997). However, the narrowing of the sex differential in life expectancy may result from factors negatively affecting the health of women. One such factor is the increase in smoking among women (Ellison et al., 1999). Another is the increased stress and reduced health maintenance activities among women as a result of the "double shift" phenomenon—that is, women increasingly working outside the home while still fulfilling most of the responsibilities of maintaining the home and family (Valentine, 1994).

Not only are males more likely to die than females, figure 4 shows that males die more often of cancer, respiratory diseases, infectious and parasitic disorders, and congenital disorders. Moreover, males are nearly twice as likely to die of injuries, accidents and suicide. Females die more often of nervous system or sense organ disorders than do males. Finally, in terms of circulatory diseases, males are more likely to die from heart diseases while females are more likely to die from vascular disorders.

In summary, males are more likely to die at all ages than females and are more likely to die from most of the common causes of death. The higher death rate for males is associated with a substantial difference in the life expectancy of males and females. Nevertheless, this sex differential in life expectancy has begun to decrease in recent years and may continue to diminish as the lifestyles and social roles of males and females become increasingly similar.

OTHER INFLUENCES ON DYING AND DEATH IN CANADA

Indicators of social class such as income, education, and occupation are associated with rates of death and therefore with variation in life expectancy (Epp, 1986; Truman and Trueman, 1995; Mustard et al., 1997). For example, Statistics Canada (1997: 5) indicates that "socio-economic status affected people's chances of survival as well as of becoming ill. Being in the lowest household income groups in 1994/95 was predictive of death before age 75, even after controlling for sex, chronic diseases, and smoking." The National Population Health Survey of 1994–5 showed an inverse relationship between income and hospitalization: the poor were more likely to be hospitalized than the rich (Wilkins and Park, 1997). Similarly, the 1990 Canada Health Promotion Survey strongly suggested that the poor have a considerably lower health status than higher income groups (Manga, 1990: 265–266). Millar's (1983) study of Canadian census data also revealed differentials in mortality by income level, with the greatest differentials between lower and upper income groups. Finally, occupation is associated with varying exposure to health risks. Aronsen et al.'s (1999) study of mortality in Canada's work force illustrated "excess" mortality from selected diseases among certain occupational groups, for example, "a high rate of laryngeal cancer deaths among male metal fitters, lung cancer deaths among female waiters, and ischemic heart disease deaths among female inspectors and foreman and male taxi drivers and chauffeurs."

Ethnicity is another factor that can contribute to life expectancy and rates of death. For example, accidents are among the leading causes of death for Aboriginal peoples of Canada (Statistics, Canada, 1997). Sheth et al. (1999) found that cardiovascular and cancer mortality varied among Canadians of European, South Asian, and Chinese origin. Chen et al. (1996) found immigrants to Canada had a longer life expectancy than native-born Canadians. The "healthy immigrant effect" (i.e., people of ill health are less likely to immigrate to another country) was thought to bring about this difference. In addition, ethnic differentials in death rates may result from genetic differences and from cultural factors such as diet and lifestyle.

Aboriginal peoples in Canada continue to have lower life expectancy and higher rates of death than the non-Aboriginal population. This is true despite increases in Aboriginal life expectancy, decreases in infant mortality, and decreases in death rates from respiratory conditions, digestive disorders, infectious diseases, and parasitic diseases (Norris, 1995). Nevertheless, Aboriginal peoples in Canada continue to have higher rates of infectious diseases such as tuberculosis and meningitis, and are thought to be facing a potentially explosive situation regarding AIDS. Furthermore, Aboriginal peoples have higher death rates from suicide, homicide and other violence, and accidents including motor vehicle accidents, accidental poisonings, and residential fires (Waldram et al., 1995). Trovato (2001) suggests that these patterns are the result of geographic isolation, poverty, and social psychological marginalization leading to high rates of social disorganization, alcoholism, and other substance abuse.

Despite higher death rates in the Aboriginal population compared to the non-Aboriginal population, the trend towards the convergence of Aboriginal and non-Aboriginal death rates suggests that there will be continuing decreases in infectious disease rates and increases in death rates from chronic diseases such as circulatory disease and cancer among First Nations peoples. At present, however, Aboriginals continue to have a lower risk of circulatory disease and cancer, except for a higher rate of cancer of the cervix. Nevertheless, Aboriginal persons who do get cancer have a lower survival rate than non-Aboriginal persons with cancer. Aboriginal persons also have a high rate of diabetes and associated problems such as chronic kidney failure (Waldram et al., 1995).

Canada is a land of climatic variation, with extremes of hot and cold weather occurring throughout the yearly cycle. More deaths occur in Canada in February and March than in other months. In fact, approximately twice as many deaths take place in February and March than during the months of August and September, which have the lowest incidence of death (Trudeau, 1997). There are several possible explanations for this seasonal variation[7] in death rate, such as a greater frequency of deaths in the winter due to an increased incidence of flu, colds, and pneumonia and as a result of falls on ice, road accidents, and overexertion from shovelling snow. The weather also undoubtedly affects health, and thus death rates, by influencing patterns of exercise, for example.

As was discussed in chapter 1, there was a pronounced trend towards the hospitalization of death during the twentieth century. The percentage of deaths occurring in hospitals reached a peak in 1994 and has since begun to decline.[8] Although it is not certain that this new trend will continue, it may be that the final days of life are taking place increasingly at home or in long-term care facilities. It is not possible, however, to determine if death has been shifting to the home, as home deaths are not reported separately in the Statistics Canada mortality data (Wilson et al., 1998).

Location of Dying and Death

An unknown number of persons who would like to die at home are dying in places such as hospital emergency departments (McWhinney et al., 1992). An analysis of Alberta's inpatient hospital data found that 19–24 per cent of all deaths in the province occurred in hospital emergency departments between 1992 and 1997, and that 17–20 per cent of all deaths in those years occurred after a single day's admission to hospital (Wilson et al., 1999).

While dying at home has its appeal, it also raises certain issues. Some authors indicate that home deaths can take place only if the family is willing and able to care for the dying person in the home (McWhinney and Stewart, 1994; Schachter, 1992). Some are concerned that unpaid female members of the family provide most of this care (Guberman et al., 1992; Pringl and Taylor, 1984; Wuest, 1993). Finally, some are concerned that there is a heavy burden of care (Bramwell et al., 1995; Brown et al., 1990).

In Britain, most end-of-life care takes place in the home; however, most deaths occur in hospital after a one- to three-day stay (Boyd, 1993; Eastaugh, 1996). In Toronto, Duffy et al. (1990) indicated that a pediatric palliative care program assisted parents who wanted to keep their dying children home as long as possible, thereby reducing the final hospital stay and also reducing the incidence of hospital deaths. Canadian research indicates that outpatient or in-home palliative care programs can help shift death successfully out of hospital (Farncombe, 1991; Gardner-Nix et al., 1995; Howarth and Willison, 1995; Levy et al., 1990; McWhinney et al., 1995). Many people believe it is likely that most, if not all, of the care needs of dying persons can be managed outside of hospitals (Boyd, 1993; Lubin, 1992; McWhinney and Stewart, 1994; Pavelich, 1992; Singleton, 1992).

In the future, death might increasingly take place in long-term care facilities. The Canadian Healthcare Association (1998) recently noted that there are a considerably higher number of long-term care beds (157,000) than acute care hospital beds (135,000 beds) in the country. Yet, in 1994–96 less than 3 per cent of all deaths in Canada took place in long-term care facilities[9] (Wilson et al., 1998). It appears, then, that seriously ill and dying long-term care residents are transferred to hospital. Unless long-term care beds are used differently, a major shift of death to long-term care does not seem likely.

Some other factors do affect the chances of dying in hospital. Deaths from accidents, injury, and suicide are much less likely than all other causes of death to occur in hospitals. In contrast, the highest rate of hospitalized death is for congenital disorders that are present at the time of birth. In 1994–96, about 95 per cent of all deaths from congenital disorders occurred in hospitals (Wilson et al., 1998). Death from congenital disorders can occur soon after a hospital birth if no treatment is possible, or later in childhood after unsuccessful treatment (Davies, 1996).

The amount of time that dying people spend in the hospital varies, but it tends to be lengthy. Levy et al. (1990) found that the average stay for dying children at the Toronto Hospital for Sick Children was twenty-nine days. In Alberta, from 1992 to 1997, the average length of hospital stay prior to death declined from twenty-eight to fifteen days (Wilson et al., 1999). These hospital stays were between two and three times longer than the average stays for all patients, most of whom were discharged alive (Alberta Health, 1992-97; Randhawa and Riley, 1995; Statistics Canada, 1998). Furthermore, frequent hospitalizations are common prior to death in hospital. Approximately half of inpatient hospital deaths in Alberta in 1996–97 were preceded by three or more additional hospitalizations in the five years before death (Wilson et al., 1999).

Although a lack of home-based caregivers could be a major factor related to dying in the hospital (McWhinney et al., 1995; Rosenberg and Moore,

1997), Statistics Canada mortality data show that married persons are more likely to die in hospital than persons who are single, divorced, and separated, suggesting that caregivers tend to take the dying person to the hospital. Similarly, males, who are more likely to have family caregivers, were somewhat more likely than females to die in the hospital (Wilson et al., 1998).

Other variables also appear to influence location of death. For instance, considerable variation in location of death occurs across Canada (Wilson et al., 1998). In 1996, the Northwest Territories had the lowest percentage of deaths in the hospital (42 per cent of all deaths) of all provinces or territories. New Brunswick had the highest rate of hospital deaths (95 per cent), followed by Quebec (87 per cent), and British Columbia (77 per cent).[10]

Summary

In summary, at the juncture of the twentieth and twenty-first centuries, dying and death in Canada typically come in old age as a result of chronic health problems such as circulatory disease and cancer. Deaths occurring early in life have come to be unexpected and have been labelled premature. Dying and death tend to come later in life for females than males. This sex differential in life expectancy increased over much of the twentieth century but has begun to converge in recent years. There continues to be a differential in the health status and life expectancy of Canada's social classes, with the poor being at greatest risk for poor health and premature death. Finally, during the twentieth century, dying and death have increasingly taken place in the hospital, and the great majority of deaths now occur in that setting.

Notes

1. For examples of such attempts, see Allard et al., 1995; Finne-Soveri and Tilvis, 1998; Gerard et al., 1996; Rubenstein et al., 1986; Vigano et al., 1999.

2. Johansen et al. (1994) found that approximately 10 per cent of hospital patients in Saskatchewan and New Brunswick were "high users," in that they were frequently hospitalized or hospitalized for long periods of time, with this group accounting for approximately half of all hospital days in the year 1989–90. "This profile of high users suggests that high medical costs are due not so much to intensive care of terminally ill patients, but to ordinary medical and palliative care of chronically and seriously ill patients" (Johansen et al., 1994: 253), and that "death in hospital occurred more frequently among high users than other users" (260). For others, ill health leads to institutionalization in long-term care facilities (Tully and Mohl, 1995). Approximately 5 per cent of Canadian seniors are institutionalized (Lindsay, 1999; Tully and Mohl, 1995) and 81 per cent of the long-term care population is elderly (Tully and Mohl, 1995; Wilkins and Park, 1998).

3. Repeat hospitalizations of a few individuals could give the impression that many more seniors suffer from the various listed diseases. It is notable, however, that Stokes and Lindsay (1996) found provincial differences in the incidence of hospitalization of seniors for specific diseases. This situation tells as much about variable access to hospitals across Canada as it does about the incidence of serious illnesses among seniors.

4. As a consequence of both a growing and aging population (Nault and Wilkins, 1995), the total number of deaths taking place each year in Canada is slowly increasing. In 1950, 123,440 Canadians died; by 1996, this number had increased to 213,171 (Wilson et al., 1998). In 1997, the population of Canada exceeded 30 million, of which approximately 12.5 per cent were seniors (Statistics Canada, 1999).

5. Aging is a gradual process. Some aspects of aging are visible, such as gray hair and wrinkles; other aspects are much less noticeable, such as senescence of internal organs. Most normal processes of senescence do not begin until adulthood is reached. Senescence is usually progressive (Beckingham, 1993). A number of theories about cellular or biological senescence exist; some emphasize the slow buildup of substances in cells which impede their functioning; others emphasize a slow loss of cells over time (Hayflick, 1980). By age sixty, most bodily organs are affected by senescence (Hazzard et al., 1999).

If a sudden injury or illness impairs the functioning of bodily organs that already have been significantly affected by senescence, then symptoms of illness are much more likely to be observed. This explains why frail elderly people may become unduly ill if they experience a common cold, flu, or another illness that would not be life threatening at an earlier age. The World Health Organization (1989) recognized this state as a loss of physiologic adaptability with aging. Given the advanced age that many Canadians reach, senescence is likely to be a common contributing factor to death. It is also possible, in some cases, that senescence is the sole factor.

6. Life expectancy can also change during a lifetime. For instance, a life expectancy of eighty-one and seventy-five years of age, respectively, was calculated for Canadian female and male babies born in 1995 (Statistics Canada, 1998). It will take most of the twenty-first century to determine if this "prediction" is correct. Many of these 1995 babies could live past their life expectancy; in doing so they will extend the life expectancy calculated for subsequent age cohorts. Although some people argue that life expectancies may become shorter in the future because of increased environmental hazards and other problems, ongoing health care developments and social advances are likely to continue to extend individual life-spans and thus enhance population-based life expectancy (Millar, 1995).

7. There is no evidence that the phases of the moon, the tides of the ocean, or other naturally occurring phenomena lead to higher or lower rates of death. Furthermore, there is no evidence to support a nursing superstition that deaths in hospital come in clusters of three. However, premonition of death, where a person accurately forecasts their own death, has been substantiated in a few cases (Burgess, 1996; Cox, 1981; Weisman and Hackett, 1961).

8. These are the first reductions since 1950. These reductions may be an outcome of a larger trend towards reduced hospital-based care. Between 1982 and 1993, Randhawa and Riley (1995) found hospital separations declined steadily in Canada. Hospital separations are the total count of all inpatient hospitalization episodes (this count excludes emergency department and outpatient department or day surgery visits). Over roughly the same period, surgery has also declined (Randhawa, 1993; Randhawa and Riley, 1995) as have the number of hospital beds in Canada since the late 1980s (Tully and Saint-Pierre, 1997). Furthermore, in the mid-1990s, approximately 25 per cent of all hospital beds across Canada were closed.

9. An analysis of the gender of persons who died in long-term care facilities across Canada from 1994 to 1996 found a 60:40 ratio of female to male deaths (Wilson et al., 1998). Lengths of stay in long-term care facilities are commonly in the range of two to three years or more (DeCoster et al., 1995; Hill et al., 1996; Stark and Gutman, 1986; Tully and Mohl, 1995; Wilson, 1991) and long-term care bed occupancy is typically 95 per cent or greater (Alberta Health, 1999).

10. All other provinces and the Yukon Territory had hospitalized death rates in 1996 that were below the national average of 73 per cent. Furthermore, it is important to note that the rate of hospitalized death has declined recently in all provinces and territories except New Brunswick. In some cases there has been a rapid decline. Manitoba was the first province to begin to reduce hospital

deaths. In 1984, Manitoba's peak hospitalization-of-death rate was 76 per cent; by 1996, the rate had declined to 72 per cent (Wilson et al., 1998).

Native-born Canadians were somewhat more likely to die in hospital than Canadians born outside of Canada (Wilson et al., 1998). Why persons who are born in Canada make more use of hospitals for dying care is unknown. Cultural differences, differences in family dynamics or structure, and many other socio-demographic influences could directly or indirectly affect location of death.

Part II

The Social and Cultural
Response to Dying and Death

Chapter 3
Dying and Death in the Context of Canadian Social Institutions

Death is a normal physiological event that occurs at the end of every life. Nevertheless, dying and death have many different meanings and implications for individuals as well as for Canadian society. Current views of dying and death, along with practices related to these phenomena, are extensively influenced by the social institutions that have developed in Canada over many years. Social institutions that are most relevant to dying and death are the family, religion, the health system, the legal system, and the funeral industry. Each of these institutions is undergoing change that has consequences for dying and death. This chapter provides an overview of how these social institutions affect dying and death in Canada. Topics such as palliative or non-curative health care, euthanasia, assisted suicide, the right to die, quality of life, sanctity of life, prolongation of life, withdrawal and withholding of life support, and advance directives are current contentious issues that constitute a major focus of this chapter.

FAMILY

Family life provides experiences that shape personal understandings of dying and death. The reactions of family members to the deaths of grandparents, family friends, or even family pets teach children much about dying and death. In some cases, children are sheltered from dying and death; they may not be taken to visit dying persons or to funeral services. In such circumstances, children may learn to respond to dying and death with avoidance, revulsion, despair, or fear. In other cases where children are more involved in the dying and death experience, they are more likely to develop positive perspectives and coping skills (Webb, 1997; Colman, 1997).

Family members often provide a great deal of support to both a dying family member and to each other. Yet not all families are able to support dying or bereaved family members. Dying and death experiences can be very stressful and can strain family relationships. Moreover, largely from lack of experience, some families may simply not know how to cope with the situation. Reduced experience with dying and death has made it more difficult for families to develop collective stances and traditions about dying and death. Smaller nuclear families and population aging have reduced the number of deaths that individual Canadians experience. In the 1960s and 1970s, Canadian families used to bury a family member every eight to ten years on average; now it is once every fifteen to eighteen years (Flynn, 1993). In this context, Webb (1997: xvii) reports that today "most of adulthood passes without personal contact with dying."

Greater geographic mobility of family members, together with the late twentieth-century trend towards the hospitalization of death, have also made it unlikely that individual Canadians have had much experience in providing hands-on care to dying family members (Charlton and Dovey, 1995; Wilson et al., 1998). Hospitalization or institutionalization in a long-term care facility is a reality during most serious bouts of illness and declines leading to death. In these settings, nurses have taken on many of the responsibilities that family members and friends used to have when home deaths were the norm (Pavelich, 1992; Pringl and Taylor, 1984; Wilson et al., 1998). Even if dying and death take place at home, home nursing care is frequently provided (Kerr and Kurtz, 1999; Wilkins and Park, 1998).

It is possible that these trends are beginning to change. The decrease in hospital deaths discussed in chapter 2 may mean that an increasing number of deaths will occur at home. Indeed, McWhinney and Stewart (1994) forecast an increase in family involvement in both death and dying: "during the next few decades, the increasing prevalence of cancer and other chronic disease and the reduced number of [hospital] beds are likely to increase the number of home deaths. Even when patients die in hospital, their length of stay is likely to be reduced, so that a longer portion of their terminal illness will be spent at home" (p. 240).

For the present, however, few families plan for a home death; the deaths of family members are unlikely to take place at home or in the immediate community of residence (Charlton and Dovey, 1995; Flynn, 1993). As a consequence, many Canadians never witness an actual death. Contact with death may be limited to attending a funeral or memorial service after death has occurred. In short, few families provide direct hands-on care to dying persons or perform the required duties that arise after death has occurred.

In some cases, decisions must be made at the time of death about organ and tissue donation. Canadians can donate up to twenty-five different body organs and tissues, including skin and bone[1] (Colman, 1997). Decisions about organ and tissue donation, and the rituals, ceremonies, and customs which follow death, vary depending on the cultural origins of the family of the deceased person (Gentles, 1988), the relationship of the deceased person to other members of the family, and changing social concepts of what is acceptable.

Following death, a funeral home or transfer service (where the body is taken directly to a cemetery or crematorium) is almost always given the responsibility of taking the body and performing death care (Kerr and Kurtz, 1999). Yet, as little as seventy years ago, around the time of the Great Depression, Canadian families commonly used their own vehicles to transport the deceased, cleaned and dressed the dead body, built coffins, used their own homes as places where family and friends could view the body, performed burials, and arranged for deaths to be registered (Colman, 1997; Ontario Coalition of Senior Citizens Organizations, 1995). Although these activities are not prohibited today, few families carry them out. Instead, they have become much more reliant upon various other social institutions to meet and to manage death. It is therefore important to consider the influences of these social institutions.

RELIGION

For centuries, religion has played a major role in dying and death. The concept of a life after death is common to many societies. Religion has also provided meaning for the dying process. For example, suffering has been considered to be important for salvation and death an avenue to eternal life (Lessard, 1991). Religion also established familiar and accepted patterns of human behaviour, and thus provided direction during difficult times. Religious representatives are often still called to death beds to support the dying person and the grieving family, and last rites remain an important religious ritual for dying and grieving Catholics.

Throughout the twentieth century, the influence of religion on dying and death declined considerably as scientific developments increasingly saved lives (Stingl, cited in Wilson et al., 1998). In the past, health care could do little to prevent death, but ongoing scientific developments in health care occurred at a rapid rate throughout the twentieth century. These developments quickly led to the rising significance of hospitals and physicians in Canadian society. The rising success and, thus, prominence of health care tended to overshadow religious conventions regarding dying and death. Furthermore, the rising significance of science during the twentieth century was accompanied by a decline in participation in organized religion (Bibby and Brinkerhoff, 1994).

Science is not the only area that has affected the role of religion in dying and death. The modern funeral industry, for example, has also constricted religion's role. Flynn (1993) observes that "most religious groups have stepped back and allowed the funeral director to define the social customs of the burial rite.... Religious leaders have not recognized the need to set clear guidelines on funeral rites, and have not educated their clergy on the financial issues surrounding death and rituals" (6–7).

This is not to say that the institution of religion and religious roles and traditions in relation to dying and death are now irrelevant in Canadian society. Some dying persons and grieving families still involve a spiritual leader in decisions over the use of life support or its discontinuation (Wilson, 1993). Furthermore, priests, ministers, rabbis, and other spiritual leaders still commonly preside over funerals. Funerals and memorial services are frequently provided in places of worship. Church groups often have visitation teams to support dying persons, and large hospitals commonly employ clergy to ensure dying individuals and their families receive assistance, if needed. Many religious-based groups offer bereavement-support groups to help families after death. Religion still has significance to individuals, but it is clearly more significant for some people than others.

Religion also influences dying and death at a societal level. Religious groups have provided leadership and advice on social policy related to death and dying. For example, in 1984 the Catholic Health Association of Canada, along with the Canadian Nurses Association, Canadian Medical Association, Canadian Bar Association, and the Canadian Hospital Association, developed guidelines on health care decision-making for terminally ill persons (Joint Statement, 1984).[2] These guidelines addressed ethical issues arising out of technological developments that increase health care workers' ability to resus-

citate patients. The guidelines stated that, although interventions with these de-
vices are often life-saving, health care professionals often feel uncertain when
deciding to resuscitate a patient for whom such an intervention would not appear to be beneficial, in that it would prolong the dying process rather than extend life" (24). Furthermore, these guidelines indicated that "palliative care to
alleviate the mental and physical discomfort of the patient should be provided
at all times" (24). In 1991, the Catholic Health Association of Canada developed written guidelines to further assist difficult health-care decision-making
in life-and-death situations. Among other things, these guidelines oppose assisted suicide and euthanasia (Blouin, 1995).

The Health System

Although all health care workers are expected to be prepared to deal effectively
with dying and death, health care workers in general may not be adequately
prepared to care for dying persons and grieving families (Kristjanson and
Balneaves, 1995; Ley, 1985; Scott, 1992b). Ambulance workers, physicians,
and nurses are the health care workers most likely to provide care to dying persons. Nevertheless, death is not an everyday event even in ambulances, hospital nursing units, or long-term care wards. Death is also likely a rare occurrence in certain health care specialties, such as pediatrics and obstetrics
(Brockopp et al., 1991).

 Of all health care workers, nurses provide the most direct, hands-on care
to dying persons. Through their work, nurses often gain different perspectives
on patient and family needs and preferences than do physicians and other persons who spend less time with the patient (Beaton and Degner, 1990;
Comartin, 1983; Lindsay, 1991; Rodney and Starzomski, 1993). Often nurses
become advocates for the patient and/or family (Van Weel, 1995). Although
nurses are the most likely health care professionals to be present during the
dying process and to be present at the time of death, personal comfort with
dying and death varies among nurses (Brockopp et al., 1991; Gotay et al.,
1985; Smith and Varoglue, 1985). This comfort or discomfort reflects, in part,
whether or not the nurse believes that the amount and type of patient care is
appropriate to the situation (Ericksen et al. 1995; O'Neill, 1978; Rodney,
1994).

 Professional detachment may buffer the personal impact of caring for seriously ill and dying persons (Beaton and Degner, 1990; Duff, 1987; Marquis,
1993). This detachment may help explain why 50 per cent of long-term care

residents at a Quebec facility believed staff were indifferent to the death of residents (Lavigne-Pley and Levesque, 1992).

Wilson (1997) found that nurses and physicians working in a large Canadian hospital frequently could not recall details about patients who had died recently while under their care. In contrast, nurses and physicians working in a long-term care facility and in two small hospitals were much more likely to recall details about the patient, the dying process, and the patient's family. This difference appears to be related to the size and type of health care institution. Health care workers in large acute care hospitals, such as nurses and physician specialists or physicians in training, usually have very little initial or ongoing contact with patients and their families. Contact is frequently limited to one hospital stay, with no additional connection outside the hospital. In contrast, small hospitals are most often situated in rural communities and less densely populated urban communities where there is a much greater chance of ongoing contact between health care workers and community residents, both in hospital during one or more admissions, and outside of the hospital.[3]

Although individual health care workers vary in their personal perspectives on dying and death, the context in which health care is provided has a powerful impact on dying and death. Medical programs, in particular, have been criticized for focusing on preserving life and for emphasizing aggressiveness in life support (Bulkin and Lukashok, 1991). For physicians, death may be perceived as a failure of medical care. Similarly, hospitals are primarily oriented to saving lives (Ajemian, 1992; Mount, 1976). The vast majority of health system funding, approximately one-half of which is devoted to hospitals alone, supports the diagnosis and treatment of illness (Health Canada, 1996). The nature of the Canadian health care system, whereby access to hospitals and medical care is ensured for all Canadians, has led to a situation whereby all Canadians can receive a wide variety of treatments to support and extend life (Roos et al., 1987; Simmons, 1996). Treatment normally continues until "nothing further can be done to preserve life" (Wilson, 1997). Curtin (1996) summed up a recent, large, multi-site investigation of end-of-life hospital care in the United States by noting that "first you suffer, then you die" (56). Suffering comes not only from the dying process itself, but also from health care treatments. There is some concern, then, with the fact that the vast majority of deaths take place in hospitals, which are oriented towards resisting death, not easing dying (Mount, 1976; Wilson et al., 1998).

There are some indications that medical approaches may be changing. Despite a ready ability to use cardiopulmonary resuscitation (CPR) to preserve life, since the mid-1970s most hospitals and long-term care facilities in Canada have developed policies that allow decisions about withholding CPR to be made in advance of death for those patients who are in the process of dying (Choudhry et al., 1994; McPhail et al., 1981; Rasooly et al., 1994; Wilson, 1996). This authorizes that CPR not be performed after the heart has stopped beating or after breathing has ceased. Wilson (1997) found that just under 3 per cent of all adults who died in four Canadian hospitals or long-term care facilities had CPR performed at the time of death. In most cases, a decision had been made shortly before death not to initiate CPR. Similarly, a large study of end-of-life care in the United States found that almost half of no-CPR orders were written on patients' charts within two days before death. Of more concern is that a third of American patients surveyed did not want CPR, yet more than half of their doctors did not know their preferences (Webb, 1997)[.4]

Hospital deaths are hidden from conscious consideration. Many hospitals carry out a practice whereby deceased persons are only removed from their rooms after visiting hours, with doors to other rooms closed, and in specially designed stretchers that conceal the body. Long-term care facilities may also down play the incidence of death among residents by transferring terminally ill and dying residents to hospital to die.

Palliative Care

Palliative care is the supportive, non-curative care of persons who are dying (Scott, 1988). Its aim is to improve the quality, not the quantity of life. This philosophy contrasts sharply with the dominant orientation in health care which is curative and life saving. Instead of emphasizing cure and the extension of life, palliative care emphasizes the management of symptoms in order to make the dying person as comfortable as possible. Palliative care is one of the most interdisciplinary and team-based health care services; it includes nurses, physicians, and many other professionals and para-professionals who work together to improve the quality of life of the dying person (Diment and Evans, 1995). Palliative care is more holistic than curative care and emphasizes the physical, psychological, and social needs of the dying person. In addition, palliative care often addresses the needs of the family of the dying person. Because of the dominance of the curative approach, there has been resistance to accepting palliative care as a health care specialty in Canada and in other countries (Calman, 1988; Scott, 1988).

The first palliative care unit in Canada opened in 1975 in a Montreal hospital. By 1985, approximately 300 hospital-based palliative care programs and 1,000 hospital beds were devoted to palliative care across Canada (Ajemian, 1990). Although such growth may seem impressive, it is far less so when compared to the over 135,000 acute care beds in some 2,000 hospitals across Canada (Canadian Healthcare Association, 1998), only a very small percentage of which are devoted to palliative care. Using acute care hospitals for palliative care has created a competition for funding between curative and palliative care in the hospital. This competition has limited the expansion of palliative care. In some cases, palliative care units have been closed following hospital funding cutbacks (Priest, 1987).

As an alternative to hospital-based palliative care, some hospitals discharge dying people to a home-based palliative care program, as was done as early as 1974 in Vancouver (Malkin, 1976). Other palliative care programs were developed in long-term care facilities, such as nursing homes (Fry and Schuman, 1986). Hospices—that is, free-standing facilities that offer palliative care—began to provide another end-of-life care option.[5] Toronto's first hospice was established in 1979 (Hailstone, 1979). In 1988, Casey House, Canada's only hospice for people dying from AIDS opened (Murrant and Strathdee, 1992). In the early 1990s, Vancouver opened the first children's hospice in North America (Eng and Davies, 1992).

More recently, the focus of palliative care expansion in Canada has been on community-based programs designed to support dying and death in the home (Canadian Palliative Care Association, 1997; Health Canada Working Group, 1997). Most community-based programs provide home nursing care and other home-based services to support the dying person at home. Some community-based programs offer respite care or day care, where the dying person goes to a care centre during the day. These allow a wage-earning family caregiver to keep working. In addition, the dying person may stay occasionally for a weekend at a care centre or stay for a few days in a hospital or long-term care facility to relieve the family of care giving, to accommodate family travel, and so on (Symons, 1992). From research comparing hospital-based and community-based palliative care programs, it appears that both types of palliative care programs benefit dying persons and their families (Downe-Wamboldt, 1985).

As the Canadian population continues to age, and the number of persons dying each year continues to increase, new developments in the organization and delivery of palliative care can be expected. An array of different palliative care programs is likely to develop, as the needs of one community can be quite different from another. For example, small remote rural communities and large urban communities are likely to develop different palliative care programs. Moreover, the palliative care needs of people who are dying can also vary considerably.[6]

Despite the ongoing need for palliative care programs, there are considerable barriers to their expansion. One of the most important is financial. Funds are limited and subject to competition in the hospital and in the community (Feser, 1992; Garner, 1976) with the result that both hospital-based and community-based palliative care programs tend to be underfunded. Another barrier is Canadian social values. Because great efforts are made, with little regard to cost, to rescue people from death and to preserve life, diverting money from programs that save lives to a palliative program that facilitates dying can be difficult to accept.

Dying people use a considerable amount of hospital resources. Hospital care is approximately ten times more expensive than care in a long-term care facility, and care in the home is usually half the cost of that in a long-term care facility (Noseworthy, 1997). Considerable savings would result from maintaining dying persons in their homes for as long a period as possible, or by using long-term care facilities for end-of-life care.

One further fiscal, as well as ethical, issue associated with hospital-based end-of-life care is the technological approach to care in hospitals. On admission, patients routinely have a number of blood tests, X rays, and other diagnostic tests done at considerable expense. Aggressive treatments are also common (Ajemian, 1992; Curtin, 1996; Wilson, 1997). When it becomes obvious that death is unavoidable and immediate, dying persons commonly are given high levels of oxygen to ease breathing, intravenous fluids to maintain hydration, two or more powerful antibiotics to reduce chest congestion, and other medications to strengthen the heart or other systems (Dush, 1993; Wilson, 1997). As a result of these interventions, dying lasts longer. Although many of these procedures cause pain or are irritating to the dying person, health care professionals and the public are reluctant to adopt a non-interventionist approach during the dying process. Apparently, few trust nature to produce a good death. Some people, however, have begun to call for a more natural death, one in which pain medication alone is used to ease suffering (Murray, 1981; Pannuti and Tanneberger, 1992; Turner et al., 1996).[7]

It is clear that the curative orientation is often ineffective and inappropriate for patients who are dying. Nevertheless, a dying person may want to be kept alive to see a child graduate, get married, or have a baby, for example. To achieve this, the dying person may accept antibiotics to combat a life-threatening infection, tube feeding to prevent physical wasting, or surgery to slow the progression of a disease or promote bodily functioning (Dush, 1993) rather than accept palliative care.

Because death is so final, is viewed with such aversion in a youth-oriented and success-oriented society, and is so painful on a personal level, the decision, by the patient or the family or both, to shift from curative care to palliative care is often delayed (Davies and Steele, 1996). While some people are more accepting of palliative care, some dying persons and family members are tremendously reluctant to acknowledge that cure or remission is no longer possible (Frager, 1996). Often this reluctance is expressed by a dying parent's children who have not seen their parent for a number of years and have not come to an understanding that their parent is dying. This situation is so common it has been labelled "California daughter syndrome." This refers to children who have moved far away from their parents and had little contact over the years, returning when their parent is facing death, but unprepared for their parent's dying. Parents are also often reluctant to accept death for their terminally ill children. Davies and Steele (1996), two British Columbia nurses, found that the parents of most dying children never consider their children to be dying, despite a shift in their treatment from cure-oriented to palliative care. Phillips (1992) has reported a need to refocus our approach to care so that it does not appear that palliative care begins when treatment ends; instead, there should be a more gradual and overlapping shift from curative care to palliative care.

In summary, dying and death typically take place in health care institutions, particularly in hospitals. In these settings, health care workers, such as nurses and doctors, provide most of the care for the dying. Although care is too often oriented towards extending life inappropriately for patients who are dying, hospitals are increasingly withholding cardiopulmonary resuscitation so as not to prolong the dying process unnecessarily. Both hospital-based and community-based palliative care programs offer an alternative to inappropriate cure-oriented care for the dying.

THE LEGAL SYSTEM

The law is becoming more influential with respect to dying and death in Canadian society. Civil and criminal law, and other legal guidelines, have often developed in Canada in response to advances in health care and changes in society. Today, most large health care facilities, as well as government departments of health, retain lawyers to provide ongoing legal advice. An organizational policy that addresses a life or death issue is likely to be formalized only after legal advice has been received. Legal advice is also frequently sought whenever there are questions about the adequacy of patient care, such as in the case of an unexpected patient death.

The Criminal Code of Canada has a very substantial impact on dying and death. The Criminal Code defines murder and assisted suicide as criminally indictable offences (Curran and Hyg, 1984). Similarly, in 1997, the United States Supreme Court announced its unanimous decision that assisted suicide was not a constitutional right (Angell, 1997; Webb, 1997). Although it would seem obvious that murder is a serious offence, mitigating circumstances influence how judges and juries in Canada and elsewhere view the crime and assign punishment. A mother in Ontario who attempted to kill her disabled six-year-old child by giving her an overdose of medication through her feeding tube was found guilty of attempted murder but was not sentenced to jail ("No jail time," 1999). Instead, she was given a two-year sentence to be served in the community. Crimes motivated by familial love or parental responsibility are often treated differently from other crimes.

It is not illegal to take your own life in Canada, but it is illegal to knowingly assist another person who is trying to commit suicide (Kerr and Kurtz, 1999) and it is illegal to intentionally cause another's death. The prohibition against assisted suicide and causing death may have unintended and undesirable consequences. For example, families may withhold strong pain killers from a dying family member for fear of being prosecuted for hastening death.[8] In the past, physicians were concerned that pain relief could lead to prosecution if it was thought that death was hastened (Bresnahan, 1993; Mount and Flander, 1996; Wood and Martin, 1995). This concern has been relieved considerably by the 1984 Joint Statement on Terminal Illness regarding health care decision-making for terminally ill persons (mentioned earlier in this chapter), the 1995 revision of the Joint Statement (CMA Policy Summary, 1995), and the publication of the goals of palliative care in Canada (Canadian Palliative Care Association, 1997). All of these statements indicate that effective care of dying persons is of paramount concern and that, although death may be hastened by comfort-oriented care as compared to curative care, the intent to relieve suffering is most important.

Withdrawing, Withholding, and Refusing Treatment

Physicians and health facility administrators have also been concerned that they might be prosecuted for hastening death by withholding or withdrawing treatment from the dying (President's Commission, 1983; Wood and Martin, 1995). For the most part, this concern has become outdated because of significant legal cases such as the Karen Anne Quinlan case in the United States. Karen Anne Quinlan's parents won the legal right in 1976 to have their brain-dead daughter's "life support" (ventilator) removed. Her case became a springboard for end-of-life law in the United States and in other countries (Webb, 1997).

Most deaths in Canada occur after one or more treatments have either been withheld or withdrawn (Cook et al., 1995; Faber-Langendoen and Bartels, 1992; Smith, 1995; Webb, 1997). In Canada, the Joint Statement on Terminal Illness (1984) supported the withholding and withdrawal of treatments if these treatments do not benefit terminally ill or dying persons. The 1995 revised statement focuses on withholding cardiopulmonary resuscitation, but notes that "a decision not to initiate CPR does not imply the withholding or withdrawing of any other treatment or intervention. A person who will not receive CPR should receive all other appropriate treatments, including palliative care, for his or her physical, mental and spiritual comfort" (CMA Policy Summary, 1995: 1652C). Despite concerns, few physicians, health care administrators, or other health care workers in Canada have been charged for withdrawing or withholding care from dying persons.

Case law developments in the area of medical care have clarified rights and responsibilities on an individual level, and set precedents for larger, societal level rights and responsibilities. In 1992, an Ontario physician was found guilty of assault and battery for insisting that blood be given to a woman of the Jehovah's Witnesses faith (Malette v. Schulman, 1992). The physician knew that the injured woman had signed a card indicating she did not want to receive blood. The ruling in favour of the plaintiff, whose life was likely preserved by the transfusion, identified personal autonomy in health care decision-making as legally binding and morally compelling. In this and subsequent cases, the physician's judgment as to what is beneficial for the patient was not considered the key factor in decision making. Instead, what the patient considered to be acceptable or appropriate treatment was deemed more important.[9]

The <u>Malette</u> decision, which supported the withholding of life-sustaining treatment at the patient's request, was quickly followed by another major legal precedent, this time in regard to withdrawing treatment. In this case, a judge was asked to grant a request by a young woman, Nancy B, who lived in a Montreal area long-term care facility and wanted to have her life-supporting ventilator removed. After it had been determined that she was fully aware of the consequences of her decision to stop this life-supporting technology, her request was granted, and Nancy B died (Campion, 1994; Sneiderman, 1993). Still more recently, a mother in British Columbia was not prosecuted for allowing her ten-year-old daughter to die after the mother refused tube feeding and other medical treatments ("No charges," 1999). The daughter had been suffering from Rett syndrome, a rare and fatal neurological disease. It was presumed that the daughter understood her choice and its ramifications.

Thus, while criminal law in Canada continues to prohibit euthanasia and assisted suicide, a dying person who is mentally competent has the right to refuse treatment, which may be withheld or withdrawn even though death results. Under these circumstances, withholding or withdrawing treatment is not defined as euthanasia or assisted suicide, and, therefore, does not trigger prosecution under the law.

Care Decisions and Living Wills

Most terminally ill persons can have their lives extended by health care. Furthermore, persons in comas, near-comas, or persistent vegetative states (PVS) can be kept alive for years and even for decades. For example, Karen Anne Quinlan was kept alive for ten years, with tube feeding, after her parents won the legal right to have her "life support" equipment removed (Webb, 1997).

Right-to-die groups, such as the Hemlock Society in the United States and Dying with Dignity in Canada, have raised questions about the appropriate time to withdraw and withhold life-supporting treatments. The Hemlock Society was founded in the United States in 1980 by Derek Humphry who wrote a best-selling book *Final Exit* in 1991. On the other side of the debate, right-to-life groups, including groups who represent disabled persons and the unborn, such as Campaign Life Coalition, are becoming more organized and vocal about their concern that life is too easily ended.

Much of the debate over the use of life support to prolong life and over the withholding or withdrawing of life support, hinges on questions of human rights, most notably on informed consent. In the past, physicians made many, if not all, health care decisions (Webb, 1997). Since the 1970s, greater awareness of the need for personal autonomy, punctuated by significant case law developments, has brought about a remarkable change in health care decision-making (Ott and Nieswiadomy, 1991). Today, competent persons can make their own health care decisions.

Physicians and other persons still tend to influence many treatment decisions. Physicians may unilaterally make decisions; indeed, some people want the physician to make the difficult "medical" decisions (Storch and Dossetor, 1994). Alternatively, some choose to refuse treatment against physician advice, while others demand treatment against physician advice. Nevertheless, health care professionals in Canada are not obliged either to offer or to provide futile care (CMA Policy Summary, 1995; Joint Statement, 1984). Who defines futility is no doubt an issue for future development.

Living wills allow competent persons to indicate their preferences for care before care is actually needed and in anticipation of circumstances where the person might not be able to make decisions. In other words, living will laws enacted in some Canadian provinces enforce the right of persons to direct health care even after they become incompetent. Living wills are also called advance directives, personal directives, representation agreements, health care directives, power of attorney for personal care, mandates, directives, or authorizations (Kerr and Kurtz, 1999). Although living will statutes vary across Canada, most allow one or more substitute decision-makers to be named and allow instructions about health care to be left for those decision-makers as well as for other health care decision-makers such as nurses and physicians. In provinces with a living will law, the instructions in the living will must be followed, providing that the requested action is legal. Thus, living wills can direct that treatment be withheld or withdrawn but cannot ask for euthanasia or assisted suicide. These instructions take precedent over the preferences of family or health care professionals. Even where there is no law, "there is a good chance that the instructions in a living will will be followed" (Kerr and Kurtz, 1999: 19).

Living wills ensure that personal care preferences are carried out if individuals lose the ability to direct their own care. Most, if not all, dying persons lose consciousness near death and so lose the ability to direct their care (Wilson, 1997). Unfortunately, few people actually have a living will. In the United States, for example, less than one-quarter of adults have a living will

(Landry et al., 1997). Even people whose death is imminent often do not have living wills (Heffner et al., 1996; Teno et al., 1997). One study in British Columbia found that only half of people suffering from AIDS had a living will (Osgood, 1994).

Withdrawing or withholding care from the dying should not be confused with euthanasia or assisted suicide. Several legal commissions, as well as the Supreme Court of Canada, have upheld a ban on euthanasia and assisted suicide. In the early 1980s, several law reform commissions recommended against legalizing euthanasia (Curran and Hyg, 1984). Furthermore, in 1994 the Supreme Court of Canada was asked to consider Sue Rodriguez's request for assistance in ending her life. Rodriguez's situation is discussed in more detail in chapter 5. The major point here is that the Supreme Court, in a five to four ruling, upheld the prohibition against assisted suicide for a terminally ill person. Following this ruling, a Senate Committee was set up to study the issue of euthanasia and assisted suicide (Blouin, 1995). The subsequent report of the Senate Committee on Euthanasia and Assisted Suicide (1995) contained a number of recommendations, one of which was that palliative care should become more accessible to dying Canadians. The committee assumed that dying persons would not request euthanasia or assisted suicide if their symptoms were managed so that they were comfortable. It has not been established, however, that access to or experience with palliative care necessarily deters people from asking for assisted suicide or euthanasia.

Voluntary and Non-Voluntary Euthanasia

Despite losing her case, Sue Rodriguez was helped to die at her home in British Columbia. Her death is an example of voluntary euthanasia, or assisted suicide. The circumstances surrounding Rodriguez's death can be contrasted with non-voluntary euthanasia, as illustrated by another controversial Canadian court case. Robert Latimer, a Saskatchewan farmer, was found guilty of murder after he confessed to using carbon monoxide to kill his severely disabled daughter, Tracy, who was mentally incapable of consenting. While some considered his actions to be a "mercy killing"—to save Tracy from further surgery and daily suffering—others felt he did not have the right to make the ultimate decision for his daughter. Yet, even if Tracy had been able to give consent and had done so, Latimer's act of euthanasia would still have been against the law.

Another example of non-voluntary euthanasia involves a physician in Toronto who was found guilty of giving inappropriate medication prescriptions to two people who had AIDS. The prescribed medications were intended to hasten death, with the physician alone making these decisions (Foot, 1997). A perhaps more perplexing case involved Dr. Nancy Morrison, a physician in Halifax, who was charged with first-degree murder for hastening the death of a dying intensive care patient. The patient who was dying of oesophageal cancer after eight months in hospital, had just been granted his pre-stated request to be taken off life support. After his life support was terminated, he did not die, and instead continued to struggle to breathe. Dr. Morrison is thought to have ended his life a number of hours later with an intravenous injection. The charges against her were later withdrawn, but only after a considerable amount of time and effort to evaluate the evidence and the context of the case (Hamilton, 1997; Robb, 1998).

It is not known how often assisted suicide or euthanasia occurs in Canada. Some data are available for Holland where 3 per cent of deaths were found to result from euthanasia (Van der Maas et al., 1996). The Northern Territory of Australia legalized euthanasia between July 1996 and March 1997, during which time four persons were euthanized (Kissane et al., 1998). In the first year following the legalization of euthanasia in the state of Oregon in February 1997, fifteen people died of lethal prescriptions (Chin et al., 1999). In June 1990, Dr. Jack Kevorkian helped Janet Adkins, a fifty-four-year-old Portland music teacher and Alzheimer's patient, die (Webb, 1997). During the 1990s, Dr. Kevorkian helped many more patients to die by assisted suicide, with each person voluntarily taking his or her own life, using the aids provided by Dr. Kevorkian. This method protected Dr. Kevorkian from conviction until he deliberately ended the life of a disabled person who was not able to carry out his own suicide. Dr. Kevorkian was subsequently convicted of murder.

In summary, in Canada, a competent person can request that life support be withheld or withdrawn, even if this hastens death. Similarly, a dying person who has become incompetent may have expressed his or her wishes in a written advance care directive, which can then justify the withholding or withdrawing of treatment. Nevertheless, a person cannot ask any other person for active euthanasia or assisted suicide, both of which are illegal in Canada.

THE FUNERAL INDUSTRY

The final stage of the dying process is an important time when most families want to be together with the dying family member. Following death, families typically gather to demonstrate respect for the deceased person and to provide support to each other.[10] Funeral and memorial services do much to assist those who grieve. They provide an opportunity to reflect upon the life of the person who has died and to publicly and collectively acknowledge the person's death.

One of the most profound changes in the death industry is that more cremations are taking place. Cremation uses a very hot fire to reduce the body and usually the coffin to only a few kilograms of ash (Colman, 1997). In 1982, only 23 per cent of bodies in Canada were cremated; by 1992, this figure had risen to 36 per cent (Nault and Ford, 1994). The incidence of cremations varied greatly across Canada in the early 1990s, ranging from lows of 3 per cent and 4 per cent in Newfoundland and Prince Edward Island, respectively, to a high of 68 per cent in British Columbia (Nault and Ford, 1994). Cremations have long been performed by certain religious or cultural groups. In contrast, other religious and cultural groups consider cremation to be disrespectful to the deceased person (Kerr and Kurtz, 1999). At present, some people choose cremation because they are disturbed by the thought of the body decaying in the ground after burial (Flynn, 1993). Cremation may also be chosen as a consequence of media reports of full and crowded cemeteries and of cemetery vandalism.

Cremations are becoming more common in Canada for a variety of practical reasons. One very significant reason is reduced cost. The average funeral in Canada costs $5,000 (Kerr and Kurtz, 1999). There are charges for every service received, including transporting the body, preparing the body for burial, the casket in which the body is buried, the burial (cemetery) plot or tomb (crypt) in a mausoleum, and the funeral service. Cremations and memorial services typically cost less than half what a funeral costs (Flynn, 1993).[11]

Cremation allows for flexibility. Funerals usually take place soon after death—in some cases within one day, but most often within three or four days. Families typically are widely dispersed geographically, and gathering family members together quickly for a funeral can be difficult. Not only is the cost of travel on short notice very high (despite special travel discounts, such as a reduction on airline tickets for close family members flying to a funeral), but childcare may have to be arranged, leaves of absence from work or study obtained, and many other personal circumstances attended to during the time of bereavement. Cremation allows for flexibility, as the urn containing the ashes of the deceased person can be easily transported to any location. A memorial service can thus take place at any location, and any time, convenient to the family (Flynn, 1993). There is less urgency, as well, in taking the ashes to their final resting place or in scattering the remains, in comparison to a body, which must either be buried within a few days of death, kept "on ice" until a later burial, or embalmed.[12]

The funeral industry itself is an important social institution. The funeral or death industry provides many persons with an income through employment or investment. Caskets and urns have to be made; bodies need to be prepared for embalming, burial, or cremation; funeral parlours and crematoria have to be built and kept in good repair; and cemeteries and mausoleums have to be developed and maintained. In addition, other businesses benefit, as notices of death are usually published, flowers sent, donations to charities made, and travel undertaken to attend the funeral or memorial service. Flynn (1993) considers this industry to be virtually recession proof.

It should not be surprising that the death industry in Canada is a large, highly profitable business. In North America, approximately nine or ten billion dollars a year were grossed in the early 1990s by businesses that provided death-related services (Flynn, 1993). One of the most noteworthy facts about the death industry is that the local, family-owned funeral home was largely replaced during the 1980s and 1990s by huge corporations with billions of dollars in assets (Flynn, 1993; Kennedy and Milner, 1999). Today, a small number of large corporations supply most of the North American "death market." Service Corporation International (SCI), located in Houston, Texas, is the largest. In the early 1990s, SCI had 758 funeral homes and 184 cemeteries/crematoria internationally (Flynn, 1993).

Until recently, Loewen Group Inc, based in British Columbia, was Canada's largest funeral company and the second largest funeral business conglomerate world wide (Flynn, 1993). Created in 1985, the company was worth $US4.3 billion by the fall of 1996 (Hasselback et al., 1999). By 1998, their holdings included 1,172 funeral homes and 628 cemeteries in North America and Britain (Kennedy and Milner, 1999; Waldie and Kennedy, 1999). A year later, however, Loewen filed for bankruptcy protection. Too rapid expansion was blamed for their bankruptcy. Another factor may have been competition from firms that had begun to sell "wholesale" caskets and "no-frills" funeral services, thereby reducing demand for expensive, full-service burial (Bourette and Milner, 1999; Waldie and Kennedy, 1999).

Despite Loewen's demise, high prices, together with effective marketing to promote services, have made the death industry profitable. Flynn (1993) has expressed concern with the ethics of industry: "the funeral industry has learned to use religious customs against the consumer for financial exploitation. How else does one explain the fast-paced rise in profit for an industry that used to be service based and is now profit driven?... Funeral practitioners have failed miserably to provide an open and honest line of communication to customers so they can make a knowledgeable decision on a purchase. All these factors create an industry in which a clientele is rushing out to make major purchases without adequate knowledge and very little experience—a salesperson's dream" (6-7).

According to Flynn, "one-stop shopping," whereby families use one service provider to make all funeral arrangements, coupled with an increased range of services have led to spiralling funeral costs. The amount of disposable income available to the family impacts which ceremonies are held and which customs are followed (Flynn, 1993). In a time of intense difficulty and pressure, families must choose between a traditional, full-service funeral or an "alternate" funeral for which there is no standard format. In addition, families must choose how elaborate the service and the casket or urn will be. The latter is a concern since there is a 100 to 400 per cent mark-up on these items (Flynn, 1993). Some other common decisions that need to be made include: whether to have a closed or open coffin; whether to permit visitation or calling at the funeral home to see the body; whether to hold a funeral with the casket present or hold a memorial service at a later time; and also whether the body will be buried, cremated, or entombed in a mausoleum (Flynn, 1993). Given all these considerations, it is prudent to pre-plan a funeral to lower costs and ensure that important rituals and customs are upheld (Flynn, 1993). Various associations assist dying persons and their families in planning the funeral, in preparing for death, and in times of bereavement (see Appendix).

In summary, the funeral industry has become big business, offering a wide range of services to the family of the deceased. Funeral arrangements can be made in advance and prepaid. When this has not been done, the family of the deceased must make a large number of decisions quickly at a time when decision-making tends to be difficult. In such circumstances, the bereaved may pay more than they need to or purchase more services than they can afford. Cremation has become more common in recent decades, given that it tends to cost less than burial and may be becoming more culturally acceptable.

SUMMARY

While dying and death typically take place in the context of the family and the health care system, the course of dying and death is also shaped by religious, legal, and economic considerations. As social institutions have changed over time, so also have dying and death changed. In particular, the primary location of dying and death has shifted from the home to the hospital, and the primary caregivers for the dying have shifted from family to health care professionals. The hospitalization and professionalization of dying is characterized by attempts to cure illness, prolong life, and deny death. More recently, palliative care has recognized the limits of medicine and emphasizes the acceptance and management of the dying process. At the same time, there may be a trend towards moving dying and death back to the home and family, who once again may become the primary caregivers, functioning with the assistance of health care professionals, in providing home care. Other social changes such as secularization, mean that religion tends to play a lesser role in dying and death than in the past. Legal developments have legitimized the advance care directive, or living will, and, elsewhere in the world, have begun to legitimize active euthanasia and assisted suicide. The funeral has moved from the home, church, and community to the profit-driven funeral industry, where death processing has been professionalized, bureaucratized, and corporatized. These social changes have implications for the meaning of dying and death for both individuals and society as a whole.

Notes

1. This practice could have implications for an open-casket funeral, but it has other more important implications. As a result of organ donation, family members may actively search for news of successful heart or other transplants. This was the case in Alberta recently, as a grieving mother reported to the media that she was grateful her son's heart had saved a young woman in desperate need of a heart transplant. Although personal information identifying donors and recipients is never exchanged by the hospital or health care professionals, this does not stop grieving families from hoping that premature deaths were not in vain, and that another person may live through their "gift of life."

2. These joint guidelines were revised in 1995 (CMA Policy Summary, 1995).

3. For residents in continuing-care facilities, long lengths of stay also usually allow relationships to develop between health care workers and residents (Wells, 1990). In some cases, relationships between health care workers and families develop, especially when long-term care residents are unable to communicate well. Dementia, conditions that impair speech and cognition, and other serious health problems are common among long-term care residents (Burke et al., 1997; Hill et al., 1996; Lindsay, 1999; Ostbye and Crosse, 1994). In other cases, health care workers develop a relationship with the resident and not the family, as the family does not live nearby or does not visit frequently (Rutman, 1992). In still other cases, no relationships develop as the length of stay is short due to death or transfer of the resident to another health care facility.

4. Some long-term care facilities in Canada have recently enacted a blanket no-CPR policy. In these facilities, CPR is not available to any resident (Kane and Burns, 1997; Kerr and Kurtz, 1999). This no-CPR policy may have arisen from the numerous studies that indicate a low success rate with CPR (Awoke et al., 1992; Gordon and Cheung, 1993; Kerr and Kurtz, 1999). Furthermore, CPR may not prevent damage to the brain and other tissues (Gordon and Cheung, 1993; Kerr and Kurtz, 1999). Other long-term care facilities have developed a policy that CPR will be performed only on certain residents if those residents want CPR and are likely to benefit from it (Kane and Burns, 1997; Kerr and Kurtz, 1999).

5. If the palliative care movement in Canada had been initiated in free-standing community centres as it was in the United States, then it is more likely that the term "hospice" would be used in Canada to describe this type of care. Hospices became a growth industry in the United States following their initiation in 1971 (Lack, 1978; McCann, 1988; Mor and Masterson-Allen, 1987), and the word "hospice" was copyrighted to protect the integrity of the concept. In

many ways, hospice and palliative care are the same, as both focus on meeting the broad-based needs of dying persons and their families. However, a ruling that a terminal illness is one that will result in death in six months or less has significant funding implications for American hospices and dying Americans (Webb, 1997).

6. Most hospital-based palliative care programs in Canada have provided care almost exclusively to people dying of cancer (Bruera et al., 1990), who often present many symptom-management challenges.

7. It is notable that the largest study of end-of-life care in the United States, which ended in 1995, found of all conscious patients, half were in pain some or all of the time (Webb, 1997). Other investigations have found that pain is not adequately addressed (Groft, 1992). In short, the philosophy of palliative care has not yet been adequately implemented.

8. Other unnecessary fears include concern that the dying person might become too sedated or addicted (Kerr and Kurtz, 1999).

9. Similarly, in the United States in 1982, the President's Commission for the Study of Ethical Problems in Medicine and Biomedical and Behavioral Research indicated that health care decisions ultimately rest with competent patients.

10. Entire communities may recognize the death of certain persons. Generally, communities note the passing of a prominent public figure, but other less prominent persons may also be mourned communally. For instance, the funeral of an abandoned infant, having captured the attention of an entire community, may be attended by a considerable number of persons.

11. Donating a body to science is another cost-saving option, although the family may have to pay to have the body transported (Kerr and Kurtz, 1999).

12. Embalming is a semi-surgical process which replaces body fluids with liquid chemicals (such as formaldehyde and methyl or wood alcohol) to disinfect and preserve the body. Embalming is not required unless the body is to be shipped across national or international borders or transported by public carrier (Flynn, 1993; Kerr and Kurtz, 1999). Bodies that have been embalmed and then buried have been exhumed twenty years later, and found relatively unchanged.

Chapter 4
Dying and Death in the Context of Canadian Culture

This chapter explores cultural constructions of the meaning of dying and death and the resulting social responses to dying and death in Canada. Cultural constructions are evident in various forms including literature, television, everyday language, and folklore, as well as in the processes of medicalization, professionalization, and bureaucratization. Responses to dying and death include making sense of death, distinguishing between different types of death, stigmatizing dying and death, and observing social rituals accompanying death. Finally, there are ethnic variations in these cultural constructions and social responses.

It has been argued that Canadian culture, along with that of other western societies, became a death-denying culture in the twentieth century (Becker, 1973; Ariès, 1974 and 1981). Nevertheless, the reality of dying and death cannot be completely denied—dying and death do come to each in turn. In a death-denying culture, reactions to dying and death vacillate between denial and awareness, fear and fascination (Joseph, 1994: 1), detachment and morbid obsession. Fascination with death is evident in cultural forms such as literature and television. Several notable Canadian authors, for example, have explored the processes of dying and the mysteries of death.

LITERATURE

Margaret Laurence published *The Stone Angel* in 1964. The book begins with ninety-year-old Hagar Shipley's reminiscences of the stone angel standing over her mother's grave in the cemetery above the fictional town of Manawaka, Manitoba. Manawaka was patterned after Neepawa, Manitoba, where Laurence was born. Through Hagar's memories, descriptions, and reflections, the reader is given a series of impressions about attitudes towards dying and death in Canada in the late nineteenth and twentieth centuries.

Hagar remembers the stone angel, other commemorative stonework, and the inscriptions in the cemetery. She remembers how strange and even amusing these things could be to a young girl. As an old woman, she remembers lives lived and largely forgotten, and observes the tendency for weeds to overgrow the cemetery, a metaphor for the tendency of time to obscure the memories of the dead.

Hagar remembers when she, as a young girl, sneaked into Simmons's Funeral Parlour with some other children to look at Hannah Pearl's pale stillborn baby in its white satin box. Told by her brother Matt that Mr. Simmons, the owner of the funeral parlour, drank embalming fluid, Hagar avoided the man, thinking of him as a ghoul.

Throughout the novel, Hagar mentions deceased ancestors—including her dead mother, who died when Hagar was born. The death from consumption (tuberculosis) of the mother of one of her schoolmates is also recalled. Hagar tells of her teenage brother, four years her senior, who caught pneumonia and died in an upstairs bedroom while asking for his mother, who had died when he was a young child.

Hagar recalls and reflects on the death of non-humans as well. She remembers the pathetic death of a fighting cock and the gruesome euthanization of some newborn chicks. As she reflects on her youthful emotions, she wonders why she could not then kill the chicks to end their misery nor comfort her dying brother. In her youth, she recoiled and distanced herself from dying and death, both human and non-human.

Even the lily of the valley, either as a flower or as the name for the eau de cologne she wears, reminds Hagar of death. As she reflects on old age, Hagar's memories often focus on death, as if past deaths are a harbinger of her own. When the minister asks Hagar if she has many friends, she observes that most of them are dead. Her parents are also long dead, as are her two brothers. Her husband and one of her two sons are dead as well. Hagar knows that her own death is near. She also knows that others, her son and daughter-in-law, her doctor and the nursing staff in the hospital where she spends her final days, are waiting, anticipating, expecting her demise. Though nobody speaks directly to Hagar of her impending death she guesses the meaning of their whispered conversations.

Laurence portrays death as both strange and familiar. While death is common and inevitable, it is also mysterious and repulsive. Laurence portrays death as something to be avoided and resisted as much as possible through cognitive, emotional, and behavioural distancing and denial. Nevertheless, she also portrays death as intimately personal and inevitable. Finally, Laurence describes the drama of mutual pretence (Glaser and Strauss, 1965) that has often accompanied dying. In this drama, everybody involved knows that death is imminent and yet nobody speaks openly or directly of dying and death. The dying person herself is discouraged from speaking of her own dying and imminent death.

W. O. Mitchell also described death in the context of early twentieth-century prairie culture. His book *Who Has Seen the Wind*, which was published in 1947, begins with a quote from Psalms: "As for man, his days are as grass: as a flower of the field, so he flourisheth. For the wind passeth over it, and it is gone; and the place thereof shall know it no more." Mitchell then provided the reader with an explanation of the meaning of the story he is about to tell. The wind he says, is a symbol of God, and the story to be told is about the mysteries of the cycle of life from birth to death.

Mitchell's classic tells the story of young Brian O'Connal, growing up in a small town in Saskatchewan in the 1930s. Brian's family consists of his mother, father, grandmother, and a baby brother. The story begins when Brian is four years of age. His baby brother is very sick and it is feared that he will die. While the baby recovers, his near death sets an ominous tone for the book. Mitchell seems to be telling the reader that life begins and continues in the shadow of death; the possibility of death at any moment and its ultimate inevitability raise fundamental questions about the meaning of life.

A baby pigeon that Brian brings home is not as lucky as Brian's brother. When the pigeon dies, it is Brian's first experience with the demise of a being who had meant something to him. Several years later, when Brian is about eight years of age, his beloved dog is run over by a horse-drawn wagon. Brian sadly buries his dog under the prairie sod and grieves.

As the story unfolds, Brian approaches ten years of age. His grandmother is now eighty years old and knows her death is near. At the same time, Brian's father gets sick and becomes jaundiced. Once again the ominous tone moves from background to foreground, and the reader anxiously wonders who will live and who will die. In the summer of Brian's tenth year, his father dies.

He is laid out in a coffin at home in the living room with blinds drawn against the light. Friends and neighbours come by with flowers, tears, and sympathy, everyone observing that the deceased was a fine man. Brian's mother is quiet, stunned; his grandmother sits, looking frail.

The minister conducts the funeral in the living room. Afterwards, Brian is sad, filled with longing, but he doesn't know what to do. He wants to cry because he feels it is the right thing to do. But, although he loved his dad, the tears are not there. He goes out to the prairie. As he thinks in his ten-year-old way of the endless cycle of the seasons, the endless cycle of birth and death, he realizes that his father is gone forever. He thinks of the irony that, although people are forever being born, at death the individual is forever gone. When he thinks of his mother grieving the loss of her husband, he cries, but his tears are for the living as much as for the dead.

Following the funeral, Brian thinks often of his father and frequently dreams that he is still alive. As time passes, Brian feels guilty that he thinks of his father less often. The family visits the cemetery frequently, and during these visits Brian tries to think of his father. He grows closer to his mother, brother, and grandmother.

The story ends with the death of Brian's grandmother. Brian has reached the age of twelve and his grandmother has lived eighty-two years. Her death is not as shocking as the death of Brian's father. Brian's father had died prematurely, in the prime of his life—his death was unexpected, shocking, tragic. The grandmother's death is expected, legitimate, bittersweet. Her long life and the frailty preceding her death justify her passing. In her own words, her time had come, writes W.O. Mitchell (288).

The story of Brian's childhood is punctuated with accounts of death and youthful attempts to make sense of life and death. Brian remembers the deaths of the baby pigeon, a gopher, his dog, a two-headed calf, his father, and his grandmother. He recalls the stench of a rotting cow. He reflects on his dead ancestors from whom his own life has come. Brian will continue to live, hunger, love, and wonder about the sense of it all.

Who Has Seen the Wind, explores the mysteries of life and death. The book suggests that death is omnipresent and yet ominous. It is mysterious, unwelcome, disturbing, distressing, and inevitable. All who live die: this observation is inescapable and yet hard to accept and even harder to understand. Mitchell suggests that if answers are to be found, they are ethereal, like the wind.

Society has its cultural and ritual ways of dealing with death. These include churches, theology, philosophy, funerals and flowers, cemeteries and gravestone epitaphs, and sympathetic, if trite, sentiments expressed to the bereaved. Mitchell describes all of these things. In the end, though, the novelist suggests that individuals must come to terms with life and death on their own, in their own way, and in their own time.

Both novels—Laurence's *The Stone Angel* and Mitchell's *Who Has Seen the Wind*—are about the culture and experience of life and death in small-town and rural settings in the first half of the twentieth century. Urban life in the second half of the twentieth century and in the early twenty-first century continues to reflect many of these earlier cultural beliefs, attitudes, and practices.

LANGUAGE

The program for the funeral service for a colleague who recently died says "In Loving Memory Of" and then states his name. Under the heading "Born," his date and place of birth are listed. Under the heading "Passed Away," the date when and the place where he passed away are listed. The word "death" does not appear in the program. It is as if people are born, but do not die. People simply pass away. Nor was this colleague buried. According to the program, the funeral service was followed by an "interment," not a burial.

Death cannot be completely denied, even in an allegedly death-denying culture, although convention can distance us from death. While one could speak directly using terms such as dying, dead, death, and burial, the conventional language of death is often indirect and euphemistic. Speaking directly seems too harsh, too cold, even cruel. The direct language refers to a harsh reality, a reality that is known, but one that people prefer to soften rather than to acknowledge explicitly.

According to Webster's dictionary, a euphemism refers to "the use of a word or phrase that is less expressive or direct but considered less distasteful, less offensive…than another." In Canadian culture, common practice indicates that it is less distasteful and less offensive to use euphemisms than to speak directly of death and related topics. Williamson et al. (1980: 434–5) present an extensive list of euphemisms for dying, death, and burial. The dead person is often referred to as the departed or the deceased; the coffin is often called the casket. When a person dies, it may be said that the deceased has laid their burden down, gone to a well-earned rest, been called home, passed on, passed over, or gone to heaven. Instead of saying the person has been buried, it might be said that the person was laid to rest. The corpse may be referred to as the body or the remains; an impersonal "the" is used instead of the personal pronoun "his" or "her." This depersonalization of the dead body disassociates the memory of the living from the evidence of death.

While the euphemisms for death tend to be tasteful, inoffensive, and sentimental, and serve to soften a harsh reality, there are other euphemisms that are, at best, humorous and, at worst, vulgar. While euphemisms can obscure the starkness of an uncomfortable reality, humour presents an alternative way of dealing with what makes us uncomfortable. Making light of something that terrifies us is one way of whistling in the dark, of convincing ourselves that we can manage our fears. Humorous terms for death include bit the dust, kicked the bucket, pushing up daisies, goose is cooked, croaked, and so on. Other slang include "cold meat" for corpse, "bone box" for coffin, "bone orchard" or "marble city" for cemetery, and "planted" or "deep sixed" for buried. In summary, by either distancing from, or making light of, death various euphemisms facilitate coping with the strong emotions that tend to accompany death.

FOLKLORE AND POPULAR CULTURE

Folklore embodies beliefs, customs, myths, legends, folk tales, stories, rumours, jokes, and sayings that are anonymously produced, collectively shared, and communicated verbally in both oral and written forms (Clifton, 1991). The following discussion examines the folklore of death in contemporary Canadian society. Note that folklore tends to reflect popular culture. As such, some may judge the following stories and jokes to be quite tasteless. Cultural constructions regarding death range from sensitive to insensitive, respectful to disrespectful, and tasteful to tasteless.

The following story has apparently been circulating on the Internet. Its origins are unknown.

A few years ago in California there was a raging brush fire. Once the fire was extinguished, the firefighters began the process of clean-up. In the middle of where the fire had been burning, they found a dead man wearing a scuba tank and wet suit. At first the firefighters were baffled as to why a man would be out in the middle of the countryside wearing full scuba gear. Upon further examination, it was determined that the man died from impact with the ground and not the fire. As best anyone can determine, this man was scuba diving off the coast of California and was accidentally picked up by one of the fire-fighting aircraft when it was refilling its water tanks offshore.

Not only are the origins of this story unknown, but there are several versions and it is not known if there is any truth to any of the accounts. Stories that are *not* true but nevertheless circulate widely and are told as if they are true are called "urban legends" (Kendall et al., 2000: 648–9). Urban legends usually deal with topics that are particularly sensational from a culture's point of view, such as death or the threat of death. While the tale told above is ironic and amusing, folklore such as this also has the potential to define and instruct. If there is a message in this story, it is that death may come unbidden, unexpected, like a macabre prank played on an unsuspecting victim.

The above story illustrates a fatalistic notion that is common in western oral culture, namely that death will find you "when your number is up." Another story concerns a middle-aged man whose car had been blown off the road and into a river during a windstorm. As the car sank beneath the water, the man broke a window, climbed out, and swam to shore, where a tree blew over and killed him. If there is a message in this story, it is that death cannot be avoided "when your time is up."

The following two urban legends were heard in Winnipeg several decades ago. Both stories concerned medical students enrolled in the University of Manitoba's medical school, and both were told by persons who swore they were true. According to the first story, some of the students from the medical school had taken an arm severed from a cadaver that they were dissecting in the course of their studies. They dressed the arm in a shirt sleeve, pasted a dollar bill to the hand, and boarded a bus. In those days, bus drivers gave change for a dollar bill (and there were still dollar bills), but as the bus driver reached out to take the money, he pulled the whole arm off and had a heart attack and died on the spot.

It is very unlikely that this prank ever actually took place. Indeed, it appears to be one of a number of similar stories that have circulated widely and been described as "cadaver stories" (Hafferty, 1988). If there is a culturally mediated discomfort with the topic of death, there is a virtual taboo against contact with dead bodies. Medical students must not only break this taboo, they must learn to control their emotional revulsion about doing so. Cadaver stories are a vehicle by which medical students can acknowledge the problem of death and at the same time claim to have transcended their difficulties with death. In these stories, the students are usually portrayed as pranksters in control of their fears of death, while the victims of the pranks are portrayed as lay persons who are shocked and horrified by death. The underlying message is that death is horrifying, although exceptional people such as doctors can and must learn to overcome, or at least manage, their horror.

The next urban legend contains a twist on the usual cadaver story. A medical student had been dissecting a corpse, starting at its feet. The body was covered with a sheet, and each part was uncovered in turn. Finally, the head was uncovered, and the student realized that he had been dissecting his recently deceased father.

In the first story about medical students, the students showed their emotional control by allegedly playing pranks on people who are easily shocked by death. In the second story, fate plays a trick on the medical student, reaffirming the horror of death. Although medical students can gain some control through strategies such as emotional distancing and depersonalization, the horror is still there and can overtake a person suddenly. The message of this story is that death is horrible and there is no escaping that horror, especially when death takes a person you love.

Legends, new and old, centring around death, are widespread in western folklore. Consider, for example, ghost stories and tales of haunted houses. Canada has its own deathly legends. The South Nahanni River in the south west corner of the Northwest Territories is a place of such legend. The back cover of *Dangerous River,* R. M. Patterson's account of his time on the Nahanni says, "The Nahanni River follows its treacherous course between Yukon Territory and the mighty Mackenzie River. One section is dominated by Deadmen Valley, so-called because of the hair-raising legends about the fate of those brave enough to enter—and unfortunate enough never to return."

In 1927, Patterson made his way by canoe from Alberta north to the Nahanni. He was told by many whom he met on his way about canyons with sheer walls thousands of feet high and treacherous currents. He was told that not many people went into that country and came back to tell about it.

> There was gold in there somewhere… Deadmen Valley was tucked away in there some place… A valley between two canyons where the McLeods were murdered for their gold in 1906. No man ever knew what happened

to them, but they were found—at least their skeletons were—tied to trees, with the heads missing… And enough men had disappeared in there since then that it was considered best by men of sense to leave the Nahanni country alone. (Patterson, 1989: 6)

Patterson was also told of the wild Mountain Men—Indians who "lorded it over the wild uplands of the Yukon Mackenzie divide and made short work of any man, white or Indian, who ventured into their country" (7). Whether the alleged murderers were the mysterious Mountain Men or not, story after story told of the gruesome end that so many had come to in the Nahanni country.

In 1946 stories of the "Headless Valley,"—that is, Deadmen Valley—appeared in the *Toronto Star* and *Chicago Tribune*. According to Hartling (1993: 94), the stories were "a blockbuster. Nahanni became synonymous with unearthly phenomena. Stories sprang up in support of the reputation: tales of hidden tropical forests, murder, head hunters, hot springs, canyons, waterfalls, and gold. Much of the reputation was based on fantasy, but an eager readership ate it up."

A year later, Pierre Berton, then a young reporter for the *Vancouver Sun*, led an expedition into the Nahanni. His reports fanned a national interest in the old legends. These stories resonate even today in the place names of the Nahanni: Deadmen Valley, the Headless (mountain) Range, the Funeral (mountain) Range, Sunblood Mountain, Broken Skull River, Hell's Gate, Hell Roaring Creek, and Headless Creek. In 1970, Prime Minister Pierre Elliott Trudeau visited the Nahanni and in 1971 it became a national park (Hartling, 1993: 99).

The stories of the Nahanni are part of Canadian folklore. They reflect the fear and fascination that people have with death. These stories also foster that very fear and fascination. While death for ourselves and our loved ones is usually unwelcome, bitter, and tragic, and while we often distance ourselves from the possibility or actuality of such death, death in general remains a topic of great interest. Finally, these stories serve as cautionary tales warning people to be careful lest tragedy befall them.

The news media report daily in great detail about death by crime, accident, disaster, and war. Visual images of death are frequent on television, in the newspapers, and in news magazines. Popular culture such as television programming, movies, and novels (consider the success of horror-story writer Stephen King) regularly deal with death. It is ironic that, in an allegedly death-denying culture, contemporary television programming is often preoccupied with dying and death. Indeed, some prime-time dramatic series are centred on health care professionals and their struggles to save the lives of the sick or injured; several others are concerned with law enforcement officers and legal professionals who seek to bring justice to unjust death.

Perhaps dying and death make good dramatic fare because of the individual and collective fear they inspire. Dying and death get our attention and can provoke deep concern and great interest. While television often captivates viewers by capitalizing on fears of death, such programming tends to offer happy endings. In the hospital dramas, dying and death are usually managed successfully, or at least humanely, and in the crime dramas, the perpetrators of unjust deaths are typically brought to justice. In short, television programming raises fears of dying and death and then calms them. The message is that, despite the chaos of illness, accident, and crime, dying and death are manageable in a world that is, in the end, patterned and purposeful.

THE SECULARIZATION, PROFESSIONALIZATION, MEDICALIZATION, AND BUREAUCRATIZATION OF DYING AND DEATH

As discussed in chapter 3, religion has played an important role historically in making death meaningful and providing guidelines for dying persons, for their family and community, and for the management of the dead body. Increasingly, however, Canada is a secularized society—that is, the importance of religion as a central social institution has declined. Church and state are separated, and weekly attendance at church has declined substantially, especially since the mid-twentieth century. Increasingly, death is defined by secular rather than religious elements of society and culture. Doctors, nurses, philosophers, ethicists, psychologists, and lawyers, for example, have tended to replace theologians as definers of the meaning of death. Similarly, officials such as medical examiners, morgue attendants, and funeral-home directors supplement or replace religious officials such as priests, ministers, pastors, and rabbis.

In addition to the church, the family and the community used to play major roles in assisting the dying, managing the dead body, and supporting the bereaved. However, during the twentieth century, dying, death, and even grieving came to be managed increasingly by professionals such as doctors and nurses, medical examiners and coroners, funeral directors, and grief workers such as psychologists and social workers. Control of dying, death, and grieving shifted from persons one knew to strangers, and from lay persons to professionals, particularly medical professionals. Furthermore, medical professionals tended to define dying, death, and grieving as medical problems to be solved by medical therapeutic intervention. They fought dying with high technology, they defined death in medical terms, and recommended the management of grieving through counselling and prescription drugs. Dying and death were removed from the context of normal life and placed instead in the context of medical institutions to be managed by medical professionals.

Cultural rules and practices develop to govern the process of dying and the individual and collective responses to death. In bureaucratic settings, these rules about dying and death are formally defined (Marshall, 1986). As noted in chapter 2, dying and death typically take place in the hospital, an elaborate bureaucracy with diverse officials and formal rules. Control over dying persons is assumed by the bureaucracy, although the requirement for voluntary and informed consent leaves the dying person with some degree of control. Death is also bureaucratized. The dead body is certified and managed by various functionaries who work in the hospital, in the medical examiner's office, and in the funeral-home industry. These functionaries perform their services according to professional and governmental rules. Bureaucratization shifts control over dying and death away from the dying person and the family and community, and towards officials who are strangers and who operate according to the bureaucratic culture rather than the individual's relevant subculture.

Kaufert and O'Neil (1991) have reported on interactions between health care professionals and Native Canadians (Cree, Ojibway, and Inuit) in Winnipeg hospitals. In the hospital, health care professionals tend to take control of the dying patient. They impose predominantly Euro-Canadian, professional, and bureaucratic rules not only on the treatment of the dying person but also on the involvement of that person's family and friends. In addition, health care professionals apply bureaucratic rules regarding the processing of the body of the deceased. The Native community tends to find these rules inappropriate and inconsistent with their own cultural guidelines. Similarly, the health care workers tend to find Native cultural norms equally inappropriate. In short, neither group understands or accepts the other (see Stephenson, [1992] for a similar discussion involving Hutterites). This impasse is alleviated by Native interpreters, who serve as language translators, cultural informants and mediators, and patient and community advocates.

Marshall (1986: 133; see also Marshall, 1980: 159; Frank, 1991) extends this argument to all Canadians. He argues that with the "bureaucratization of death and dying through such institutions as hospital death and the funeral industry," the family and community of dying persons and of the deceased have become marginal spectators of processes in which they have traditionally played central roles. Nevertheless, the grief experienced by the bereaved is not likely lessened by this marginalization, and indeed may be intensified.

Making Sense of Death

Marshall (1986: 129; 1980) observes that humans construct meanings to make sense of the world and to facilitate functioning in the world. People everywhere have tried to make sense of death. While an individual's search for meaning is a highly personal endeavour, it is facilitated by systems of meaning that exist separate from the individual. These meaning systems are components of culture. Through processes of socialization cultural meaning systems are often internalized by the individual without critical reflection. For example, a person may be raised with a particular religious belief that provides the individual with answers to questions of meaning, in particular, the meaning of life and death. Systems of meaning are also found outside religion, in philosophy, psychology, schools of thought regarding therapeutic grief counselling, and so on.

Yet, having a culturally based meaning system is no guarantee that death will be easily accepted. An individual may find that the circumstances of a particular death undermine their system of meaning. In such circumstances, the individual is suddenly forced to search for meaning and to make sense of the incomprehensible. If systems of meaning are socially constructed, they can be deconstructed. Sometimes, events in life do just this. Death, in particular, can be very destabilizing.

In contemporary Canadian culture, death is typically seen as acceptable if it comes at the end of a long life and ends a period of deterioration. Other deaths are not so easily accepted. Deaths by murder, suicide, and accident are typically seen as tragic and senseless, especially when these deaths are "premature." Braun (1992: 80-89) discusses the commonly shared beliefs, values, assumptions, and rules that make the death of a child problematic. She makes a number of observations: contemporary western culture places a high intrinsic value on children; children may provide meaning and purpose for their parents' lives; there is an expectation that life will be long and good and that death will come only in old age; there is a belief that if life is lived responsibly and correctly, then things will turn out well; and, finally, in a death-denying society, the death of a child is a taboo topic, unthinkable, obscene, and unacknowledged. In a cultural context such as this, parents will tend to lack a meaning structure through which they can make sense of the death of their child.

Furthermore, the death of a child may threaten any meaning structures that the parents do have. The death of a child may undermine the parent's faith in God. Parents who have believed all of their lives might find themselves asking: "If there is a God, and if God is good and all powerful, then why is our baby dead?" While human beings crave and create systems of meaning, these constructions can be fragile. In the face of death, most people find themselves searching for meaning. Some find meaning in the cultural constructions of their upbringing while others find themselves separated from their cultural moorings.

Different Types of Death

Death is not simply a biological event. Death is also a social and cultural phenomenon. Indeed, from social and cultural points of view, there are different types of death. The most obvious type of death is "biological death," which is the death of the body. The death of the body is accompanied by "personal death"—that is, the death of the person. However, while the dead body decays, the dead person can seem to live on. The deceased person may live on in the memories of survivors and may be believed to live on as a spirit or soul in a "life after death."

There are other types of death that may come to those who are not biologically dead. Sudnow (1967) wrote of persons who were treated as if they were physically dead when they were still alive: he called this "social death." Years ago, following a disaster at a coal mine in Nova Scotia, twelve men were trapped underground for six and a half days, and another six men were trapped for eight and a half days. Lucas (1968) records the following:

> On the fifth day a high-ranking official of the mining company publicly announced that there could be little hope that any man remained alive. The trapped miners although physiologically alive were socially dead. The wife of one of the trapped miners had ordered a coffin for her husband, had bought mourning clothes and prepared the house for his funeral. After rescue, the miner's comments on his social death were: "Well when I came home they talked about they had my casket ready, and then the wife she got sympathy cards, and when you think about all that it hurts you. [They] had you dead when you wasn't dead, you know." (2-3).

Other examples of people who are likely to be treated as socially dead include persons who are comatose, in a persistent vegetative state, institutionalized, frail, or socially derelict. The comatose can also be said to have experienced "psychological death" in that they lack consciousness (Doka, 1995). Doka also writes of "psychosocial death," in which a person is significantly changed so that they no longer seem to be the person they once were. Examples of psychosocial death include mental illness, trauma to the brain through head injury or stroke, organic brain diseases such as Alzheimer's, drug or alcohol addiction, religious conversion, and even growing up. (I found myself grieving when my son was suddenly, so it seemed, a young man and no longer the little boy that I had loved so dearly. - HN) Finally, relationships are also said to die, as when a marriage ends in divorce, or children are given up for adoption or taken into foster care.

Legal death is yet another type of death. A person who is declared legally dead may or may not be biologically dead. In wartime, persons missing in action may never be proven to be deceased but may be presumed to be so and declared legally dead (Aiken, 1991:4–5). Such declaration allows for the settlement of the missing person's property and terminates that person's legal relationships. A declaration of legal death ends a marriage relationship and makes remarriage possible for the surviving spouse.

Doka (1995) argues that cultural definitions and rules recognize some deaths as legitimate while other deaths are "disenfranchised." The biological death of a close family member such as a parent, grandparent, child, or sibling is typically recognized as legitimate, and the bereaved are offered social support such as time off work, flowers and cards, and attendance at the funeral service. The bereaved are allowed to grieve because the death is perceived as a legitimate death. The biological deaths of more distant relatives such as uncles, aunts, or cousins tend to receive less legitimization and therefore less social support. No support at all may be offered for the biological deaths of ex-spouses, homosexual lovers, extra marital lovers, roommates, friends, colleagues, clients, and pets, all of which tend to be disenfranchised. Similarly, other deaths that tend to be disenfranchised include spontaneous and therapeutic abortions, and perinatal deaths. Disenfranchised deaths tend to be neither acknowledged, publicly mourned, nor socially supported.

Non-biological deaths also tend to be disenfranchised. Social death, psychological death, psychosocial death, and the death of a relationship are all illustrated by a person in the later stages of Alzheimer's disease. On this point, a woman in a National Film Board of Canada video (McGowan and Bowen,

1990) speaks of her husband who has been institutionalized as a result of Alzheimer's.

> I feel that it is like widowhood except (pause) you know you're griev-ing but uh but there isn't any ritual. I try not to have as my only conversation my husband's illness because ... you really need to keep that part of your grieving to yourself.

As Doka (1995: 272) says, "societies have sets of norms—in effect, griev-ing rules—that attempt to specify who, when, where, how, how long, and for whom people should grieve... Each society defines who has a legitimate right to grieve." The woman in the video does not yet have the right to grieve, de-spite all she has lost. Her husband is no longer the person he was, and their marriage, as it was, has come to an end. However, without a dead body, grief is disenfranchised.

DYING AND DEATH AS SOCIAL STIGMA

A culture is a set of definitions and beliefs about reality, rules about how to behave, and evaluations about what is good and bad. These beliefs, normative rules, and values tend to be widely shared and persist over time. Some things are quite arbitrarily defined and evaluated as either good or bad. Consider rac-ism, where a whole category of people are defined as bad, inferior, and so on, on the basis of physiological characteristics such as skin colour.

Death is generally defined as bad, repulsive, contaminating, and threaten-ing. Accordingly, an ideology of beliefs has developed to justify these evalua-tions, and normative guidelines have developed to manage death. There may be good reason to evaluate death negatively. First, the smell of death—that is, the smell of rotting flesh—is highly disagreeable. Moreover, rotting flesh is as-sociated with disease and pestilence, contamination and contagion. Second, threats to life are generally feared and avoided. Finally, the death of a loved one tends to be one of life's most emotionally painful experiences.

Nevertheless, the negative evaluations of death go well beyond the obvious. In many cultures, death, the dead, and places of death such as graves and cem-eteries are feared and negatively valued because of beliefs about the danger and malevolence of departed spirits and ghosts. Furthermore, death may be feared because of what might come after—religious constructions of everlasting tor-ment in hell, for example. Even more curiously, people who are not dead but are merely associated with death may be negatively evaluated. Posner (1976) writes that the widow, the orphan, the "hangman," the processors of the dead, such as the morgue attendant and undertaker, and the aged, all tend to be negatively valued. Yet, what offence does the widow or orphan or undertaker commit? None, except they have a relationship with the dead. The widow's husband is dead, the orphan's parents are dead, and the undertaker's clients are dead. What offence do the aged commit? None, except that their age is a harbinger and reminder of death. The cultural logic seems to be: if death is bad, then anybody and anything that is associated with death is also bad. Such treatment is an example of what Goffman (1963) refers to as a "courtesy stigma"— that is, a person is stigmatized because of a stigma attached to someone with whom they are associated. Because death is stigmatized, almost anyone and anything associated with death is also stigmatized. The contamination is not literal, it is cultural (Posner, 1976).

SOCIAL RITUALS ACCOMPANYING DYING AND DEATH

Major changes in an individual's social status tend to be publicly acknowledged and celebrated in rituals known as rites of passage. Examples of rites of passage include the christening of a newborn baby, the bar mitzvah for a Jewish boy who has reached the age of thirteen, high school graduation, post-secondary graduation, marriage, retirement, and death. Regarding death, Posner (1976: 46) writes:

> In a culture such as ours which abhors death, it is not surprising to find that we attempt to deny it or at least repress the emotional responses which accompany such occasions. It is appropriate to conclude that funeral rituals represent a rather clever attempt to deal with a paradoxical situation. On the one hand, death must be denied, covered or played down at all costs. On the other hand, the occurrence of death must be tactfully disclosed so that members do not inadvertently touch upon contaminating topics.

Funeral rituals acknowledge the death of a member of the community, acknowledge the grief of those who have lost a loved one, and provide guidelines for the public display of emotion. These guidelines describe what emotions should be shown, and where and when they should be shown. Furthermore, funeral rituals provide guidelines as to how to proceed with the disposal of the dead body and how members of the community are to the provide support to the bereaved. As Posner notes, funeral rituals have a dual and paradoxical function: they simultaneously allow for the display of emotion and control emotional displays. In addition, funeral rituals simultaneously acknowledge disruption of the normal social order and provide a mechanism for re-establishing social normality. (For a discussion of the funeral industry in Canada, see chapter 3.)

Funeral rituals in Canada acknowledge both the deceased and the mourners. In many funeral services, a eulogy—a selective and idealized reconstruction of the life of the deceased—is given. Furthermore, the grief of the mourners is acknowledged. Support is offered in the form of attendance at the funeral service, flowers, sympathy cards, and verbal expressions of sympathy. In addition to the eulogy, a formal speech is often given at the funeral service that constitutes a message for the living about the meaning of life and the meaning of death. Burial or cremation typically follows the funeral service. Alternatively, a memorial service may follow burial or cremation. At the conclusion of the formal funerary rituals, community members return to their normal lives, and the bereaved are expected to return to public normality shortly thereafter.

CULTURAL CONSTRUCTIONS OF DYING AND DEATH

Funeral rituals vary from one culture to another. Culture influences personal beliefs, subjective perceptions, and the meanings that an individual assigns to dying and death. In a multicultural society such as Canada, made up of a variety of ethnic and religious groups, there are variations in cultural definitions and guidelines regarding dying, death, and grieving. The balance of this chapter examines these definitions and guidelines among several different groups in contemporary Canada.

Coast Salish

The Coast Salish are an Aboriginal people living on the West Coast of Canada. Joseph (1994) studied Coast Salish cultural values and rituals regarding dying and death. Salish people today combine traditional beliefs with Catholic and other Euro-Canadian beliefs, past with present. Furthermore, beliefs vary from one individual to another among the Salish as they do in any other community. Joseph notes that in traditional Salish culture there is a belief in the continuity of life from this world to the spirit world and in the connection between these two realms. The deceased lives on in the spirit world and is taken care of there. It is believed that the living and the deceased can communicate through rituals and in dreams, and that the spirits visit the living from time to time. These beliefs do not lessen the pain of grief, but do facilitate healing.

In her study, Joseph records the recollections of two sisters concerning the death of their father some eight years earlier following a series of strokes. The two sisters were members of the Squamish Nation living on a reserve in North

Vancouver. Joseph notes that, while one sister tended to rely on a Christian church and prayer to deal with her grief, the other sister tended to rely on traditional Salish cultural rituals, going to the Longhouse to engage in socially supported ritualized emotional expression for the purpose of healing. Other social rituals included use of water, cedar, and devil's club (a shrub) for purification, as well as the grieving circle, smudging, pipe ceremony, and burning (to send selected items to the deceased). The sister who relied on Salish traditions also received ministrations from a medicine man.

The dying of the elder in Joseph's study was described as a time for family gathering. As is customary, on the third day after the elder's death, a wake was held, where the body of the deceased was viewed. On the fourth day there was a funeral at the church followed by a graveside service. The church service combined elements of both Catholic and Salish tradition. Not long afterward, the family had a burning to send their loved one clothes and other items that they thought he would need in the spirit world.

While culture can shape and assist grieving and mourning, the sisters selected different cultural elements. Both exercised faith, although faith in different cultural elements. It is an oversimplification to assume that culture is necessarily a monolithic homogenizing force. Instead, there tends to be a diversity of cultural elements from which individuals select. In short, culture tends to shape a diversity of individual responses.

Cree

Preston and Preston (1991) note that emotional restraint is the general rule among the Cree living in Quebec near James Bay. Cultural rules require a person to say goodbye when leaving on a journey lest death intervene unexpectedly. Similarly, it is considered important that goodbye be said to a person known to be dying and that the dying have an opportunity to say goodbye as well. Saying goodbye affirms relationships and completes them should death intervene.

When death comes, it is to be met competently with composure and self-control by both the dying and the bereaved. The bereaved are informed promptly after death has occurred, and a brief intense emotional outpouring of grief is permitted at that time. Grief is shared by others and social support given. Grief is expressed periodically up to and including the burial, which is held without undue delay. It is expected that composure and self-reliance will be regained soon thereafter, and inner emotions held in check.

Dene

Ross Gray, a psychologist from Toronto, was sent by the government to consult with northern communities about suicide prevention (Gray, 1993). One of the communities he went to was Fort Simpson, near the Nahanni River area discussed earlier in this chapter. The majority of the people at Fort Simpson were Slavey Indians, who are one of several First Nations peoples collectively referred to as Dene. Gray found a cultural taboo against speaking publicly about loved ones who had committed suicide and about the strong feelings that such suicides generated. Nevertheless, many people informally sought out respected elders who had come for the consultation about suicide prevention. Gray also found that school children at the local school seemed to abandon the taboo and talk more readily about suicide than did adults.

Inuit

During his assignment as a consultant for suicide prevention, Gray also visited several predominantly Inuit communities, including Rankin Inlet, Baker Lake, and Coppermine. There, Gray observed among the Inuit "a natural leeriness of 'southern' professionals [who] come to enlighten northerners about the nature of reality" (206). Gray learned that instead of simply listening to the "expert," the people preferred to tell their stories of loss and pain, each in turn, in detail, and in as much time as the stories took to tell. Gray had to give up his time-bound agenda. He writes:

> Several people ... talk[ed] to us about the style of this consultation. They say it reminds them of the way things were in the past, when there would be much community discussion of issues, with decisions arising out of the discussions. More recently, consultations from government and others have tended to be top-down. Hierarchical notions of wisdom, with travelling experts dispatching information to needy recipients. People have become disconnected from their own wisdom. (210).

Muslim

Hebert (1998) observes that Islamic society, like Western society, is pluralistic and multicultural. Furthermore, in both Western and Islamic societies, individuals practise their religions with varying degrees of devotion and adherence to traditional beliefs. Nevertheless, it is possible to compare in a very general sense Western and Islamic orientations to death.

Hebert examines Western and Islamic cultural definitions and prescriptions regarding perinatal death—that is, death of a baby before or shortly after birth. In the West, perinatal death is generally unacknowledged and grief following such a loss tends to be disenfranchised (Doka, 1995). Hebert (1998: par. 12) writes:

> Consistent with the Muslim attitude toward life and death, the death of a fetus or neonate is not minimized as it tends to be in the West, nor does it carry with it the same onus evident in western societies—that of being an illogical, unnatural, and incomprehensible event to be quickly forgotten as soon as possible. Rather, the loss is regarded as being just as significant and meaningful as the loss of someone later on in life and the fetus is treated with the utmost dignity and respect by all.

Prayers are said at the site of death, which may be the hospital. The baby is given a name. Autopsy, cremation, and embalming, are prohibited by the Muslim faith. The family prefers to take the baby quickly for preparation for burial. This preparation may include ritual washing and shrouding. The burial takes place very soon after death, usually within twenty-four hours. Uncontrolled emotional outbursts are discouraged, as grieving parents are encouraged to accept the will of Allah. The official mourning period is three days, but unofficial mourning may go on for forty days, with visits to the grave on Fridays, the Muslim Sabbath.

Hebert (1998: pars. 27-29) describes a case involving a Muslim family and a perinatal death that occurred in a Montreal hospital. The mother had a miscarriage and lost her baby of twenty-two weeks gestational age. A bereavement support team including a social worker was called in. Following are excerpts from the case report.

> It became clear that a conflict between the two cultures (Muslim and Western) was brewing. The nurses had offered the patient [the mother] an epidural, which her husband had refused outright, and [the nurses] were becoming increasingly frustrated with the men, their loud chatter in the hallway, and their seemingly controlling and unsympathetic attitude toward their patient... The first successful intervention centred on the need to find a female physician. Once found, [the father] seemed to calm down... The mother was asked if she would like to hold the [dead] baby. [The father] refused for her, saying that it would be too painful. He, however, would hold the baby, which he did lovingly and tearfully... He was horrified when offered a snippet of the baby's hair, and likewise refused any photographs. One family member declared that there should be no autopsy, that the body should be kept, unwashed, with the placenta, and that formalin [a preservative] should not be used... The men's loud praying, once again, became disturbing to the staff and to the other patients, and the social worker had to find an empty room in which they could con-

tinue their prayers. The nurses felt that [the father], because of the time he spent with the men, was unsupportive of his wife. To make matters worse, within an hour after the delivery, [the father] was asking to take the baby home. The nursing team became extremely upset... On clarification, it was discovered that [the father wanted to take the baby] to the Islamic Centre for preparation for burial... Finally, after much negotiating and compromising, the baby was ready for transport.

These excerpts from the case report reveal the intense frustration felt by the hospital staff. The Western nurses were reluctant to set aside practices to which they were committed medically, professionally, and bureaucratically. Furthermore, while the nurses were sympathetic to the mother, they were extremely critical of the father and the other Muslim men. From the Western point of view, the men were authoritarian and overbearing, and the nurses felt that the mother was oppressed and abused.

While the case report does not portray the Muslim men sympathetically, the reader can extrapolate from the report that the Muslim men also felt a great deal of frustration. They had to fight every step of the way in order to follow their cultural and religious practices. This case study reveals how difficult interactions can be when cultures collide.

Jewish

Fishbane (1989) studied the mourning rituals of persons affiliated with an orthodox Jewish synagogue located in a major Canadian city. At the funeral home and immediately before the funeral service for the deceased, a garment is torn by and for seven relatives: father, mother, brother, sister, son, daughter, and spouse. The practice for this synagogue is to have the women tear a black kerchief while the men tear a black tie. The tearing is done on the left side of the body for a deceased parent and on the right side for any one of the other relatives who might be the deceased. The torn garment is worn for a seven-day mourning period. From the time of death until the burial ceremony, the bereaved are not supposed to shave, cut their hair, bathe, work, go to parties, or engage in the usual daily religious observances. The official mourning period begins immediately following the burial ceremony which is supposed to be held within a day of death.

A funeral service takes place before burial. There is a requirement that a minimum of ten men be present. At this service a eulogy is given and prayers are said. At the burial ceremony, a male survivor recites a special prayer.

Those present then form two lines, and the mourners walk away from the grave through the two lines which close behind them.

The mourners are transported from the cemetery to the house of the deceased. Before entering the home, the mourners ritually wash their hands and remove their shoes. They are then served a meal of condolence, consisting of bread and eggs prepared by friends or neighbours. The mourners remain at home for seven days, during which time visitors come to offer their condolences, and a minimum of ten males come regularly to offer prayers. A number of prescriptions and proscriptions—to burn candles, cover mirrors, to not bathe or cohabit—are supposed to be observed, but may not in fact be followed. (Many of the members of this orthodox synagogue are not committed observant Jews.) The seven-day mourning period ends with a walk of some distance out-of-doors to signify rejoining the community. Additional rituals are traditionally observed for more extended periods following burial.

Ethnic Viet and Lao Hmong

Schriever (1990) compares medical and religious belief systems related to dying for ethnic Viet and Lao Hmong refugees in Canada. Ethnic Viet refugees (not to be confused with ethnic Chinese refugees from Vietnam) arrived in Canada from Vietnam in the late 1970s. About the same time, Hmong refugees arrived from Laos. Both groups place a strong emphasis on family genealogy—that is, on one's ancestors.

Schriever discusses the intricacies of the traditional Viet and Hmong beliefs and practices regarding dying, death, and mourning. She observes that it is not clear to what extent these refugee groups in Canada continue to maintain their traditional beliefs and practices and to what extent they have incorporated Western beliefs and practices. In a multicultural society, there is a tendency for one culture to borrow from another. This fusion of differing belief systems is known as *syncretism*. It follows that individual Viet and Hmong immigrants may be traditional, syncretic, or Westernized. Schriever encourages Western professionals involved in the process of dying to ascertain the belief system of their clients rather than proceeding on the basis of stereotypes or limited understanding.

In her study, Schriever offers a number of suggestions for workers providing palliative care to dying Viet or Hmong patients. She recommends using bilingual and bicultural interpreters, including extended family in care, and not isolating the patient from the family. The worker should expect that the patient and family will use dual medical systems (traditional and Western) and should not assume that traditional remedies are inconsequential. The workers should not dismiss accounts of dreams or encounters with spirits as having no meaning or relevance, and should be aware that emotional distress may be reported in physiological terms. It is important to note that the individual's surname is often placed first instead of last. Several gestures may be inappropriate. For example, it is rude to touch an adult's head, to show the bottoms of one's feet (shoes), to snap one's fingers, or to beckon with an upturned finger (fingers should be pointed down instead). Referring to the deceased by name may also be inappropriate. Invasive procedures such as drawing blood, surgery, and autopsy should be avoided. The workers should be prepared to facilitate dying at home, as this may be preferred to hospitalization. Finally, it is important to note that Western notions regarding grieving and emotional release may be inappropriate.

Western European and Euro-North American
Philippe Ariès (1974; 1981) has surveyed portrayals of death in western European culture from the Middle Ages to the present. He suggests that until the early Middle Ages (through the twelfth century), death was "tame," omnipresent, familiar, and accepted as the natural order of things. Later, death became "wild" and it was increasingly feared and resisted. By the twentieth century, death had become dirty, ugly, shameful, hidden, and denied.

Stroebe et al. (1995) have characterized nineteenth-century Western culture as romanticist. Romanticism emphasized the soul or spirit, love, and enduring commitment to intimate human relationships, even after the death of a loved one. Accordingly, "To grieve was to signal the significance of the relationship, and the depth of one's own spirit. Dissolving bonds with the deceased would not only define the relationship as superficial, but would deny as well one's own sense of profundity and self-worth" (Stroebe et al., 1995: 237). From the romantic perspective, grief could legitimately last a lifetime.

In contrast, these authors characterize twentieth-century Western culture as modernist. Modernism emphasizes efficiency, progress, and rationality rather than emotionality. From the modernist point of view, "bereaved persons need to break their ties with the deceased, ... form a new identity of which the departed person has no part, and reinvest in other relationships" (234). From the modernist perspective, grief is to be gotten over.

Postmodernism takes the view that romantic and modernist conceptualizations of death are products of cultural and historical processes—that is, they are socially constructed (Stroebe et al., 1995; see also Marshall,

1986). It is not clear that one perspective is more correct than the other or that one perspective has better therapeutic outcomes than the other. Each perspective defines death differently and each prescribes different courses of action for the bereaved. What is defined as appropriate in one culture may be inappropriate in another. What "works" for the individual often depends on that person's cultural frame of reference. It follows that the meaning of death for the individual and the individual's reaction to death must be understood in cultural context. It also follows that, when support or therapy is offered to an individual, the support must be tailored to the individual and must fit with that person's cultural point of view. In an increasingly heterogeneous society like Canada, death has different meanings for different subcultures, and reactions to death will vary depending on subcultural frames of reference.

Part III
The Individual Response to Dying and Death

Chapter 5
Individual Perspectives on Dying and Death

Death presents an existential problem for the living: as an individual becomes more and more aware of the inevitability of death, questions arise about the meaning and purpose of one's existence. How should one live, given that life ends in death? What is the meaning of life? What is the meaning of death? Furthermore, for those persons who are in the process of dying and who face imminent death, questions arise about how one should die and how dying itself can be made meaningful.

EXPECTATIONS OF DYING AND DEATH

The possibility of dying can be assessed in both statistical and psychological terms. Statistically, babies born in Canada a hundred years ago had a much higher likelihood of dying in infancy or early childhood than do babies born at the present time (Gee, 1987: 269; Marshall, 1986: 132). Today, death typically comes in old age, and the death of a child is unlikely.

In psychological terms, very young children tend to have a limited awareness of the possibility of dying. At birth, a newborn child cries when it experi-

Dying and Death in Canada

ences cold, hunger, thirst, pain, and fear. Crying expresses the baby's discomfort and distress and typically elicits caregiving responses from persons in the baby's social environment. In other words, the baby has an innate capacity for dealing with threats not only to its comfort and well-being but also to its very existence. Nevertheless, it will be some years before the young child can fully conceptualize dying and death (Aiken, 1991: 3, 162-167).

Children and young adults give little thought to the possibility of dying. For young people, their own death is a distant possibility. Nevertheless, fear of death may underlie distancing from death (Aiken, 1991: 167-169, 190). Thus, while young people may rarely think of death, they may fear dying when they do think about it. Because young people perceive death to be removed from them, they can simultaneously fear death and put it out of their minds. In contrast, middle-aged and older persons, who because of their age are closer to death, are more likely to think about dying and death (Aiken, 1991: 191). Yet, older persons are less likely to fear death than are middle-aged or young adults (Novak, 1997: 297; Aiken, 1991: 198). It appears that proximity to death in old age motivates one to think of death (Marshall, 1986), but not necessarily to fear it.

Death has come to be unexpected, except in old age. When a colleague dies at fifty-seven years of age, it seems inappropriate, premature, too early. When a child dies, it is incomprehensible and unacceptable (Martin, 1998). Some years ago in Canada, death was more expected. Consider a man and a woman born on the Prairies in 1912 and 1922, respectively, married in 1946, and who in the early 1950s bought three grave plots, two for themselves and one for a child that they expected to lose to early death. Eight children and fifty years later, the extra grave is still unused. Earlier in Canada's history, it seemed prudent to expect death at any time. Now Canadians generally do not expect death, except in old age.

DYING TRAJECTORIES   In one sense, we all begin to die from the moment we are born. However, relatively healthy children, adolescents, and young adults do not think of themselves as being on a trajectory ending in death. While awareness of one's mortality does tend to become more acute in middle age, the healthy middle-aged do not think of themselves as dying (Marshall, 1986: 137–8). The everyday phrase "over the hill" reflects the perception that one has reached the midpoint or zenith of one's life and has begun the inevitable decline into old age and,

108

ultimately, death. Nevertheless, the concept of the dying trajectory is reserved for those who are perceived to have a disease or condition with an explicit terminal prognosis—that is, death is clearly anticipated as the end of the person's present circumstances.

The dying trajectory refers to the course that a person follows over time as they move from a healthy state to death. Glaser and Strauss (1968) note that there are various dying trajectories. In unexpected death such as sudden infant death syndrome (SIDS), accidental death, homicide, suicide, or heart attack, the dying trajectory is precipitous and brief: death comes quickly. Alternatively, the dying trajectory may be long, as with Alzheimer's disease, for example, and may be complicated with remissions and relapses, as can be the case with cancer.

The shortest possible trajectory resulting in quick death is generally preferred over a long, lingering dying trajectory (Aiken, 1991: 204). Indeed, the ideal death is often described as a healthy and happy old age that ends suddenly and painlessly in one's sleep (Aiken, 1991: 196). This ideal reflects the so-called "natural" death from "old age." It can be illustrated by an anecdote told by a hairdresser whose father had been a barber. One day a gentleman in his early nineties came in for a haircut. After the man had been in the chair for a while, the barber noticed that his client seemed to have drifted off to sleep. In fact, he had quietly died. He had peacefully passed from life to death, and his hair cut turned out to be for his funeral. Stories like this illustrate the preferred way to die and can be contrasted with accounts of ways of dying that are less preferred.

As discussed in chapter 4, Lucas (1968) interviewed men who had been trapped underground for days in a coal mine disaster in Nova Scotia. The miners had no food, had run out of water and batteries to power their lights, and were surrounded by their dead and dying co-workers. The men began to speculate that death would come to them either from starvation, thirst, or suffocation from deadly gas or lack of oxygen. The miners had little fear of death itself but were more concerned about how they might die. The men hoped to die painlessly, to just "go to sleep." They seemed to expect that poisonous gas would come eventually and, indeed, gas was the preferred mode of death. The miners knew that when the gas came, they would just go to sleep, and death would follow quickly and painlessly.

PREFERENCES FOR DYING AND DEATH

As mentioned in chapter 3, the death of Sue Rodriguez received a great deal of public attention in the early 1990s (Wood, 1994; Bartlett, 1994; Ogden, 1994). In 1991, Rodriguez, an athletic woman who was just past forty years of age, and who was the mother of a young son, began to experience symptoms that would eventually be diagnosed as amyotrophic lateral sclerosis (ALS). This disease leads to a progressive loss of muscle control, ending in paralysis, with death often coming from suffocation. Told by doctors that she had from two to five years to live, Rodriguez said that at first she felt panic, then numbness, and shock. She began to notice seniors, envying them because she would not get to experience old age. Although she was briefly defiant, thinking that she would beat the disease or at least live longer than predicted, the relentless progression of the disease soon put an end to such thoughts. Instead, she decided she would commit suicide at some future time when the quality of her life was sufficiently compromised. As she became increasingly dependent, however, she realized that she would need help to die, and so began a much-publicized campaign for the legalization of doctor-assisted suicide in Canada.

The CBC-TV program *Witness* (Bartlett, 1994) followed Rodriguez through her final eighteen months of life. The program intimately revealed to viewers the person and the devastating effects of her disease. Rodriguez assessed her situation in a straightforward manner. She did not want to die, and, had she not gotten ALS, she would not be seeking to end her life. However, she observed that ALS is an awful disease to live through, and is a gruesome and unfair way to die. She wanted some control over her destiny and wanted a better death than the one that the disease promised.

Early in 1994, completely dependent and barely able to speak, Rodriguez achieved her better, though still illegal, death with the assistance of an anonymous person. She was forty-three years of age at the time of her death, having lived not quite three years from the time she first experienced symptoms.

Like Sue Rodriguez in Canada, Professor Morris Schwartz, an American, died of ALS. As did Rodriguez, Schwartz faced his disease with great courage and dignity and with a desire to make his death meaningful. He spoke of the lessons learned in dying, lessons shared with and recorded by a former student. Indeed, the professor and the student collaborated on a book about the professor's experience with dying, his "last thesis" (Albom, 1997). As was the case with Sue Rodriguez, Morris Schwartz's dying became public. In 1995 he came to the attention of Ted Koppel, host of the American television program *Nightline,* and interviews with Professor Schwartz were aired on three different occasions as his disease progressed and death approached. The book about his dying and death, entitled *Tuesdays with Morrie*, became a best-seller and was made into a movie starring Academy Award winner Jack Lemmon.

Unlike Sue Rodriguez, Morris Schwartz did not campaign for assisted suicide. While both Rodriguez and Schwartz sought to gain control over their dying, they did so in different ways. Rodriguez sought to control the final moment through assisted suicide; Schwartz sought control by managing his emotions, acknowledging and then setting aside negative emotions such as self-pity and concentrating on positive emotions such as love. Schwartz accepted a natural death, and made no effort to control the time or cause of death. In contrast to Rodriguez, who died at home from assisted suicide, Schwartz died at home from the suffocating end of ALS, an end that Sue Rodriguez had described as gruesome and unfair.

Although most people would say that ALS is not a good way to die, both Rodriguez and Schwartz could be cited as examples of good deaths. It is their manner of dealing with their terminal illness, rather than the illness itself, that tends to be applauded and portrayed as exemplary. As discussed earlier, however, dying peacefully in one's sleep in old age might also be considered a "good" death. In this scenario, there is only death—no dying, no pain, no suffering, no need for coping, and no test of character. It is an ideal death because it is an easy death.

Dying with ALS is not easy: it is a dying that tests, shapes, and reveals one's character. Cultural ideals value dignity, fortitude, courage, endurance, self-control, and making the best of the worst situation. Public accounts of people such as Rodriguez and Schwartz are designed to move others emotionally and to provide moral inspiration. Dying is not simply a biological process; it is also a process with psychological, social, moral, and spiritual dimensions. Public accounts of persons who die exemplary deaths are designed to remind us of these various dimensions and to describe and define the various pathways to a "good" death.

Austin, in an article originally published in the Toronto *Globe and Mail* (July 16, 1997), described the dying and death of his mother. Three years before her death, she "began her journey to death" when she experienced sudden liver failure at the age of seventy. Her unexpected recovery from that initial event "led to a three-year celebration of life in the shadow of death." Austin wrote that his mother "continued to laugh and shop" and that "she chose to gauge the quality of her existence by the joy she found every day in her interaction with others." She resisted death, and even near the end said resolutely "I am not going." Noting that dying with dignity does not necessarily mean a quick and quiet death, Austin concluded that "Mom died slowly, but she died well" (quoted in McPherson, 1998: 364–5).

Austin's account shows that dying, despite its many drawbacks, can be a rewarding and meaningful time for the dying person, the family, and for others such as professional caregivers whose lives are touched by the dying person. Austin's account also illustrates a particular style of coping with dying. In this case, the coping style involves living life to its fullest extent, given the circumstances, and resisting death by fighting the good fight and never giving in. In this regard, Austin's mother illustrates a cultural ideal: the person who exercises her will to live, to extract as much meaning as possible from life, while holding death at bay for as long as possible. The notion that will power can extend life is part of our cultural mythology and reflects the social expectation that a person should make every effort to resist death. Austin's mother chose her own way of coping with her dying. Although we cannot know the extent to which she was influenced by cultural prescriptions, the telling of the story tends to reinforce these prescriptions.

The notion of dying well, as evident in the stories of Schwartz, Rodriguez, and Austin, is not solely a manifestation of Euro-Canadian values. The Cree living in Quebec near James Bay also value self-control and composure in the face of death (Preston and Preston, 1991). One evening, Jimmy Moar, an old and blind Cree man, announced his impending death by saying to his daughter, "I'm almost falling off from my chair. That's all I can sit here. I am very tired." He then told his daughter how much he loved her and his granddaughter, put on his best clothes, went to bed, and died (Preston and Preston, 1991: 142). This story is told as an example of a good death. Goodbyes were said, relationships were affirmed, and death was met with dignity and quiet competence.

FEAR OF DYING

The preference for a quick death suggests that dying is perceived to be distressing, even more than death itself (Lucas, 1968; Lévy et al., 1985: 31; Frank, 1991: 43; Aiken, 1991: 198). Although people generally prefer living to dying and prefer life to death, a person on a dying trajectory, such as Sue Rodriguez may find dying so unpleasant that the dying person asks for death. Indeed, following their demise it is commonly said of such persons that death was a "blessing" for the deceased because it brought their suffering to an end. In short, people tend to fear the process of dying more than they fear death itself.

Fear of dying is driven by concerns about loss and suffering (Lucas, 1968; Frank, 1991: 43), and it tends to focus on the possibility of a long and lingering dying trajectory. As a person enters such a dying trajectory, the person faces loss of health, loss of control and independence, loss of competence and dignity, loss of status and social roles, loss of future plans and goals, and impending loss of life. Furthermore, fear of dying is motivated by concerns about prolonged suffering and, in particular, about pain (Lucas, 1968; Frank, 1991: 43).

AWARENESS OF DYING

Persons who are dying may be unaware that they are dying, either because they have not been informed of their terminal prognosis or because they are in denial. According to Glaser and Strauss (1965), persons who are aware that they are dying have two options. On the one hand, a drama of mutual pretence may be enacted in which the dying persons and the people around them do not speak of the dying process or of impending death. On the other hand, people may prefer to discuss the terminal prognosis openly. Today, dying persons are more likely to prefer to talk openly of dying and death (Novak, 1997: 304), although some ethnic groups have social norms that discourage open communication (Kastenbaum, 1998: 297). Not speaking of dying and death maintains denial, hope, normalcy, and avoids unpleasant topics and issues. On the other hand, openly acknowledging dying facilitates the obtaining of information, allows for the expression and sharing of feelings, helps decision-making, and allows one to settle one's affairs and make final arrangements (Novak, 1997: 305).

THE DYING PROCESS

Dying is a process that takes place over variable lengths of time. Elisabeth Kübler-Ross (1969) interviewed dying persons and, from these interviews, constructed a theory that suggests that dying persons typically go through stages in the course of their dying. This model is a generalization and does not necessarily apply in all aspects to any given individual. Furthermore, the model has been misused as a prescription about how one should feel in the course of dying and about how one should proceed through the process. Kübler-Ross's model states that a typical initial reaction to a terminal diagnosis is denial. As reality overcomes denial, anger is a typical second reaction. A third stage tends to involve "bargaining" for more time. In the fourth stage, depression sets in as the person reacts to their many losses and prepares for further losses. Finally, cognitive and emotional resistance give way to resigned acceptance. In other words, the stages might be characterized in the dying person's voice as "Not me!" "Why me?" "Not yet," "Poor me," and finally "I give in."

PERSONAL ACCOUNTS OF "BRUSHES WITH DEATH"

Occasionally people have an experience where, for a short moment or for some time, they come to think that they might be facing dying and death. A middle-aged man told the following story.

> In my early thirties, I began to experience frequent, extreme, and unexplainable fatigue often accompanied by anxiety, depression, and difficulty coping with everyday tasks. Visits to the doctor produced no explanation. Indeed, visits to the doctor were so unproductive and frustrating that at one point I swore I would never go back to a doctor again. I assumed that I was under stress from my employment and needed to develop better stress management strategies. However, nothing seemed to help.
>
> Things got worse over several years. I thought I might be losing my mind. In time, I became convinced that I was dying. The thought that I was dying came as a clear and certain realization. I remember being surprised that I felt no emotion attached to this realization. I was neither afraid nor angry. I was dying, most likely, and that was that. Indeed, I felt so miserable that death seemed to be the solution and dying seemed to be the explanation. I still wondered exactly what was wrong with me, but nevertheless, whatever was wrong, I felt that it was killing me.
>
> I was pretty desperate when my wife made a doctor's appointment for me with a new doctor and told me that I was going to see him or else. I went. The doctor told me that I was probably losing my mind but agreed to do some blood tests. A week later he diagnosed Hashimoto's Thyroiditis and shortly afterwards a specialist diagnosed pernicious anemia as well. I had a double whammy.
>
> It seems melodramatic now to say that I was dying. These diseases are perfectly treatable today. But I was dying. A hundred years ago, I would have gone mad and then died. It would have been an unpleasant death for myself and for those around me, in particular for my wife and young children. While these two diseases will not kill me, I find myself wondering what will. Some day, sooner or later, I will get another diagnosis and next time I may not be so lucky. (Personal communication, 1999)

For this storyteller, personal self-diagnosis was a cognitive exercise rather than an emotional one. While there was much emotional turmoil in his life, the storyteller exhibits an emotional detachment as he assesses his health status, concludes that he is dying, and attempts to deal with that realization. This story also reminds us that death has a certain capriciousness about it: many who are now reading this would already be dead if born at an earlier time in history or in some place where modern health care was not available. So many of the diseases that killed our ancestors are now either preventable or treatable. Similarly, those diseases that today are most likely to kill us at some time in our lives may yet be rendered impotent. When we die and how we die is in part a function of our time and place in history. Yet, the storyteller himself did not dwell on such academic observations. His concerns were more pragmatic: his perception was that he was dying, and his concern was what to do about it.

Persons who confront dying are often said to show anger, revealed, in part, in the form of questions such as "Why me?" or "Why now?" (Kübler-Ross, 1969). Such questions imply resistance and an unwillingness to accept fate. The storyteller above seems to be more fatalistic. It is as if his reaction is a bemused acknowledgment that these things happen haphazardly, and so "Why not me?" and "Why not now?"

A woman in her thirties told the following story.

It all started four and a half years ago driving home from a family ski trip with my husband and our two school-age daughters. I felt an itch behind my right ear and as I was scratching I felt something unfamiliar to me. It felt like three bumps. My mind started to wander. Being an emergency nurse was not helping. I was thinking the worst. What if these were cancerous tumours?

It was a long trip home. I needed to get a proper look behind my ear. I was horrified to see the lumps. They were not anything I had seen before as a nurse (and believe me, I had seen it all). [The next day] I phoned my family doctor. I told the receptionist that I needed to see my doctor that day. They got me in to see him later that afternoon.

My doctor was not able to explain the lumps. His facial expression said it all and then he started asking me a lot of questions. Questions I had heard over the years from my nursing experience. Questions that centred around signs and symptoms of cancer. I asked him bluntly. Is it cancer? He said he wasn't sure what they were but he didn't like what he saw. In his attempt to be reassuring, he said, "If it is Hodgkin's disease, you are lucky. It is one of the best types of cancer to get. You could have up to a ten year survival rate." Why was it that I wasn't feeling too lucky? Ten years did not seem like such a long time when I had one daughter in Grade two and the other in Grade three.

[The next day] I had an appointment with a surgeon. I was due to work the night shift but I called in sick. The charge nurse knew something was wrong immediately. She called me back at home and asked me what was wrong. In telling her my story, I broke down crying when I told her that the following day I was seeing a surgeon to see whether or not I had cancer. She was very understanding.

The next day was as fearsome and tense as the day prior. Waiting. Always waiting and wondering. I saw the surgeon. Again, the visit was not very encouraging. He thought the lumps looked suspicious. The only way to get a diagnosis would be to have a biopsy [of the lymph nodes in my neck. The surgeon] said he would schedule me for day surgery.

You may be wondering what was going through my mind these long days and nights. Well, I guess the first thing was fear. Not fear for myself, but fear for my daughters. If the news ends up being bad (malignant) what will happen to my girls? My husband works out of town which means that they would have no mother and would see their father infrequently. Essentially they would be raised by a stranger (perhaps by a nanny). This is not something I wanted for my daughters. So I guess I was scared that my children would suffer tremendously if something was to happen to me.

Another concern was how to tell my children if the lumps turned out to be malignant. How do you tell your school-age daughters that their mom has cancer and may die within ten years? How do you prepare them for that? Well my girls were very perceptive. They had never seen Mom quite so emotional before. I was crying all the time. Every time I saw them, my eyes would swell with tears. My voice was shaky and my mind fuzzy. I was definitely not my cheerful, upbeat, optimistic self. I was a stranger in my own body. My girls and I have a very open and honest relationship so I decided to tell them the truth. "Mommy is having minor surgery to see if these lumps on my neck are cancer." They took the news very well. No tears were shed, but many questions were asked. Not once did they let on that they were scared for me. It was only weeks later that one of the girls' schoolteachers told me that my youngest daughter was very concerned about me. Now I realize that they were trying to be strong for me. Strangely enough, I did not give the process of dying a second thought.

The waiting game wasn't over. My surgery was two weeks away. Two more weeks of thinking and trying to prepare myself for the worst case scenario. I couldn't cope with working so I called the nurse manager. She agreed that it would be best if I took the time off until the biopsy was done. Once again, I had a lot of understanding from my immediate supervisors. But the support given to me by my husband was different.

I don't want to say that my husband wasn't supportive, I guess he thought I was getting myself all worked up for nothing. "Wait until we see what the results are. It may be nothing." My husband didn't go with me to either of my doctor appointments. I guess he thought that he wouldn't be much use to me. After all, I was the health care professional, not him. He wouldn't know what the doctor was saying anyway, so why miss a day's work. He also did not go with me to the hospital for my surgery. Again he felt that we wouldn't find out the results that day and he wouldn't be able to go in the treatment room so he chose once again to go to work. My mother knew that this would be a difficult day for me and drove me to the hospital, waited in the waiting room (picked my girls up from school while I was having my biopsy done), and drove me home. She cared for me like when I was a little girl. I know my mom was as worried about the outcome as myself. I don't think my mom knows how much that meant to me having her there and I also don't think my husband knows how hurt I was *not* having him there.

[After the biopsy] I still had anywhere from four to seven days to wait for the results from the pathology report. On the fourth day following the biopsy, I phoned the surgeon. No results as yet. I phoned every day until the results were in. It took a full week.

What was frustrating during that week was the attitude of the surgeon. I knew he had no idea what I was going through emotionally and mentally. What was equally infuriating was that when my results did reach the surgeon's desk he shuffled them aside when he saw that the diagnosis was benign. He did not call me with the results. He waited until I called him. When I asked him if he had the results he said yes, but couldn't remember what the report said. As he shuffled through the reports on his desk, he finally found mine. Oh ya. The news is good. Nothing to report.

Does the story have a happy ending? The diagnosis was benign and I wasn't going to die from Hodgkin's disease. But the story is not over. It will never be over. The surgeon told me to be continually checking my lymph nodes because even though they were benign that day, that may change in the future. The obsession continues. Every time I feel a lump I feel the same anxiety I did four and a half years ago. The scar behind my ear is a constant reminder of those very stressful few weeks in my life and of my mortality. (Personal communication, 1999)

A casual reading of this story suggests that the storyteller was afraid that she might have cancer and might die. Her story highlights the anxiety and fear that she felt while waiting for a diagnosis. But what is the storyteller really afraid of? She indicates that she did not give any thought to the process of dying, nor did she seem to give any thought to death in purely personal terms. Instead, her story focuses on relationships with her children, her family doctor, her supervisor at work, her surgeon, her mother, and her husband. Her greatest fear is that her young daughters will be left motherless, will be raised by a stranger, and might suffer because of the loss of their mother. She is also worried about how to tell her children about her health and about how this will affect them.

In her story she goes on to discuss her other relationships in the context of the time she waited for a diagnosis. She describes the women in her life as being very supportive: her daughters, her supervisor at work, and her mother are all sympathetic, understanding, and helpful. Her male family doctor sees her almost immediately and tries to be reassuring. The other men in the story are not perceived as being supportive. Her male surgeon does not acknowledge her concern or her need to know her diagnosis. Her husband minimizes the situation, refusing to get upset over something that "may be nothing." Not only does he distance himself emotionally from the situation, he distances himself physically by going to work.

The differences between the males and the females in this story can be explained in part by sex role socialization. Social norms for females tend to legitimize emotional expression and nurturing responses (Aiken, 1991: 246). In contrast, social norms for males tend to define emotional displays as deviant and unacceptable (Haas, 1977; Lucas, 1968). Consequently, males are less likely to show their emotions and are less likely to acknowledge the emotions of others.

The storyteller ends her account by pointing out that, while the initial lumps were benign, she nevertheless has to be continually on guard for new lumps. In the end, the experience serves as an ongoing reminder of her mortality. This event brought death into focus in a very close, personal, and threatening manner, when previously death had been only a distant eventuality. Death had become threatening because the storyteller wishes to raise her young daughters herself, an agenda that death would prevent. Death for this storyteller means suffering, not for herself, but for the daughters she would leave behind. For this reason, death is feared.

Another story about people who thought they were likely to die focuses on the Nova Scotia coal miners referred to earlier in this chapter. Trapped underground, for the first three days the men tried to dig their way to safety. When their battery-powered lights gave out, they waited in total darkness. They would either be saved or they would die.

Before becoming trapped in the mine, the miners in their daily routines had not discussed death with each other and said that they seldom thought of it individually, although they knew that coal mining was dangerous work.[1] Even when trapped in the mine, the men maintained a psychological distance from dying and death by directing their lights away from the dying and dead and by speaking of the dying as if they were already dead, thereby using social death as a substitute for physical death. Furthermore, the miners knew that they were expected "to die 'like a man' with little expressive outcry, but with stoic determination" (Lucas, 1968: 16). Social norms against the expression of fear of dying are strong in male-dominated subcultures and may also exist in female-dominated work subcultures such as nursing (Reutter and Northcott, 1994).

The miners did express to each other in the mine certain regrets about dying. They spoke of things they had planned to do but would have to leave undone. They mentioned their roles as husbands, fathers, and providers, and expressed concern about not being able to fulfil these roles, and the consequences that this might have for the survivors. In this regard, the miners were like the mother in the earlier story who worried more about the daughters she would leave behind in the event of her death than about herself. Finally, the miners engaged in a review of their lives in an attempt to affirm "that their achievements were creditable" (Lucas, 1968: 13). In summary, the miners who faced death did not express fear about their own impending deaths. They did express concern about how they might die, hoping for a quick and painless death, and about the consequences that their death would have for those they left behind.

Arthur Frank, a professor at the University of Calgary, published a personal account of his own experiences with two very different "brushes with death" (Frank, 1991). When he was thirty-nine years of age he had a heart attack, and at forty he was diagnosed with cancer. He survived both life-threatening illnesses and wrote to tell his story.

Frank notes that serious illness takes a person to the edge of life. He refers to life-threatening illness as a "dangerous opportunity" to clarify what is important about life. The danger, of course, is that one might die; however, there is opportunity as well as danger. Standing at the edge of life, at the boundary between life and death, tends to change one's perception of both life and death. When death becomes personal, an immediate and real possibility, questions are raised about how one has lived one's life and how one should live one's life in the future should the illness not prove fatal.

Recovery from his heart attack meant that Frank returned to his previous life "as if nothing had happened." Of course, something had happened, but his inclination was to put the whole experience behind him. The diagnosis of cancer was different. The sense of being in remission rather than fully cured, coupled with the lengthy and demanding experience of cancer treatment, was transformative. Neither Frank, nor his wife, nor his life, nor their life together was the same again.

In analysing his relations with his doctor, Frank observes that their communication involved a detached language of medical objectivity rather than the language of personal experience and subjective perceptions. In other words, communication was "cool" rather than emotional, impersonal rather than personal. Furthermore, the interaction focused on the management of the disease rather than on the experience of it. In short, both doctor and patient conformed to cultural rules that emphasize professionalism and technical and personal competence. In our society, emotionality is associated with incompetence. As a result of this association, persons facing death tend to be denied legitimate expression of their fears, frustrations, and experience.

Frank also wrote about the coherence and incoherence associated with serious illness. Incoherence is the loss of order in one's life and the loss of connection with others whose lives are ordered. Illness, pain, and dying separate a person from the normal biological and social order of lives. Because perceptions of order help a person to make sense of life, incoherence involves loss of a sense of understanding and meaning. Coherence involves (re-)gaining a sense of order, connection, and meaning. Frank observes that communication with others can facilitate the construction and maintenance of coherence. However, he distinguishes between communication in the form of detached medical talk, which tends to promote a sense of incoherence, and the communication of personal experience to sympathetic others which tends to promote a sense of coherence.

Antonovsky (1987) has argued that a sense of coherence is very important to health and well-being. Coherence, he suggests, has three components: comprehensibility, manageability, and meaningfulness. Comprehensibility refers to the ability to make sense of things, to understand, to explain and to predict.

Although things may be either good or bad, it is helpful if they are at least understandable. Manageability refers to the perception of having adequate resources and supports to deal with problems. Meaningfulness refers to the ability to make things meaningful and to find purpose and motivation. Life-threatening events, terminal illnesses, and the death of others can undermine a person's sense of coherence. From the perspectives of both Antonovsky and Frank, the challenge for the person facing death is to hang on to or to re-create their sense of coherence.

Frank describes the experience of a potentially terminal illness as alienating. One is separated from future plans and goals, from past health, from roles and relationships, and from "innocence"—that naive sense of security that persists as long as death remains distant and abstract. Frank notes that all of these losses must be mourned. Yet, society tends to dictate the terms of mourning, and these are not always consistent with the needs of individuals who grieve for their losses in their own way and in their own time. Similarly, Frank complains that the medical system tends to take control of one's body, disease, identity, and even experience. One's identity becomes the disease; one's personal experience, expressed in subjective terms, is treated as largely irrelevant. The challenge for individuals facing death is to hang on to their personal identity and to acknowledge their personal experience in their own terms.

Robert Hughes, a regular contributor to *Time* magazine, described his brush with death in a severe automobile accident that occurred in Australia (Hughes, 1999). Although he does not remember the collision itself, he remembers the hours he was trapped in the wreckage. Gasoline was leaking, and he begged a friend to shoot him if the car caught fire. Hughes preferred to be shot to death rather than face a fiery death; nevertheless, he wanted to live. He writes: "At one point I saw Death… I looked right down his throat, which distended to become a tunnel. He expected me to yield, to go in. This filled me with abhorrence, a hatred of non-being. In that moment I realized … that the 'meaning of life' is nothing other than life itself, obstinately asserting itself against emptiness. Life was so powerful, so demanding, and in my concussion and delirium, even as my systems were shutting down, I wanted it so much."

Hughes's story gives voice to the common assumption that individuals have a strong will to live, find death repugnant, and accordingly resist death. Indeed, it has been argued that, in a non-religious age, the terror of death and the fear of non-being have led to the widespread denial of death (Becker, 1973). Nevertheless, Hughes's story also points out that some types of death are preferred to other types of death, in order to avoid unacceptable suffering, for example.

The story of the car accident contrasts in many ways with the other stories reported above. Hughes's brush with death is sudden. In the other stories, the storytellers have more time to contemplate death's approach. In Hughes's story, death is hated and resisted because of the threat of "non-being." His concerns are immediate and personal. He has little time to come to terms with death. The other storytellers, perhaps because they have more time to contemplate death, tend to come to terms with their own death but resent death more for the disruption that it will cause the loved ones they will leave behind.

FEAR OF DEATH

In Kübler-Ross's model of the dying process, denial is the initial reaction to learning that one is dying. This suggests that, initially, death is unwelcome and unthinkable. In the last stage of Kübler-Ross's model, however, the dying person accepts death (Kübler-Ross, 1969: 118). People who are closer to death often fear it less than persons more removed from death. Furthermore, dying may be feared more than death itself. Nevertheless, for most people most of the time, death is an unwelcome eventuality.

According to Ernest Becker (1973), fear of death is fundamentally motivating and at the same time denied. Becker rewrote the Freudian thesis by arguing that awareness of one's mortality, rather than one's sexuality, is the fundamental human motivation. Furthermore, because awareness of one's mortality gives rise to terror, it is also the fundamental repression: Becker argues that people repress their awareness of their mortality so that they can avoid the anxiety that this awareness provokes.

Becker argues that an awareness of one's mortality provokes terror not only because it ends the individual life but also because it potentially invalidates the life lived. The individual prefers to believe that life is significant and has meaning and purpose. In Becker's terms, people have a need to see themselves as "heroes." The eventuality of death creates a problem for heroism, in that it calls into question the value of the individual life. In other words, awareness of one's ultimate demise creates an existential crisis centring on questions about the meaning of life. To deal with these unsettling questions and emotions, Becker argues that individuals either search for answers of their own creation or, more often, find answers in the form of socially constructed solutions, such as religion, notions of romantic love, or cultural prescriptions about how one can live a good and respected life. These ready-made answers provide direction and rationale that help the individual gain a sense of heroism, a sense that their life is meaningful.

Becker's thesis is hard to prove. If people admit that they fear death, then there is support for Becker's thesis that death provokes terror. However, if people say that they do not fear death, then there is support for Becker's thesis that death is denied. Heads Becker wins; tails he still wins. Nevertheless, his work has some merit. Death is widely "denied" both individually and collectively in contemporary Anglo-Canadian culture (Ramsden, 1991). Young people act and feel immortal (Aiken, 1991: 169). Death has been removed from polite conversation in the home and community (Aiken, 1991: 161; Ariès, 1981). Furthermore, death does seem to raise existential questions and anxieties. The dying person typically attempts to make sense of their impending death and to make sense of their life in the face of death (Marshall, 1986).

THE RELIGIOUS SOLUTION

The religious solution to the problem of death was identified by Becker as the most pervasive and enduring socio-cultural mechanism for defining death in terms that reduce anxiety. However, this solution may be irrelevant for those persons who do not have faith. Furthermore, the religious solution to the problem of death and the meaning of life has been undermined by secular trends. Interestingly enough, people who have strong religious beliefs and people with no religious beliefs tend to report less fear of death than persons with weak religious beliefs (Novak, 1997: 298; Aiken, 1991: 200; Mirowsky and Ross, 1989: 108–111). It appears, then, that the religious solution can make death palatable for those who firmly believe; those people with no religious faith whatsoever also seem to be able to come to terms with death. Death seems to pose the greatest difficulty for those persons who are unsure about what lies beyond death.

THE SPIRITUAL SOLUTION

In a secular era, religion has little force in the lives of many individuals; yet some individuals continue to emphasize spirituality, even in the face of secularization. While spirituality may reflect religious discourses, at the beginning of the twenty-first century it is often linked with non-religious constructions that are designed to assign special meaning and significance to selected experiences such as dying and death. Durkheim ([1915] 1965) observed that things and experiences can be defined as ordinary or special or, in Durkheim's terms, as profane or sacred. Thus, to construct a definition of something as special is to define it as sacred. Once something is defined as sacred, then this thing tends to elicit reverence, respect, and deep consideration. Even in a secular society, there is a tendency to define life as sacred and to give the end of life special consideration. Perhaps the search for meaning and for significance in dying is inherently a spiritual quest.

RISKING DEATH

Gerald Kent (1996) describes himself as "yuppifying rapidly: 33 years old and somewhat paunchy; four young children; a ten-year marriage; a passion for golf and curling; and a busy law practice in Cranbrook, British Columbia." He writes: "I needed a weekend away! The stress and strain of home and practice was calcifying my soul" (81). His weekend away involved climbing Little Robson, a rock outcropping part of the way up Mount Robson, the highest peak in the Canadian Rockies. This was his first experience at rock climbing.

"After the descent," Kent writes, "the relief and happiness of being alive flooded my soul and I initially vowed never to return. I would stick to golf and curling and succumb to domestication at home with a thankful heart... Life was too precious to risk" (81). However, a year later he attempted a dangerous solo ascent of Mount Robson. He worried about leaving his children without a father and wondered how to deal with those who would ridicule him for risking his life. So why did he make the climb? He explains that he thought it "a great way to protest our society's obsession with physical health and security and its willingness to wink its eye at everything that is destructive to spirit and soul" (82).

Paradoxically, and metaphorically speaking, the moral of the story is that one can lose one's life while living it and find one's life by risking the loss of it. Kent was engaging in edgework—that is, in voluntary risk-taking (Lyng, 1990). Note that Kent characterizes his quest in spiritual terms, as an activity to free the spirit and to decalcify the soul. The experience is transcendent. The edgeworker transcends his or her own limitations and the petty circumstances of everyday life. Becker (1973) suggested that an awareness of our mortality undermines our sense of heroism or our definition of ourselves as significant. Ironically, in edgework, coming face to face with mortality by purposely risking one's life is a means of achieving heroism and finding significance for one's life.

Edgework is evident in the current trend towards extreme sports, including skydiving, hang gliding, auto racing, dirt bike racing, triathalons, mountain climbing, mountain biking, whitewater kayaking and rafting, scuba diving, downhill skiing, heli-skiing, ice climbing, and bungy jumping. Edgeworkers acknowledge the risk of dying. Part of that acknowledgment typically involves making the sport as safe as possible. There is no death wish operating here. Edgeworkers want to live—they want to *really* live! They risk death because it makes them feel alive.

Choosing Death

While some persons risk death in order to affirm their life, some choose death voluntarily and purposely. The affirmation of life through edgework highlights the value of life both for the individual and for others in general. The choosing of death, on the other hand, may suggest that life has no value. Because others tend to think of life as inherently worthwhile, it can be particularly difficult for persons who have lost a loved one to suicide to understand and accept the decision of the person who chooses death.

Why would a person choose death over life? As noted above, dying tends to be feared more than death. In death, there is no life, no living, and therefore no pain, suffering, humiliation, and so on. Dying is feared when it involves living with pain and suffering. In such a situation, the dying may prefer to "get it over with," and death may be viewed as a relief and a blessing.

While dying may involve suffering, living may also involve suffering to the point where life does not seem worth living. Suicide ideation—that is, thoughts about suicide—are common and tend to occur in times of sickness or stress (Aiken, 1991: 70, 73). People who are not otherwise facing death may prefer to actively seek death for a variety of reasons: depression, mental illness, grief, loneliness, unhappiness, chronic illness, pain, guilt, shame, low self-esteem, or feelings of failure (Kastenbaum, 1998: 175–205; Aiken, 1991: 76–77). Alternatively, death may be chosen to escape social sanctions such as imprisonment or public humiliation.

Not all persons who attempt or commit attempt suicide want to die. For some, suicidal behaviour is a desperate attempt to obtain help. For others, motivations may include getting attention or seeking revenge (Kastenbaum, 1998: 195–196; Aiken, 1991: 76). Suicide can even be "accidental" (Kastenbaum, 1998: 197): a person may intend to survive their suicide attempt but miscalculate the lethality of the means employed, or may expect to be rescued but not be found in time. Suicide may also result from a momentary impulse when, for the most part, the victim would seem to prefer living. In summary, while some who commit suicide suffer chronically and reject a life without quality, others who commit suicide appear to be more ambivalent about the relative merits of life over death.

In 1984, the National Film Board released a video entitled *The Last Right* (Fortier, Grana, and Howells), a docudrama based on a true story. The video introduces us to three generations living together as an extended family. The grandfather develops a progressive dementia (formerly referred to as senility) resulting from hardening of the arteries in the brain. His behavioural and psychological symptoms include disorientation, memory loss, intermittent periods of lucidity and confusion, wandering, occasional outbursts of anger, and a sense of his own decreasing competence. The video depicts tender family moments and difficult times. There are tense family discussions about whether or not the situation is good for the two young children in the family and whether the grandfather should be placed in a nursing home.

One emotional discussion concerns whether the family should follow the grandfather's wishes. He had previously expressed his wish that if he got really sick he wanted the family to just let him go. He said that he did not want to become a "zombie." He did not want to die like his brother, who had died a long, slow death. When the grandfather indicates that he has decided not to eat any more, the family members have an emotional discussion about how to respond. In the end, the grandfather does stop eating and after three weeks he dies quietly at home.

This video raises questions about whether people should have some control over their dying. Does a person have a right to say how and when they will die? In this video, the grandfather decides to stop eating and thereby hastens his death and determines its cause. His final decision, implemented in his demented condition, is justified in terms of his earlier decision expressed before the onset of his dementia. It had been his expressed will that his life not be prolonged in such circumstances. In short, this video anticipates the so-called living will, more recently referred to as an advance directive (Novak, 1997: 305–308).

In addition, the video focuses on the question of a "better" death. Is it better to die at home or in the hospital? Is it better to die under the care of loved ones or under the care of professionals who are strangers? Is it better to have some say in your dying or should control be given completely to others? The message in this video is that a person's last right is the right to have some say in dying, to exercise some control, and to have personal decisions respected.

PREFERRED LOCATION OF DYING AND DEATH

A "good death" has a number of characteristics. Individuals tend to prefer a quick and peaceful death. Dying individuals may prefer to be conscious, informed, and free to openly express themselves and to exercise some control by participating in the decision-making process. Finally, a good death may be seen as one that takes place at home, where one's surroundings are familiar, comfortable, and meaningful, and where family and friends can freely congregate (Des Aulniers, 1993: 45). Such deathbed ideals have been enshrined in pre-twentieth-century literature and art (Ariès, 1974: 12; 1981). However, as discussed in chapter 2, in the course of the twentieth century, the rise and successes of modern medicine resulted in dying and death being moved from the home to the hospital (Aiken, 1991: 161, 215; Ariès, 1974: 87 -89; Ariès, 1981: 570 -571). In the twentieth century, the hospital has generally been perceived as a good place to be saved from death, but not as a good place to die. The medical community has increasingly questioned the appropriateness of the acute care hospital for the dying. Furthermore, those contemplating dying have tended to characterize a hospital death in negative terms, using adjectives such as cold, technological, antiseptic, and impersonal (Aiken, 1991: 161, 215, 221).

At the beginning of the twenty-first century, the preferences of the dying and their caregivers are resulting in dying being returned to the home and to more home-like institutional environments such as palliative care units and hospices (Aiken, 1991: 221–215; Kastenbaum, 1998: 119–145). As discussed in chapter 3, palliative care, which administers to the dying person's physical, emotional, psychological, spiritual, and social needs (Novak, 1997: 300-304), is increasingly preferred over futile attempts to maintain life. The dying are typically more interested in comfort, dignity, and social support than they are in prolonging their life when prolongation means additional suffering, indignity, and impersonal care.

In this vein, in 1980, the National Film Board of Canada (NFB) released a video entitled *The Last Days of Living* (Gilson and Daly, 1980), which deals with the palliative care unit (PCU) established in 1975 at the Royal Victoria Hospital in Montreal. This unit, which was established to treat the terminally ill, was the first of its kind in Canada (McPherson, 1998: 366; Novak, 1997:

301–302). The PCU serves not only the dying person but assists the bereaved as well, offering services both in the hospital and in the patient's home.

The video features a number of PCU clients who were dying from cancer, including elderly and middle-aged men and women as well as a man in his early twenties. The filmmakers try to show the needs of the dying and the caregivers' response to those needs. The patients' responses to terminal illness range from angry questioning and discouragement to philosophical acceptance. A middle-aged woman who has had a mastectomy cannot fully accept what has happened to her. "It is just not right," she says. One elderly man declines an invitation to go out on the patio on a sunny day. He says that it holds no interest for him and that it won't do him any good. Another elderly man says that he feels lousy and complains that he can't even change his position in bed a half an inch. "You ask for death," he says, meaning that he feels his life is so circumscribed he wishes to die. A young man has decided to forego further treatment in the hospital and go home to die. He talks matter-of-factly about his impending death, observing that he finds it easier now that he knows that he will die, in comparison to the "roller coaster" phase when he and his family lived with uncertainty and vacillated between hope and despair. We are all going to die, he says, and it is only the how and the when that differ. As he expressed it, "There is no right age to die; any age is the right age." His parents observe that his dying has scared his friends away—they have stopped visiting. The video shows the young man and his parents sharing meaningful time together until his death at home.

The Last Days of Living has two central messages. The first is that death comes to us all and comes in its own time: it can come early in life, in middle age, or in later life. The prominence in the video of the young man who dies at home emphasizes the capriciousness of the timing of death and highlights the vulnerability of persons of any age. Furthermore, his story suggests that dying at home can be a positive experience for all involved. This is the second central message of this video—that is, the video can be seen as an attempt to describe the good death, or at least a better death. Dying with the assistance of palliative care, whether in the PCU or at home, is implicitly contrasted with dying in the hospital's intensive care unit while enduring heroic attempts to prolong life. Although this contrast is not made explicit, it is shown that palliative care can make dying less painful and less lonely, thus helping the dying achieve a better death.

LIVING WITH DYING

Two other videos from the NFB show that living with dying can be a long process with both positive and negative aspects. In the video *Living with Dying* (Dolgoy and Phillips, 1991), the audience is introduced to Albert and Margaret Kerestes. Mr. Kerestes was in his early sixties when he was told by a cancer specialist that he was terminally ill and had weeks or perhaps months to live. Mr. Kerestes says that it is difficult to learn that you have only a couple of months. He notes that, initially, he was emotionally upset, but he got over it. Despite his acceptance, this was a difficult time for Mr. and Mrs. Kerestes. Their calendar was full of appointments at the cancer clinic, at the hospital, and with doctors. The medical appointments and regimens took control of their lives. They were glad when this phase came to an end and they were able to go home and regain some control over their own lives. Their home-care nurse emphasized the importance of people having a sense of personal control in such situations.

Mr. Kerestes's dying trajectory did not go as expected: his cancer went into remission. Although he still suffered many limitations and his prognosis was still terminal, he was now living with dying, and the time of his dying was no longer predictable. The home-care nurse described him as a chronic palliative care client. Her initial focus had been on managing pain and symptoms and providing needed physical aids such as a wheelchair. During Mr. Kerestes's long remission, she shifted her focus from active care to surveillance.

Mr. Kerestes benefited from the care received from doctors and hospitals. At home he benefited, in particular, from the care of Mrs. Kerestes, and from the visits of the home-care nurse. The local pharmacist helped make arrangements with Blue Cross to facilitate payments for medications. Other supports included the Kerestes' extended family (grown children, grandchildren, siblings), friends and neighbours, church officials and fellow parishioners, their faith, prayer, and a move to a government-subsidized senior citizen apartment, which charged a fixed percentage of the Kerestes' income for rent and which was at ground level with no stairs to negotiate. Family and social gatherings and activities were frequent and enjoyable. The Kerestes indicated that they never felt alone.

Mr. Kerestes had expected to die and the remission of his cancer was unanticipated. He lived for years following his original diagnosis before finally dying. His home-care nurse said in the video that he wanted to live, and that his wife and family wanted him to live. She noted that he defied the experts and stayed alive because he was a fighter.

This reference to the will to live is common in discussions about dying, reflecting a widespread belief that people have some control over the course of their dying and can will themselves to live or to die. There is some risk in making this assertion. For example, those who live tend to be congratulated for being a fighter and for their strong will to live, while those who die may be blamed for giving up or for lacking in will power. Both congratulation and blame may be misplaced. They both demonstrate our tendency to psychologize death—that is, to overemphasize the power of psychological processes and to underemphasize the power of biological processes. In terms of Mr. Kerestes, other considerations besides will power—social supports, medical treatments, divine intervention, or the capriciousness of the disease—could be credited with prolonging life.

In any case, the reasons for the remission of Mr. Kerestes's cancer are not a particular concern of the filmmakers. Rather, the video shows that, while living with cancer and a terminal diagnosis has its pain and sorrow, living with dying can also have many meaningful and pleasurable moments. Another NFB video, *My Healing Journey: Seven Years with Cancer* (Viszmeg and Krepakevick, 1998), reinforces this point.

In 1991, Joseph Viszmeg was in his mid-thirties when he was diagnosed with adrenal cancer and told that he would likely die within a year. Seven years later he directed, wrote, and edited a video describing his experience. The video shows him in 1991, a filmmaker and a single parent raising a daughter. He is newly diagnosed with terminal cancer. Saying that his first reaction was disbelief, he then speaks of feeling cheated because of the anticipated shortness of his life. He told his daughter that he had a tumour, but did not mention cancer at that time. A risky surgery went well, and a large tumour was removed. A year later Viszmeg married, and the year after that he and his wife, Rachel, became parents to a baby boy.

Following his initial diagnosis and surgery, Viszmeg spoke of the many things he tried in an attempt to promote his health—Native healing practices, spirituality, macrobiotics, transcendental meditation, yoga, and shark cartilage. Nevertheless, many tumours grew back and by 1993 he once again expected that he did not have long to live. He treated his time as a gift and concentrated on the moment. The new baby brought much joy.

Then, unexpectedly, the cancer went into remission, which lasted for several years but was not permanent. In 1997, Viszmeg had surgery again and almost died. His recovery was slow, and he wondered how much time the surgery bought. Acknowledging all the difficulties, he said that sometimes he thought that it would have been better to have done nothing.

Finally, Viszmeg tried chemotherapy which he had previously resisted because of its harsh side effects. At that point, he knew there was almost no chance of cure, but he hoped for relief from his constant pain. In 1991 his newly diagnosed cancer seemed like a novelty; seven years later, it had become "a drag." He said he was bored with it, bored with the pain and nausea and weakness. He wanted the cancer to end. This did not mean that he wanted his life to end. He liked his life and wanted more: he just wanted the cancer to end. At the end of the video, he spoke of the importance of loving and of the wonderful events and people in his life. He died the following year, in 1999.

CONCLUSION

Death inevitably raises questions about meaning—the meaning of life and the meaning to be found in dying and death. Proximity to death because of terminal illness or old age tends to motivate an individual to reflect on the meaning of life and death.

A century ago, death was expected more than it is today. At the beginning of the twenty-first century, death is not expected, except in old age. The premature death of a child, a young adult, or a middle-aged person has become unexpected and difficult to accept.

While individuals generally do not wish to die, some deaths are preferred over others. The ideal death occurs suddenly, without pain, in a familiar setting, and in old age following a life lived to its fullest extent. People tend to fear the process of dying, with its potential losses, indignities, and suffering, more than they fear death itself. People facing death often express more concern for the loved ones that they will leave behind than they do for themselves.

This chapter has focused on perceptions of dying and death from the point of view of the person facing death. In the next chapter, the focus is on the perceptions of those persons who lose a loved one to death—that is, on survivors' perceptions of dying and death.

Notes

1. Haas (1977) observed the same behaviour among the curiously named "high steel ironworkers," who erect the superstructures for high-rise buildings.

Chapter 6

Survivor Perspectives
on Dying and Death

This chapter examines perspectives on dying and death from the point of view of those persons who grieve the loss of a loved one. We begin with some brief comments on health care professionals. The primary focus of the chapter, however, is on the family and friends of the deceased.

Dying and death generally take place in a social context involving both professional caregivers and family members. While the health care system tends to take control of dying and death, health care professionals are not always willing participants in the process of dying. As we discussed in chapter 3, doctors, who are generally trained to cure, have a tendency to view death as evidence of failure. Similarly, health care professionals of all kinds working in acute care hospitals typically emphasize the curative model and may not be equipped organizationally or psychologically to deal with dying, palliative care, and death (Aiken, 1991: 216–217).

Health care workers, especially younger workers, may find caring for the dying stressful (Gow and Williams, 1977). Some health care workers are threatened psychologically by death. Those who choose to work with the dying—in palliative care, for example— may be better suited and have better attitudes for dealing with the dying and the death of their patients (Aiken, 1991: 222–223; Novak, 1997: 301–304).

Some health care workers may fear contamination and death as a result of working with persons dying from infectious diseases. Reutter interviewed thirteen nurses who cared for persons dying from AIDS in an active treatment hospital in western Canada (Reutter and Northcott, 1994). While the risk of contracting HIV/AIDS at work is very small, the nurses expressed concern because of the life-threatening consequences should they become infected. The nurses employed behavioural and cognitive strategies to gain a sense of control. They came to perceive risk as manageable by using precautions such as gloving and masking, reappraising risk as minimal or normal, and using distancing strategies including denial and avoidance of threatening thoughts and situations. The nurses in Reutter's study also accepted risk through finding meaning in their work (Reutter and Northcott, 1993). A sense of meaning was created by accepting the AIDS patient as a person who needs and deserves care, by finding work enjoyable and worthwhile, and by emphasizing professional commitment to care. The notion of risk as meaningful and manageable gave the nurses interviewed by Reutter a sense of security. However, when nurses were exposed to HIV-infected blood or body fluids, their feelings of security dissolved (Reutter and Northcott, 1995). They were instantly reminded of their own vulnerability and mortality.

Professional caregivers who work with the dying are reminded daily of the mortality of others and presumably of their own mortality. Health care workers who care for the dying must "come to terms" with dying and death if they are to provide quality care without undue personal distress.

GRIEF AND BEREAVEMENT

A precise vocabulary has developed to describe the loss of a close friend or family member. Persons who lose a loved one are often referred to as the bereaved and are said to go through a period of bereavement. The bereaved typically experience grief—that is, intense suffering—and go through a process of grieving. Bereaved persons who display their grief publicly are often referred to as mourners and are said to mourn or to be in mourning. If a distinction is to be made between grieving and mourning, it would be that grieving is personal and spontaneous while mourning tends to conform to social and cultural norms (Counts and Counts, 1991; Aiken, 1991: 239).

Some people may suppress emotions that they feel; others may express emotions that they do not feel. In other words, there is not a one-to-one relationship between private and public grieving. Cultural rules describe what emotions can be expressed and when and where they can be expressed. These rules shape the grieving process and can both facilitate and impede grieving. Although cultural rules can legitimate feelings and their expression, these rules also define what is appropriate, and the person who grieves too long or too intensely tends to be defined as abnormal, deviant, pathological, or a danger to self or others (Counts and Counts, 1991).

While individuals may be moved emotionally by the evening news, with its frequent accounts of tragedies around the world, the death of strangers is typically not associated with grief, mourning, or bereavement. It is the death of a significant other, a person with whom one has a personal relationship, that is distressing. In one sense, death ends the relationship; in another sense, death only transforms the relationship. While the deceased is no longer physically present, the relationship continues, transformed, evident in survivors' memories, thoughts, feelings, conversations, and behaviours.

The extent of grief and the course of grieving are influenced by a number of factors. Grieving may be influenced by the timing of death—that is, whether death is sudden and unexpected or occurs at the end of a long dying trajectory (Aiken, 1991: 204, 246). Grieving is also influenced by the nature of the death. Death from suicide, accident, or homicide may be seen as preventable, senseless, and tragic, while death from cancer or Alzheimer's disease may be seen as unpreventable and a "blessing" that brings an end to suffering (Aiken, 1991: 215; Marshall, 1986: 142; Kastenbaum, 1998: 334–335).

Grieving is also influenced by the characteristics of the deceased, such as age. Inasmuch as death is expected in old age, it is generally more difficult to lose a loved one who is young than to lose one who is old (Marshall, 1986). Furthermore, grieving is influenced by the characteristics and personality of the survivor. A parent who has one child, for example, may have more difficulty losing that child than would a parent who has several children (Martin, 1998: 24). Someone who has never experienced the loss of a loved one may have more difficulty than a person who has experienced such a loss, although multiple losses can also be very difficult (Norris, 1994). Males may grieve differently than females (Kastenbaum, 1998: 324–326; Martin, 1998: 18 -19; Martin and Elder, 1993: 81; Fry, 1997: 135; Aiken, 1991: 246–247), and the young may grieve differently than the old (Kastenbaum, 1998: 290–292, 333—336).

Finally, grieving is influenced by the relationship the survivor had with the deceased. Grieving may differ for a parent who loses a young child, an adult who loses an aged parent, a wife who loses her husband, a husband who loses his wife, or an adult who loses a friend. Furthermore, while it may be difficult to lose someone with whom one had a good relationship, it may also be difficult to lose someone with whom relations were strained (Aiken, 1991: 247–249).

In the context of the family, the loss of a loved one results in a change in social status and social roles. A wife who loses a husband becomes a widow, a husband who loses a wife becomes a widower, a parent who loses an only child becomes a non-parent, and a child who loses a parent becomes fatherless or motherless while a child who loses both parents becomes an orphan. These changes in status and role imply changed relationships, changed circumstances, and alterations in personal and social identity. Adjustments following the death of a loved one involve coming to terms not only with the loss of the loved one but also with all of the associated disruptions to the survivor's life.

LOSS OF A CHILD   In the past, the death of a child was a frequent and expected event. Throughout the twentieth century in Canada, the death of a child became an increasingly rare event (Marshall, 1986: 132). Today, children are expected to grow up and grow old. Indeed, the death of a child at any age has come to be unexpected, and parents assume that they will predecease their children (Fry, 1997).

Partly because of the unexpected nature of the event, it is particularly difficult for a parent to accept the death of a child (Martin, 1998:4-5). Braun (1992) interviewed ten Canadian mothers who had each lost a child. At the time of their death, the deceased children ranged from five months gestation to twenty-five years. Braun wanted to understand how bereaved parents develop an understanding of their child's death.

Braun (1992: 62–63) focused on the parents' existing "meaning structure" at the time of their child's death. Meaning structure refers to a person's understanding of the nature of life, including their beliefs and assumptions—a construction of reality that gives life meaning and purpose. For some parents, their existing construction of reality was able to provide a meaningful explanation of the death of their child. Other parents experienced disorientation when their meaning structures could not provide an adequate explanation. Disorientation took the form of a deconstruction of existing beliefs. Adjustment involved a process of reconstructing meaning. Braun (1992: 89) points out that parents who ask "why?" are indicating that they do not have a readily accessible meaning structure in place which they can use to make sense of their child's death.

A person who believes that whatever happens is a manifestation of God's plan has an explanation for a child's death while a person who believes that God should be looking out for the innocent has a problem. Similarly, a person who believes that there are no guarantees in life has an explanation of a sort, while a person who believes that being a good parent will protect a child has a problem. A child's death can raise questions about whether there is a caring God and whether life is just, fair, safe, meaningful, manageable, predictable, purposeful, and ordered. Furthermore, because a child can give a parent's life meaning and purpose, the loss of that child can then be particularly difficult.

According to Braun, loss of meaning resulting from a child's death is associated with guilt, placing blame, anger, incomprehension, feeling disconnected from the world, a wish for their own death, or thoughts of suicide, Loss of meaning is reflected in loss of a sense of security, hope for the future, motivation, and interest, as well as loss of a sense of personal control and purpose. The process of adjustment involved searching for an explanation for the child's death and searching for a new sense of meaning and purpose in life.

Martin (1998) studied the reactions of Canadian parents to the loss of their child as a result of sudden infant death syndrome (SIDS). In this situation, parental grief tends to be particularly intense because SIDS takes the life of a baby, occurs suddenly without warning, has no known cause, and is investigated by legal authorities including the police and the medical examiner.

Reviewing the existing research on SIDS, Martin noted that bereaved parents manifest a wide range of individual grief reactions including emotional manifestations such as shock, numbness, sorrow, depression, anxiety, anger, and fear. Cognitive reactions include "flashbacks" to the moment of discovering the deceased baby, obsessive reviewing of the circumstances prior to baby's death, preoccupation, difficulty concentrating, dreams about the baby, self-reproach, guilt, and difficulty controlling thoughts. Physical reactions include problems sleeping, headaches, stomach problems, fatigue, dizziness, chest pain, and loss of appetite. Regarding spiritual reactions, some parents rely on their faith while others question or lose faith. For some, life loses meaning and purpose. Behavioural reactions include crying, restlessness, moving to a new residence, losing interest in social activities, difficulties at work, ineffective functioning, taking medications, and increased smoking or drinking. Some consider or attempt suicide.

The studies that Martin reviewed also showed that spousal relationships are affected by the loss of an infant to SIDS. The husband and wife may grieve in different ways, and their grieving may follow different timelines. These differences can be a source of marital strain. Yet, while some couples experience increased marital difficulties, some marital relationships are strengthened.

When there are other children in the family, SIDS takes a baby away from its parents and its older siblings. The other children may feel guilt that they are somehow responsible for the baby's death. They may show anger or anxiety, have nightmares, ask repeated questions, and have behavioural problems. The loss of the baby also affects the relationships among the surviving children and their parents. Both the parents and the surviving children are changed because of their grief and loss. The siblings have to cope with changed relationships with their grieving parents and the parents have to cope with their children who are also grieving each in their own way. Sometimes children become angry with their parents. Parents can become distant from their children or, alternatively, can become overprotective.

Martin's own research featured in-depth interviews with nine couples and another three mothers, each of whom had lost a baby to SIDS. The deaths ranged from as recently as less than one year prior to the study to over twenty-five years ago. In reviewing the wide range of reactions of individual parents to the loss of their baby, Martin concluded that underlying these various individual reactions was the undermining of the foundation upon which the parents had built their lives. The baby's death abruptly and substantially altered the parents' lives. Not only was the baby suddenly gone, but the seeming randomness of SIDS undermined the parents' sense that the world is ordered, comprehensible, predictable, manageable, just, and meaningful. Accordingly, the baby's death lead to a "search for reason" in an attempt to find the cause and meaning of the baby's death. Parents sought to make sense not only of their baby's death but of their own lives once again.

Grieving for a deceased baby involves emotional pain, but searching for the reason for the baby's death is also a reaction to cognitive, intellectual, and spiritual pain (Martin, 1998). Death occasions various kinds of pain and various responses to suffering. At a cognitive level, Martin observed that some parents were able to reconcile the loss of their baby with their previous world-view. Other parents constructed a new world-view, some "for the better and some for the worse." Still others were unable to make any sense of their baby's death. The perspective that parents took "made the difference between eventual healing or continual hell" (Martin, 1998: 219).

Martin (1998: 229–232) described five phases of the grief process. Parents who had lost a baby spoke of the loving attachment that had developed prior to the baby's death. They then spoke of being devastated, trying to carry on while struggling for control, learning to let go, and being changed. She argued that "being changed" does not necessarily imply recovery, resolution, or healing. Indeed, she challenged "the myth" that people can ever fully recover. According to Martin, "Since some people improve and some people never function well again, I propose that we stop using the word 'recovery' to describe the goal of the grief process. We need to start talking about how traumatic experiences can change survivors. My study clearly shows that the death of a child changed the parents, some negatively and some positively" (232). She concludes by commenting on the power and potential of the human mind to construct interpretations of devastating events such as the death of a child, constructions that often help the bereaved deal with their grief.

The following is an account written by a father who experienced the unthinkable—the unexpected loss of two of his four children in separate fatal accidents.

"When a loved one dies, a part of you also dies." This cliché is in fact, true. The moment someone close to you dies, you are a changed person. Instantaneously. Your whole being transforms the moment a close one departs from his or her earthly existence. They exit, and in reality, your being as you knew it also exits. You immediately become a different person. Whether you like it or not, or wish to acknowledge it, it's true. If you don't believe it, a perception check of those immediately around you should make you aware of this fact. The world's perception of you changes. This truism is all the more pronounced when one loses a close one tragically. Instantaneously. One second a loved one is here. A second later gone. Your total world goes numb. You hope that it is just a bad dream, a nightmare, that you will awake from and get on with normal living. Deep down you know this is only wishful thinking. Your world, as you knew it, has changed forever. You walk around in a daze, put up a brave front, and proceed to do all the normal things like nothing has happened. Pick up the mail, wash the dishes, all the while fighting a deep depression that totally engulfs your whole being, from the tips of your toes to the bristling hairs on your head. You reflect on how life was a few moments ago, a few days ago, and yearn for the clock to be turned back just enough to by-pass the tragedy you are now faced with. But in your heart you know you have to somehow muster the strength to deal with the situation at hand, impossible and unreal as it might seem.

No one has prepared you for this moment. You read about it happening to other people; the sudden loss of a child—It sent shivers down your spine, made you feel totally uncomfortable and vulnerable. Something to quickly forget. A parent's worst nightmare; sudden death of a child. Now it has happened to you. Not once, but twice, in the matter of a couple of years. Moments earlier, your daughter was healthy and alive. Now the policeman, in your living room, at three o'clock in the morning, tells you she is dead. How can this be possible? Two years later, one o'clock in the morning. Two policemen on your back step. Your son has been in an accident, they're working on him, we'll drive you to the hospital. Body language and the words of the police tell me that our son is indeed dead. We drive to the hospital and meet reality face to face. Another child suddenly departed. Without warning. How does one cope; where is one's statute of limitations on grief and pain? Numbness, depression, a longing for moving the clock back, just a couple of hours.

Years earlier, the phone rang at approximately five o'clock on a Saturday afternoon in early February. A relative is on the other end. "There's been an accident, your mother is dead." I was introduced into the real world of grief, pain, and coping with loss. Anxiety, depression, and sense of loss. Ongoing. How to muster enough energy to get through a day; this was an ongoing battle. Now two children dead in the short span of just over two years. When does one's reservoir run dry? I remember, at this time, using the quote attributed to William Irwin Thompson: "The future is beyond knowing, but the present is beyond belief."

When our daughter died, I felt that I was regressing in grief and despondency. After six months I felt worse than after the first week. I was fortunate that a counsellor gave me some materials on "coping with loss." I then recognized the grief cycle I was going through; first six months, a year, and so on. It didn't make it easier, but at least I became aware that there are some usually predictable happenings in the grief cycle, and one usually has to go through the full grief cycle before one can return to cope with a "normal" life again. Not dealing effectively with grief can leave one stranded in "grief limbo" endlessly fighting a futile battle until the end of one's mortal existence.

What coping mechanism worked for me? I have no magic answer. Daily, I have to deal with memories, an enormous sense of loss. However, I feel that part of our difficulty in dealing with the death of close ones, and those others in our immediate environment, is that it puts us in direct touch with our own mortality. Realizing this, one has to acknowledge the minute shortness of time one has on earth. To live to 80, or 8, the time spent on earth in comparison to eternity is minuscule. I look around, and death is continuous. A close friend, a neighbour, a relative. Everyone dies a mortal death. Thus, it makes it all the more important that we make the most of the few minutes we do have on earth. We should not become a victim of a close death; by martyring oneself to the memory of a departed close one, we in fact also become a victim of the initial death. However, it is much easier said than done. Our emotions, our sense of loss can be overwhelming.

A close friend of mine passed away, shortly after my daughter's death. A couple of years ago I saw his widow on the street. I asked her how she was doing. She said, "it's okay to remember, but not to dwell."

I found that co-workers, friends, neighbours, and acquaintances have difficulty in acknowledging your dilemma. We are all good at sending cards, flowers, and attending the immediate functions such as the funeral and luncheons. Then it is over. You are on your own, to grieve your loss in a vacuum. Very few want to enter this domain. It becomes your own personal battleground. Everyone gets back to their life, their worries, their concerns. You feel isolated, despondent, abandoned. The pain of loss is usually too much for "outsiders" to comprehend. It is better to stay a safe distance away. Most everyone wants to be "associated" with someone who "lady luck" shines down on; the sweepstakes winner, the person who visibly is on a positive track in life. The opposite holds true for those perceived to be "down on their luck." Whether we like it or not, there is a general perception that we are in control of our destiny; we reap what we sow. Death is not where it's at. Avoidance of the situation is most prudent for most concerned. I have no problem with that—when I was younger I tried to avoid thinking of death—a casket was cause for concern. However, the reality is that death is a major part of life. No one can escape it. We must all some day face death head on.

Personally, I sincerely believe that on earth we are but travellers, passing through a transition period. A very short trip in an eternal spectrum. But a very important trip. We are not human beings having a spiritual experience. We are spiritual beings having a human experience. In my mind, this belief brings reason to an otherwise meaningless existence.

How does one really cope with extreme grief? With great difficulty. I found that some very close friendships can add some comfort, family pets, physical activity such as weights and tennis, walking, a strong belief in the "hereafter," a loving wife, a sense of humour, and most of all the avoidance of the word "why?" As other factors/individuals played significant roles in the demise of our two children, I was initially adamant that these said parties formally acknowledge responsibility for their actions. In both cases, neither party was willing to do so. I have accepted this as something I have no control over, and life must go on. However, I think it indicates a common significant human factor in coping with the sudden death of a loved one; someone or something is perceived to be totally or partially responsible for the tragic sudden ending. Surely it is more than just "chance."

Also, I found that in the cases of all three deaths [mother, daughter, son], I felt a strong urgency to have their memories live on. It seems that the moment a person dies, he or she becomes a nonentity to the rest of the earthly living population, with the exception of the immediate loved ones. Therefore, any dedication to their memory was and is most important to me. I find that most people have trouble talking about the "dead."…It is like a pretence that they never existed. I find this disheartening. These departed individuals are still family. The fact that they have departed earth a few minutes before me does not change their status. They are still loved ones, my family members.

Death, tragic or otherwise, of loved ones, weighs heavily on the minds and souls of those left behind. Coping is an ongoing process. And like a member of Alcoholics Anonymous, the survivor must take one day at a time. Grief can overtake one instantaneously, if one leaves the door open. Honour those that have gone before you, and fill your remaining days on earth with good works. (Personal communication, 1999)

This father's story of the deaths of his daughter and son contains four themes: change, personal feelings of grief, personal coping, and social reactions. The father notes that the loss of each child brings change. He feels that part of him has died, his world as he knew it has changed forever, he feels different, and he believes that others see him differently. Yearning for life as it was before tragedy struck, for his normal life, he nevertheless recognizes that his previous life is irretrievable. For friends and neighbours, disruption is temporary. The father's life, however, is permanently altered. There is no going back, and going forward involves coping with grief.

The second theme is personal feelings of grief. The grieving father experiences a range of emotions including numbness and feeling dazed, yearning and longing, depression and despondency, isolation and abandonment, pain, and a sense of loss. He writes of feeling worse months after the initial tragedy and of going through the motions of daily living while fighting deep depression. Keeping the memories of his deceased children alive becomes a goal. He suggests that one never fully recovers from grief, for it can intrude again in an instant.

With regard to the third theme, the father describes coping as an ongoing process. He writes about putting on a brave front, mustering strength and energy to deal with immediate situations, and *acting* normal as if nothing has happened. His coping is facilitated by his wife, some close friends, his pets, physical activity, and a sense of humour. Although he notes that going through the "full grief cycle" helps one to cope, at the same time he observes that grief is ongoing and can surface and overwhelm at any moment, "if one leaves the door open."

In the process of coping, he is initially adamant that the people who were directly involved in the tragedies acknowledge the part they played and accept responsibility for their actions. Otherwise, he explicitly avoids asking "why?" Indeed, he adds (personal communication) "that I have always felt that it is pointless to pose the question 'why' when a death occurs—I feel strongly that part of my survival gear for coping is to never let 'Why did this happen?' be part of my repertoire." Instead, he finds assurance in his beliefs in spiritual existence and eternal life. From his beliefs, he gains a sense that human life and, therefore, human events ultimately happen for a reason and have meaning.

In addition, he uses an intellectual strategy to normalize death. He comments on the pervasiveness of death: sooner or later everyone dies. He himself has experienced the death of loved ones; he knows others who have lost loved ones; he acknowledges his own mortality. This normalization of death, tied to his beliefs in eternal life, renders death more acceptable.

Finally, this father comments on the social reactions to his family's losses. He makes three points, all of which relate to the concept of stigma. First, he notes that the world's perception of him has changed. He is now seen as one of the unlucky, one of the unfortunate. In this new social status, he receives sympathy, but also blame, reflecting the tendency for people to assume that the unfortunate are in some way responsible for their misfortune. This social reaction is both victim-blaming and stigmatizing, and supports the argument of Posner, discussed in chapter 4, that people associated with death are stigmatized because death itself is stigmatized. The father acknowledges this lack of social acceptance when he notes that people tend to avoid the unlucky and unfortunate.

Second, the father recollects a widow saying to him, "it's okay to remember, but not to dwell." He interpreted this comment positively. He understood her to say (personal communication) that "it is important and okay to remember a dearly departed one, but one should not dwell on the memory to a point that one gets depressed and regresses into deep depression." The widow's comment conveys encouragement and advice and reflects society's rules for the bereaved. The widow encourages him to remember but also to be careful not to wallow in self-pity.

Third, the father observes that, after the initial events of tragedy and funeral, others go back to their normal lives and distance themselves from the grieving family. These people have difficulty acknowledging or participating in the family's grieving. Indeed, avoidance is the typical response. On this point, the father says: "I find that most people have trouble talking about the 'dead.'…It is like a pretence that they never existed." This avoidance indicates social stigma. When people are faced with social stigma, they tend to experience discomfort, distance themselves, use avoidance, and act *as if* nothing is wrong. The father finds this social response disappointing and unsupportive.

Turning now from parents to grandparents, when parents lose a child, grandparents lose a grandchild. Fry (1997) studied 152 grandparents in Alberta who had lost a grandchild in the previous three years. Although, most of the grandchildren were under nineteen years of age at the time of their deaths, some were young adults. Fry found that grandparents often reported survivor guilt—that is, they felt that it was their turn to die and that the grandchild should not have died. Fry's analysis of responses to an open-ended questionnaire and to in-depth interviews shows the multidimensionality, complexity, and diversity of the grief reactions of grandparents to the loss of a grandchild. Finally, Kastenbaum (1998: 332) observed that, when grandparents lose a grandchild, they grieve not only for the deceased grandchild but also for their own child who is the grieving parent of the deceased.

LOSS OF A SPOUSE
Many marriages end with the death of one of the spouses. Because women have a longer life expectancy than men and tend to be younger than their male partners, the husband is more likely to die before his wife, leaving her a widow. Indeed, in Canada there are currently about five widows for every widower.

Widowhood typically occurs in the older years and the likelihood of being a widow or widower increases with age (Matthews, 1991: 2–7; Northcott, 1984).

The loss of a spouse tends to be experienced as a particularly stressful event, although for some persons other events may be more stressful (e.g., the death of a child). In some cases, a widowed person may view the death of a spouse as a positive thing, e.g., as in the case of the death of an alcoholic or abusive spouse (Matthews, 1991: 17–19). Vezina et al. (1988; see also Ducharme and Corin, 1997) studied older persons who had lost a spouse and found that, while bereavement tends to be generally stressful, some of the bereaved were at greater risk for depression and anxiety than others. Widowhood later in life tends to be more "expected" than early in life (Matthews, 1991: 20; 1987). There is a complicated relationship between the timing of widowhood (i.e., early or late in life), anticipation of the spouse's death (i.e., whether widowhood is expected or not), the intensity of grief, and the resolution of the grieving process. Some evidence indicates that widowhood is most stressful when it is unexpected and occurs early in life (Matthews, 1991: 19–23, 25).

In marriage, spouses tend to develop a shared identity and a shared life. The loss of a spouse undermines this identity and transforms the life of the surviving spouse. Furthermore, the social status of the surviving spouse is devalued, even stigmatized to a degree. Widowhood then tends to be psychologically and socially disorienting. Adjustment for many widowed persons—both male and female—tends to occur within several years. Some even come to see widowhood as an opportunity for growth and a time of autonomy, independence, and freedom (Matthews, 1991: 23–29, 33–34, 119; see also Gee and Kimball, 1987: 89–90).

Widowhood may affect men and women differently. Women are more likely than men to be economically disadvantaged by the loss of their spouse. Further, men and women may have different coping strategies and tend to have different social support networks, which they access differently. Although it may be experienced somewhat differently, the loss of a spouse may be equally difficult for both men and women (see Norris, 1994; Matthews, 1991: 89).

Van den Hoonaard (1997) analysed ten published autobiographical accounts of widowhood written by widows in Canada and the United States. Most of the authors lost their husbands after long illnesses. The stories of their marriages and the dying of their husbands were integral parts of these stories of widowhood, indicating what was lost and how it was lost. Despite long dying trajectories and the anticipation of death, the women experienced shock at the time of their husbands' deaths.

Because they were written for an audience, mostly other widows, these accounts are both descriptive and instructive—that is, the stories are descriptive personal accounts with which a reader can empathize and, at the same time, the accounts provide guidance for a reader who is seeking to know what to do in a similar situation.

Van den Hoonaard's analysis of these accounts of widowhood yields common themes relating to loss of identity and its reconstruction. In a process that van den Hoonaard terms "identity foreclosure" the loss of the husband and of social interactions (including friendships) that depended on being a couple undermined the widows' sense of self. At the death of the husband, the old identity as a wife and as a couple became obsolete. The widows described themselves as no longer knowing who they were nor how they fit into society. A new identity as a widow was thrust upon them, an identity that was not chosen, not welcomed, and that was perceived as a devalued social status. Being called a widow or filling out a form and having to select "widow" for one's marital status for the first time became "identifying moments" in which the wife's new status as a widow was often shockingly and painfully driven home. In these moments, the widows came to know that their identity had been transformed and that they were viewed differently by society. These widows were made to feel that they were different, and they were treated differently in a couples-oriented society.

According to van den Hoonaard, the transformation of identity is a process in which the previous identity as a wife is lost and replaced with the socially imposed identity as a widow. The loss of the old identity is disorienting and the imposition of the new one is distressing. In time, however, a new and positive identity is created. The authors of these stories tend to describe themselves as becoming "new women" with new characteristics such as greater self-reliance and increased independence.

Widowhood can be real or anticipated. Sometimes a spouse has a "brush with death" that leads her or his partner to contemplate the possibility of loss and the life that would result from that loss. For example, a woman in her thirties tells about her reaction to her husband's brush with death:

> I have been married to my husband for fifteen years. My husband spends about 50 per cent of the year out of the country on business, leaving me and our three children alone to cope without a husband or a father. Need-

less to say, I have become a part-time single parent. I have gotten used to this over the years but never did I think that part-time single parenting could potentially become full-time single parenting. Last week my husband had a brush with death that would have left me a widow and our three children without a father.

My husband travels frequently to Taiwan on business, experiencing small earthquakes on almost all of his trips. So, I didn't get too hysterical when I was told of another earthquake in Taiwan, this time registering 7.6 on the Richter scale. My friend, who informed me of the most recent Taiwan earthquake, was surprised that I was so calm. She wondered if I was in a state of shock. But I knew that what you heard on the radio or saw on TV was the worst damage caused by the earthquake and that my husband was probably just fine. Meanwhile, my husband left voice mail on our answering machine that he was alive and well.

When I received his message, I returned his call immediately. I was relieved to hear that he was well, but didn't really expect that I would hear any differently. My husband told me to call all our family to let them know that he was fine should they watch the evening news and panic. Being in the middle of the day most of our family were working so I just left messages on their answering machines. My voice was cheerful and reassuring. But when I got a live person on the end of the phone, that's when my whole outlook changed.

When I talked to my husband's sister I fell apart. She started the conversation by asking (as she always does), "How are you?" That's when it happened. I fell apart. I could hardly get a word out. I was crying uncontrollably. I could hardly speak between sobs. I guess it was at that point in time that I realized I could have been a widow at a very young age. I wasn't prepared to be a widow and a single mother of three children. The possibility of becoming a widow was terrifying. I was used to being alone and a part-time single mother, but I always knew that this was a temporary situation. In a few days or weeks, my husband would be arriving home and we would share the parenting role once more. It took about ten minutes before I gained some sort of composure.

LOSS OF A PARENT

Within minutes another one of my friends phoned. Once again, my tears took me by surprise. So why was this happening now? I concluded that it must be because at the time I was talking to my husband I was just grateful that he was all right. I didn't really think about the "what ifs?" I didn't really think about potentially becoming a widow until I started talking to more and more people.

This emotional period was short-lived. In the end, I realize that I have no time or energy to dwell on the "what ifs" and therefore, my fleeting thoughts of widowhood were just that, fleeting. (Personal communication, 1999)

At first, the storyteller cognitively assesses the odds of her husband being killed in the earthquake and concludes confidently and unemotionally that everything is most likely all right. Concern expressed by others, however, cues her and leads her to re-evaluate her own level of concern—to consider the "what ifs," as she puts it. This draws out an intense, although brief, emotional reaction.

Why did the what ifs upset her? A family is a set of relationships, roles, circumstances, and patterns, and all of these are disrupted by the death of one of its members. In this story, the person who might have been killed occupies the roles of husband and father, roles that would have been vacated and left unfilled by his death. The family's circumstances and patterns would have been disrupted, and the survivors' roles and social statuses would have been transformed—from wife to widow, from part of a parenting couple to a single parent, and from children with a father to fatherless children. These transformations were things that the storyteller had not really considered previously, was not prepared for, and found terrifying. Death is disruptive. While death is the final disruption of the life of the deceased, death also disrupts the lives of the surviving family members. The family, as it had been, no longer exists. The family is transformed and the survivors have to adjust to a new life.

The preceding storyteller describes her husband's brush with death and her thoughts about being left a widow. The storyteller's two eldest daughters, aged twelve and thirteen, also described their reactions to the question "What if Dad had died?" Nina,[1] aged twelve writes:

As my mom was explaining that my dad was in a near death experience (Taiwan earthquake), the question "What if my dad were to die" flashed through my mind. Shortly after she was done talking and said that my dad was all right I stopped thinking about it. I thought about the question for about one minute and, after that, I thought about it a bit occasionally, but after I found out he was okay all the questions just slowly disappeared. Although I only thought about it a little while, I still cared just as much as someone who couldn't get their mind off it (Personal communication, 1999).

While the question "What if my dad were to die?" flashed into her mind, Nina was quickly reassured. Her dad was safe, so there was no reason to get upset. She did not dwell on what might have happened but instead focused only on what did happen. Her last comment suggests slight defensiveness, as if she felt that she might be criticized for her reaction. However, she saw no reason for concern, reminding the reader that this does not mean that she does not care.

This story contains a twelve-year-old's honest report of her reaction and, at the same time, an acknowledgment of her awareness that others may have expectations about how she should react. As people age, it perhaps becomes increasingly difficult to distinguish one's unique personal reactions from one's socialized reactions that reflect one's understanding of society's expectations.

Nina's thirteen-year-old sister, Mackenzie, also gives her thoughts on the question "What if my dad had died?" She writes:

> "Do you want the good news or the bad news first?" was my mom's question introducing the terrible disaster that happened. My mom told my sister and me that my dad was okay, however, he was in an earthquake. A million questions went through my mind at that time. Such as, how big was this earthquake? How many lives did it take? I was relieved that my dad was all right but couldn't help but wonder how many kids had lost their dads. After my mom said that dad was all right I didn't think much of it. I thought about it but it wasn't on my mind every waking moment. People kept calling and asking how I was feeling and if I was okay. My dad was fine so what more did I have to worry about? I feel bad for people that lost someone close to them.
>
> "What if my dad had died?" That is a question that I thought about a little more than once. It was weird to think my dad wouldn't come home after work and say hello to all of us. Or that I would never get to spend time with him again or even talk with him because he would be gone. The last words that I said to my dad was to go away and turn off the lights. I said that because it was like 6:00 AM and I was half asleep. If my dad was to die then I wouldn't want those to be my last words to him. That was probably what I thought about the most. I thank God for sparing my dad's life. I pray for all of those who lost someone close to them. (Personal communication, 1999).

Mackenzie, who, like her sister, is quickly reassured that her dad is fine, and sees no reason to get upset. Nevertheless, she identifies and sympathizes with children who did lose their fathers. She acknowledges that, if her dad had died, it would have been "weird" —that is, her life would have been transformed by the loss of both her father and the familiar pattern of her relationship with him. She would also have regrets. For example, she would regret the last words that she said to him when he woke her early in the morning to say goodbye as he left for his business trip. Mackenzie recognizes that the loss of a loved one implies not only the loss of a relationship but also the loss of the familiar and the necessity of adjusting to a new and unanticipated life.

Silverman, Nickman, and Worden (1995) studied children aged six to seventeen who had recently lost a parent to death. They found that the children constructed connections to the deceased that helped them maintain a relationship with their dead parent. Five things helped the children to create and maintain this connection to the deceased. First, the children tended to locate their dead parent, often in heaven. Second, they experienced the deceased in dreams or in feelings—for example, feeling that the parent was watching them. Third, the children reached out to the dead parent by visiting the cemetery, perhaps, or by speaking to the deceased. Fourth, the children thought about and remembered the parent. Finally, they held on to certain objects that served as reminders of the deceased.

While the connection that the child constructs with the deceased parent tends to evolve over time, it does not end. Silverman et al. write: "Bereavement should not be viewed as a psychological state that ends or from which one recovers... The emphasis should be on negotiating and renegotiating the meaning of loss over time, rather than on letting go" (269).

LOSS OF A FRIEND A young adult woman was asked if she had had any experience with dying and death. She answered with the following account about the death of a school acquaintance.

> When you first asked if I had experienced death in my life I initially thought of family situations, of which I have no close experiences. It surprised me when I remembered that a friend, Joyce, died when I was in high school. For all the time that I had known her she had leukemia. We met in junior high school when her family moved [to the city] to be closer to the hospitals for her sake. She never really seemed sick. Except for the initial rumours that circulated when she first came to our school, none of us really thought about it much.
>
> I got to know her well in high school as we had English class together. We talked about a lot of things including her illness. I remember her being a lot of fun and very strong willed. During that same year her

cancer started to progress. I don't really know all of the medical things that were happening to her. Some friends and I went to visit her in the hospital; she seemed in great spirits. We never really thought that anything bad was really happening. We all got sick; we all got better.

Things progressed pretty quickly. She slipped into a coma and was put into intensive care. Then we arrived at school one day and her closest friend came up to us in tears and we knew that she had died. The first class I had that day was English. During the announcements they informed us that she had died and we had a moment of silence. One girl in the class started sobbing and I remember a guy in the back saying something like, "I don't know why she's crying she didn't even know her." I didn't cry. I remember wondering why since I had known her pretty well. I continued going to classes through the day until someone told me that people who had known Joyce were in the guidance counsellor's office. I went because I wanted to make sure that some of my other friends were okay. A number of them met me in the hall because they had been looking for me. Many were crying but I still wasn't.

It was very surreal. None of us really knew what to do. We decided that we should go to the funeral home. So the night before the funeral we decided to go together. One thing that sticks out clearly in my mind was that we did not know what we were supposed to do. It was strange because Joyce's mom was the one that took us under her wing and led us into the room where the casket was laying.

The casket was closed because she had wasted [away] a great deal and the family thought it would be better. As we stood around the casket I was wishing that the casket were open so that I could really believe that she was gone. It was difficult to really believe it. I stared at the picture of Joyce on the casket and thought over and over again how it was her lying inside, that we would not see her again. That was when the tears started to come. It was overwhelming. I don't think I had ever really sobbed in my life, but I was right there in front of a bunch of strangers, but I wasn't thinking about that at all. My crying touched off the rest, so the five or six of us stood there sobbing our hearts out for a good long time. Joyce's mom and aunt were comforting us. They seemed to want to take care of us.

One of our friends had experienced death in her family a great deal more than the rest of us. We looked to her for guidance. There was a kneeling bench in front of the casket, so I whispered to ask her if it was for praying. I knelt and prayed for Joyce's family and for us. After our tears had dried up we went to the lounge and talked together. I think everyone felt very badly for us. We decided to go back to my house together because my parents were away. We just wanted to be together for awhile. We just talked, watched some TV and played Twister. I think we wanted to laugh. We talked about Joyce a bit but mostly we chatted about nothing.

The next day was the funeral. I had a lot of anxiety because the only nice clothes I had were light colours and I thought that was sacrilegious but I wore them anyway. I remember a lot of detail from that day even though it was seven years ago. I remember Joyce's mother, brother, and sisters coming in along with Joyce's boyfriend. I remember the minister's eulogy, how we laughed at Joyce's aggressive basketball skills but also reminisced about her tender concern for others. Everything about the funeral was new to me. I think it was the very first funeral I had ever been to. Again, I didn't cry. I think that [may have been seen] as a sign that I didn't really care but it was more that I don't cry very often. The outpouring at the funeral home was a great shock to me.

The reception seemed strange to me. To be sitting around eating, laughing, joking, chitchatting while Joyce was dead. It was awkward for me. After the funeral we talked about Joyce less and less. I would think of her in English class, wishing she was there so we could gossip in the back row, but life went back to normal quickly for us. When there was a write-up about Joyce in our graduating yearbook, two years after she died, I wondered why it was there. Nobody seemed to remember her. She would have accomplished a lot in her life; she had accomplished a lot by the time she died at fifteen. I suppose some of that came from knowing that she had a terminal illness.

I'm not sure how much of my grief was for Joyce and how much was over the fact that someone my age was dead. Her opportunities were over. As I think about all this now I am wondering what if. What if she had lived to be twenty-three years old, as I have? What would she be doing now? Would she be proud of me? Have I used the years wisely that she didn't have? It's hard to think about those things; perhaps that was why she was so far from my consciousness when we discussed my experience with death. (Personal communication, 1999)

The storyteller, who faced dying and death for the first time in her relatively young life, speaks of the strangeness of dying and death. At first the schoolmate who died is not perceived to be sick, despite her terminal illness, and the storyteller indicates that nobody really thought of the possibility of her dying. Even when the girl is obviously sick and in the hospital, her schoolmates still assume that she will recover. Death is not known: it is a stranger to these young people.

When death does come, the storyteller describes the situation as surreal, as dreamlike and without context. Accordingly, Joyce's schoolmates did not know what to do. Once again, death is described in terms of its strangeness. The one schoolmate who had experience with death was looked to for guidance by those who were not experienced.

The storyteller speaks of her and her friends' intense, though brief, outpouring of grief. While the grief was because of Joyce, it seems to have also been occasioned by a loss of naivety—that is, by the realization that a young person can die and that so much unlived life can be lost. A moral is taken from the story focusing on the value of life and the importance of living life wisely.

Finally, the salience of another's death tends to recede from active consciousness as survivors get on with the business of everyday life. While the story of Joyce is not a memory that the storyteller visits every day, it was nevertheless a significant event, a socializing event in the sense of providing instruction about dying and death, and a memory that the storyteller calls upon when she thinks of dying and death and their meaning for her.

A SECOND-ORDER ACCOUNT OF DYING

This young woman's story of her experience of the death of another is a personal account—that is, an account of the first order. First-order accounts of dying and death take the form of Y's account of Z's dying and death. For example, a wife's account of her husband's dying is a first-order account, which gives the wife's version of how she experienced the dying and death of the loved one.

Second-order accounts, on the other hand, take the form of X's account of Y's experience of Z's dying and death. X's account may be a more or less accurate representation of Y's experience. Accurate or not, X's account reveals X's subjective understanding and often evaluation of Y's experience. Consider the following second-order account provided by a young woman.

> I am really concerned about my aunt. My uncle is dying with stomach cancer. It was a great shock when he was diagnosed last year and the doctor determined that he would not survive. Over the year he has been in and out of hospital a great deal undergoing a number of surgeries to relieve some of his pain and to help his digestive system. I have been pretty removed from the whole situation; even though I was living very close to

my aunt and uncle I only saw my uncle once since he was diagnosed and saw my aunt only a few more times than that.

My aunt has spent a lot of time trying to deny the fact that her husband is dying. She didn't tell their children for a time after she found out that his cancer was terminal. Each time my uncle has had to return to the hospital it serves as a reminder that he is dying but then when he is again released it seems that she tries to forget the end prospect. She has done very little planning for a future without him; I recently found out that a will has not even been signed. When I think of the difficulties that she has been dealing with and will have to deal with I wonder how she will get out of bed every day.

She is my father's sister and is relying on him for a great deal. Any time she has a crisis he is the first one she calls. When I speak with him on the phone I notice the toll that it is taking. My aunt is expecting when my uncle dies that my father will make all of the funeral arrangements and bail her out of the difficulties of not having a will, etc. All this time I think that my father is facing his own fears of death. I think that for him cancer is very frightening and stomach cancer the most frightening of all. His grandfather died of stomach cancer; he fears that he is in line as cancer can be hereditary. Watching the suffering of my uncle is no doubt bringing back memories as well as touching on a great fear for his own health. (Personal communication, 1999)

While this woman's account of her aunt's reaction to her husband's dying is empathetic, it is also critical. The storyteller indicates her concern for her aunt. However, while acknowledging her aunt's distress, shock, and denial, and her difficulty facing the dying and impending death of her husband, the storyteller is critical of her aunt. The niece feels that her aunt should face reality, plan more adequately, cope better, and be more self-reliant. The aunt is portrayed as overly reliant on her brother (the storyteller's father). Finally, the storyteller is concerned for her father, whom she perceives to be overly burdened by his sister's difficulties and distressed by concerns for his own health, which are exacerbated by his brother-in-law's dying of a feared disease.

Accounts such as the one above are both descriptive and prescriptive. On the one hand, they describe the storyteller's perception of the facts of the situation. At the same time, in describing the difficulties a distressed spouse is having in the face of her husband's dying and the problems that inadequate coping brings, the storyteller prescribes how the distressed person *should* respond. The telling of such stories serves more than the simple communication of a person's perceptions of a distressing situation; the telling also creates and reinforces collective norms about how one should cope with the dying of a loved one.

PATHWAYS FOR THE GRIEVING

Clark (1993) studied six persons from Alberta who were having difficulty with their grieving. The subjects of this study were: a young woman who had lost her sixteen-year-old sister in a motor vehicle accident; a man who had lost his seventy-nine-year-old father in a motor vehicle accident; a man who had lost his wife at the age of fifty-two to breast cancer; a woman who had lost her daughter at the age of thirty-four to a diabetic coma; a woman who had lost her mother at the age of seventy-seven to complications following surgery; and a man whose sixteen-year-old son had been murdered. The death of most of the loved ones had occurred from one to three years prior to the study; in one case the death had occurred seven years earlier.

Difficulties with grieving arose for various reasons. One subject had difficulty coming to terms with her loss of connection with her sister. She also experienced the loss of her sense of security because of the nature of her sister's sudden, unexpected, and horrifying death. A son had difficulty because his love for his father was intertwined with resentment towards the man who had never made him feel loved and respected. A husband suffered intensely following the loss of his beloved wife and the life that they had shared. A mother felt that there must have been something she could have done to save her daughter. A daughter felt that there were things health care professionals could have done to save her mother or at least to have given her mother more dignity in dying. A father remained confused about how to deal with the various emotions he felt regarding his son's death.

The subjects expressed various emotions, including intense sorrow, anguish, depression, bitterness, anger, rage, regret, self-blame, guilt, loneliness, pessimism, hopelessness, despair, confusion, emptiness, and numbness. They experienced fatigue, lack of motivation, low self-esteem, feelings of failure, a sense of personal vulnerability, loss of faith, loss of meaning, and loss of purpose. Alienation from other surviving family members was not uncommon. Some turned to thoughts of suicide, looked forward to their own death, or displayed inappropriate behaviour. Clark (1993: 149–151) points out that each person's grieving is, to a degree, personal and unique and reflects the particular circumstances of that person's life, the relationship with the deceased, the circumstances of the death, and the survivor's coping style and resources. In a sense, each person follows his or her own path in the course of grieving.

Martin and Elder (1993) wrote about "pathways through grief." The use of the plural, "pathways," emphasizes the uniqueness and the individuality of grief. Martin and Elder suggest that each person tends to grieve in a unique way and to find his or her own pathway through grief. They acknowledge that, while there are commonalities among individuals, there are always differences as well.

Despite Martin and Elder's phrase "pathways *through* grief," they argue that grief is not a process with a beginning, an ending, and well-defined steps between the two. A person does not necessarily ever get "through" grief, in the sense of being done with it or getting beyond it. Instead Martin and Elder proposed a figure-eight model of grief. In this model there is no end point and an individual can return to a "place" where they have been before. The "places" in the model include protest, despair, and detachment in one half of the figure-eight, and exploration (of ways to rebuild a disrupted life), hope, and investment in new relationships in the other half.

At the intersection of the two circles, the authors located meaning, their central concept. Meaning refers to interpretations individuals use to define and make sense of their loss and of their lives. Different individuals take different meanings, and the meanings taken influence the pathway that an individual then follows.

Following bereavement, intense grief may dissipate and return, rise and fall. Martin and Elder's model allows for the cyclical nature of grief. It also acknowledges that some people follow better pathways than others. Regardless of the pathway, however, grief is never truly over.

CONCLUSION

It is hard to lose a loved one to death. While, in one sense, death ends the relationship with the loved one, in another sense death transforms the relationship, which continues in the survivor's memories, thoughts, feelings, conversations, and behaviours. Because the relationship continues, albeit in a transformed way, grieving for the presence of the deceased is ongoing. While the intensity of grief tends to wane over time, grief does not completely disappear. It comes and goes and returns again.

To the extent that our lives are made up of our relationships with others, the death of a loved one transforms our own life. Part of us dies with the deceased. Life is never completely the same again. We grieve for the deceased and we grieve for ourselves, for what we have lost of ourselves. Nevertheless, out of loss and despair, many find meaning, purpose, and hope. To paraphrase the father who lost two children to unexpected and premature deaths: we can remember the dead and honour them, we can accept our own mortality as the natural order of things, and we can do good works while we are among the living.

Notes

1. In the previously unpublished accounts of personal experience with dying and death, names and other identifying material have been changed to protect the privacy of individuals.

Conclusion

Dying and death reflect the material and social conditions of society. In the pre-contact era, living conditions for Aboriginal peoples in Canada were such that life expectancy was perhaps thirty to forty years, about the same as in Europe at that time. While death often came early in life for Aboriginal people, some individuals survived to old age. Nevertheless, dying and death were common, visible, and expected occurrences. Aboriginal social practices and cultural definitions reflected these realities and, in turn, shaped the experience of dying and death.

Contact with Europeans brought devastation to the Aboriginal peoples of Canada. Infectious diseases previously unknown in North America increased death rates and decimated whole populations. The gradual destruction of Native economies and ways of life further contributed to high rates of death. In addition, European culture, brought by missionaries and traders, had an impact on Aboriginal social practices and cultural definitions and tended to transform the social and personal experience of dying and death. Christian religious views of life and death sharply contrasted the values common among First Nations. For Aboriginal peoples, death was more likely to be a natural or unavoidable part of life, explained by Native cosmology and given meaning by Native spirituality. Death began to take on a new significance when viewed in the Christian context of heaven and hell.

While the infectious diseases brought to Canada by the Europeans were especially devastating for the Aboriginal peoples, they were also devastating for the European explorers, traders, and settlers. The harsh climate, rough pioneer existence, low standards of living, and unsanitary practices contributed to many early deaths in the colonies. Infant mortality was high, as was maternal mortality, and life expectancy, in general, was low. Health care was relatively ineffective and the few hospitals that existed were considered to be places of death. It was not until the late nineteenth century that the newly emerging public health movement began to have a positive impact on health and life expectancy by improving sanitation and the safety of food and water. Subsequent advances in health care in the twentieth century brought dramatic improvements in life expectancy. The causes of death shifted from infectious diseases to chronic diseases. The timing of death shifted increasingly to later life. The care of the dying was transferred from family members to health care professionals, and dying and death was moved from the home and community to the hospital. Death, which had been common and familiar, became unfamiliar and expected only in old age.

At the beginning of the twenty-first century, the most common causes of death were circulatory disease and cancer, although causes of death vary depending on personal characteristics such as age, sex, and social class. For example, the most common cause of infant death are congenital disorders. Young adults are most likely to die of accidents, injuries, and suicide. In the older age groups, cancer and circulatory disease dominate as causes of death. The timing of death has become noticeably discrepant for males and females, with females outliving males by a number of years on the average. This gender differential in life expectancy emerged during the twentieth century but in recent years has begun to decrease. The disadvantaged social classes and relatively disadvantaged groups such as Aboriginal people continue to have life expectancies below the Canadian norm. Nevertheless, deaths occurring early in life have come to be unexpected and have been labelled premature. Finally, dying and death have increasingly taken place in the hospital, and the great majority of deaths now occur in that setting.

Views of dying and death, along with practices related to these phenomena, are influenced by social institutions such as the family, religion, the health care system, the legal system, and the funeral industry. Families have become much less likely to be involved as primary caregivers for the dying. Increasingly, professional caregivers attend to the dying, often in an institutional setting rather than in the dying person's home. Furthermore, families have become much less involved with the processing of the dead body. Instead, processing of the dead body and the management of the funeral rituals are now typically provided by the funeral industry.

Religion has played a significant part in giving meaning to dying and death and continues to do so for those who maintain a religious commitment. Furthermore, religion continues to play an active role in social debates about end-of-life issues such as euthanasia and assisted suicide. Nevertheless, the influence of religion for many has been undermined by secular trends.

The successes of twentieth century medicine in curing disease and forestalling death led to the dominance of the curative model in modern medicine. This model emphasized cure and tended to resist death, viewing death as failure. Towards the end of the twentieth century, the palliative care movement gained momentum emphasizing the quality of life for the dying by focusing on managing symptoms rather than engaging in futile attempts to cure. This movement has raised legal questions, and while the Criminal Code of Canada continues to define active euthanasia as murder and assisted suicide as illegal, there is a trend towards legalizing advance directives which authorize the withholding or withdrawing of treatment and care.

Finally, the funeral industry has become "big business" consistent with a general trend towards the corporatization, bureaucratization, professionalization, and secularization of dying and death. Increasingly, the funeral ritual has moved from the home, community, and church, to the profit-driven funeral industry.

Despite the twentieth century trends towards the hospitalization, bureaucratization, and professionalization of dying and death, there appears to be a trend towards moving dying and death back to the home and to the family, who once again may become the primary caregivers, functioning with the assistance of health care professionals, in providing palliative home care.

There is a diversity of views as to what death is and what it means. For some, death is a transition to a better life. Others view death as the final end. For many, death is a mystery or, as Shakespeare put it in *Hamlet*: "the undiscovered country from whose bourn no traveller returns" (Act III, Scene I). People facing death tend to interpret it, to give it meaning, but the specific meaning assigned to death tends to vary from one individual to another. Similarly, those facing death tend to engage in a review of their life, to examine their biography and give it meaning in the face of death. Just as the specific meaning assigned to death tends to vary from one individual to another, so does the meaning assigned to one's life. Because each individual's biography is personal and unique, the construction of life's meaning and the construction of the meaning of dying and death are both personal and unique.

The dying tend to view the process of dying as more distressing than the prospect of death itself. Pain and suffering are not welcome. Furthermore, the dying do not welcome the various losses that they face in the course of dying, including losses of health, future, competence, independence, social roles and status, and personal relationships. The dying often express concern for those who will survive them and for the relationships that will be disrupted by their death. Nevertheless, death itself may be welcomed as an end to suffering.

There are many different kinds of deaths and many different ways of dying. Similarly, there are many different ways to grieve. While shock and numbness often attend the sudden loss of a loved one, and while sadness commonly is experienced by the bereaved, different people grieve in their own way and in their own time. While *intense* grieving tends to end, grieving may nevertheless last a lifetime.

Losing a loved one means losing a relationship with that person, a relationship that is part of oneself. It follows that the loss of a significant other involves a loss of oneself to some degree. Loved ones are not forgotten; they are remembered from time to time with varying degrees of emotion. In that sense, grieving does not end. Furthermore, the process of making sense of loss and of finding meaning in death and in life tends to be ongoing. Nevertheless, over time personal grieving tends to become less "disruptive" to one's personal and social functioning.

While dying and death, bereavement and grieving are intensely personal experiences and reactions vary from one individual to another, nevertheless, society and culture tend to provide definitions and guidelines for grieving. When personal grief violates these guidelines—for example, when a person continues to grieve intensely beyond the time allotted for grieving—then such grief tends to be defined as complicated, prolonged, chronic, unresolved, deviant, abnormal, pathological, or as a sign of individual failure and weakness. Definitions such as this fail to legitimize individual differences in grieving and put pressure on persons to hide their personal grief while in public.

People may manage their emotions and behaviours in public to conform to social expectations, showing grief or hiding it when appropriate. Public displays of either grief or non-grief should not be mistaken for the private and the personal. Similarly, the homogeneity of public displays should not blind one to the heterogeneity of personal experiences. Dying and death, bereavement and grieving are, in the end, highly personal experiences.

Appendix:
Sources of Information
on Dying and Death

There are many sources of information on dying and death. Some of the most overlooked sources are family and friends, clergy, and nurses and other health care professionals who may have had extensive or recent experience with dying and death. Some published and electronic sources of information are better than others. It is always important to check one source of information against another. Care should also be taken to safeguard your personal information (name, address, and credit card numbers) when communicating with persons or companies via the internet or telephone. Following are some of the best sources of information at the time this book was written.

The Division of Aging and Seniors at Health Canada has information on palliative care and other services for seniors. It's address is:

> Division of Aging and Seniors
> Health Promotion and Programs Branch
> Health Canada
> Address Locator #1908A1
> Ottawa, ON K1A 1B4
> phone (613) 952-7606
> fax (613) 9579938
> http://www.hc-sc.gc.ca/seniors-aines

In addition, some provinces and territories have regulatory boards and legislative acts governing the death industry, which provide various assurances and forms of assistance to the public. For instance, in the authors' home province there is the Alberta Funeral Services Regulatory Board. Most provinces also have living will/advance directive laws. Free information about preparing a living will/advance directive is usually available from provincial departments of health and seniors' groups.

Most areas of Canada have either provincial memorial societies or local memorial societies that provide information on funerals, including how to pre-arrange a funeral. Telephone directories provide a current source of information on these societies. One of the largest is:

> Memorial Society Association of Canada
> 55 St. Phillips Road
> Etobicoke, ON M9P 2N8
> phone (416) 241-6274

Long-term care facilities, hospitals, churches, and other such organizations may have a bereavement group or provide information about one.

The Canadian Palliative Care Association can provide information about local palliative care groups. The national association's address is:

> The Canadian Palliative Care Association
> 43 Bruyere Street
> Room 131B, Ottawa, ON K1N 5C8
> phone (613) 241-3663 or 1-800-668-2785
> fax (613) 241-2989
> www.llysne@scohs

The Hospice Palliative Care Movement in Canada, phone (877) 203-4636, is an affiliated organization. Revenue Canada can provide information on tax credits for caregiving.

A variety of associations, support groups, or information groups, focus on one illness (such as AIDS, cancer, etc.). There are provincial or territorial organ donor programs (program names vary across Canada and most large hospitals will have this information).

One of the most prominent right-to-die groups in Canada is:

> Dying with Dignity
> East Eglinton Ave, East, Suite 705
> Toronto, ON M4P 1G8

phone (416) 486-3998
fax (416) 489-9010
http://www.web.net/~dwdca/index.html

Although it tends to focus more on birth issues than death issues, one of the most prominent right-to-life groups in Canada is:

Campaign Life Coalition
53 Dundas Street, East
Suite 305, Toronto ON M5B 1C6
http://www.lifesite.net/

Scholarly journals are available in university libraries, provincial/territorial departments of health libraries, and large hospital or public libraries. Some of these journals may be online as well. Some journals focus specifically on death and dying: Journal of Palliative Care; Journal of Pain and Symptom Management; Hospice Journal; Death Studies; American Journal of Hospice and Palliative Care.

Books and videos are available in bookstores and libraries. It is best to use current Canadian sources such as M. Kerr & J. Kurtz, *Facing a Death in the Family* (Toronto: John Wiley & Sons, 1999) or D. Flynn, *The Truth about Funerals: How to Beat the High Cost of Dying (An Insider's Perspective)* (Burlington, ON: Funeral Consultants International Inc., 1993).

Relevant internet sites include:

www.cemetery.org
www.deathclock.com (a controversial web site which predicts your death date)
www.dlcwest.com/~jacques.law/LvgWills.html
www.funerals.org/famsa
www.gov.edmonton.ab.ca/cemetery (other cemeteries are also online)
www.hon.ch/ (health information on the net)
www.hospicecare.com/Directories/NorthAmerica.htm
www.meetingofhearts.com (a bereavement-support site)
www.net-globe.com/chac/eng/papers/advdir.html (Catholic Health Association)
www.nfb.ca (National Film Board of Canada)
www.pallcare.org (an Ontario palliative care group with links to others)
www.vaxxine.com/pallcare/whatis.htm (palliative care information)

www.who.org/programmes/ncd/cpl/cpl_home.htm (World Health Organization)

www.worldgardens.com

http://home.istar.ca/~vandee.index.shtml (index of prolife organizations)

http://iyop-aipa.ic.gc.ca/english/projects5.htm (International Year of Old Persons home palliative care project)

One of the most comprehensive art galleries and museums on dying and death is in the United States:

> National Museum of Funeral History
>
> 415 Barren Springs Drive
>
> Houston, Texas 77090
>
> phone (281) 876-3063 or 876-4403

References

Agnew, G.H. (1974). *Canadian Hospitals, 1920–1970*. Toronto: University of Toronto Press.

Aiken, L.R. (1991). *Dying, Death, and Bereavement* (2nd ed.). Boston: Allyn and Bacon.

Ajemian, I.C. (1990). Palliative care in Canada: 2000. *Journal of Palliative Care*, 6(4), 47–58.

Ajemian, I.C. (1992). Hospitals and health care facilities. *Journal of Palliative Care*, 8(1), 33–37.

Alberta Funeral Services Regulatory Board. (1998). *Fundamentals of Funeral Planning*. Edmonton, AB: Author.

Alberta Health. (1992–97, 1999). *Annual Report*. Edmonton: Author.

Albom, M. (1997). *Tuesdays with Morrie*. New York: Doubleday.

Allard, P., Dionne, A., and Potvin, D. (1995). Factors associated with length of survival among 1081 terminally ill cancer patients. *Journal of Palliative Care*, 11(3), 20–24.

American Heart Association. (1994). *Advanced Cardiac Life Support*. Dallas TX: Author.

Amyot, G.F. (1967). Some historical highlights of public health in Canada. *Canadian Journal of Public Health*, 58(8), 337–341.

Angell, M. (1997, July 11). Lawmakers bully the dying. Patients in agony should have the option of overdose. *Edmonton Journal*, A18.

Antonovsky, A. (1987). *Unraveling the Mystery of Health: How People Manage Stress and Stay Well*. San Francisco: Jossey-Bass.

Ariès, P. (1974). *Western Attitudes toward Death: From the Middle Ages to the Present*. Baltimore: The Johns Hopkins University Press.

Ariès, P. (1981). *The Hour of Our Death*. New York: Alfred A. Knopf.

Aronson, K.J., Howe, G.R., Carpenter, M., and Fair, M.E. (1999). Surveillance of potential associations between occupations and causes of death in Canada. *Occupational and Environmental Medicine*, 56(4), 265–269.

Audette, A. (1964). Nursing care in cardiovascular surgery. *Canadian Nurse Journal*, 60(3), 259–268.

Awoke, S., Mouton, P., and Parrott, M. (1992). Outcomes of skills cardiopulmonary resuscitation in a long-term-care facility: Futile therapy? *Journal of the American Geriatrics Society*, 40(6), 593–595.

Barbeau, M. (1958). *Medicine-Men on the North Pacific Coast*. Ottawa: Department of Northern Affairs and National Resources.

Bartlett, S. (Director and Producer). (1994). Who owns my life? The Sue Rodriguez story. From the television series *Witness* [Video]. Canadian Broadcasting Corporation.

Baumgart, A.J. (1992). Evolution of the Canadian health care system. In A.J. Baumgart and J. Larsen (eds.), *Canadian Nursing Faces the Future* (2nd ed., pp. 23–41). Toronto: Mosby.

Baylis, F., Downie, J., Freedman, B., Hoffmaster, B., and Sherwin, S. (1995). *Health Care Ethics in Canada*. Toronto: Harcourt Brace.

Beaton, J.I., and Degner, L.F. (1990). Life and death decisions: The impact on nurses. *Canadian Nurse Journal*, 86(3), 18–22.

Beauchamp, T.L., and Childress, J.F. (1994). *Principles of Biomedical Ethics* (4th ed.). New York: Oxford University Press.

Beauvoir, Simone de (1973). *Old Age.* (trans. Patrick O'Brien). London: Deutsch

Becker, E. (1973). *The Denial of Death*. New York: Free Press.

Beckingham, A.C. (1993). Aging in Canada. In A.C. Beckingham, and B.W. Dugas, *Promoting Healthy Aging: A Nursing and Community Perspective* (pp. 3–49). St. Louis: Mosby.

Belliveau, J., and Gaudette, L. (1995, Spring). Changes in cancer incidence and mortality. *Canadian Social Trends*, 2–7.

Bettman, O.L. (1956). *A Pictorial History of Medicine*. Springfield, IL: C.C. Thomas.

Bibby, R.W., and Brinkerhoff, M.B. (1994). Circulation of the saints, 1966–1990: New data, new reflections. *Journal for the Scientific Study of Religion*, 33(3), 273–280.

Bigue, C., and Paplauskas-Macdonald, R. (1968). Heart transplants in Canada. *Canadian Nurse Journal*, 64(10), 34–39.

Birch, S., and Gafni. A. (1992). Cost effectiveness/utility analyses. Do current decision rules lead us to where we want to be? *Journal of Health Economics*, 11(3), 279–296.

Black, C., Roos, N.P., Havens, B., and MacWilliam, L. (1995). Rising use of physician services by the elderly: The contribution of mortality. *Canadian Journal on Aging*, 14(2), 225–244.

Blishen, B.R. (1991). *Doctors in Canada: The Changing World of Medical Practice*. Toronto: University of Toronto Press.

Blouin, M. (1995). Care-in-dying: A call to action. *Catholic Health Association of Canada Review*, 23(1), 23.

Boisvert, C. (1967). Intensive care unit in cardiovascular surgery. *Canadian Nurse Journal*, 63(1), 36–38.

Bourette, S., and Milner, B. (1999, June 2). No-frills funerals changing an already evolving industry. *Globe and Mail*, B11.

Boyd, K.J. (1993). Palliative care in the community: Views of general practitioners and district nurses in East London. *Journal of Palliative Care*, 9(2), 33–37.

Bradley, L.O. (1958). The changing role of hospitals. *Canadian Nurse*, 54(6), 550–558.

Bramwell, L., MacKenzie, J., Laschinger, H., and Cameron, N. (1995). Need for overnight respite for primary caregivers of hospice clients. *Cancer Nursing*, 18(5), 337–343.

Braun, M.J. (1992). *Meaning Reconstruction in the Experience of Parental Bereavement*. Unpublished masters thesis, University of Manitoba, Winnipeg.

Bresnahan, J.F. (1993). Getting beyond suspicion of homicide: Reflections on the struggle for morally appropriate care of the dying under high technology medical care. *Trends in Health Care, Law and Ethics*, 8(1), 31–38.

Brockopp, D.Y., King, D.B., and Hamilton, J.E. (1991). The dying patient: A comparative study of nurse caregiver characteristics. *Death Studies*, 15(3), 245–258.

Brown, J.S.H. (1980). *Strangers in Blood: Fur Trade Company Families in Indian Country*. Vancouver: University of British Columbia.

Brown, J.J., Potter, J.F., and Foster, B.G. (1990). Caregiver burden should be evaluated during geriatric assessment. *Journal of the American Geriatrics Society*, 38, 455–460.

Bruera, E., Kuehn, N., Emery, K., and Hanson, J. (1990). Social and demographic characteristics of patients admitted to a palliative care unit. *Journal of Palliative Care*, 6(4), 16–20.

Bruera, E., Miller, M.J., Kuehn, N., MacEachern, T., and Hanson, J. (1992). Estimate of survival of patients admitted to a palliative care unit: A prospective study. *Journal of Pain and Symptom Management*, 7(2), 82–85.

Bruera, E., Suarez-Almazor, M., Velasco, A., MacDonald, S.M., and Hanson, J. (1994). The assessment of constipation in terminal cancer patients admitted to palliative care unit: A retrospective review. *Journal of Pain and Symptom Management*, 9(8), 515–519.

Bryce, G. (1902). *The Remarkable History of the Hudson's Bay Company* (2nd ed.). London: Sampson Low Marston.

Buckley, S. (1988). The search for the decline in maternal mortality: The place of hospital records. In W. Mitchinson and J.D. McGinnis (eds.), *Essays in the History of Canadian Medicine* (pp. 148–163). Toronto: McClelland and Stewart.

Bulkin, W., and Lukashok, H. (1991). Training physicians to care for the dying. *American Journal of Hospice and Palliative Care*, 8(2), 10–15.

Burch, E.S. (1988). *The Eskimos*. Norman: University of Oklahoma Press.

Burgess, K. (1996). The influence of will on life and death. *Nursing Forum*, 15(3), 238–258.

Burke, M.A., Lindsay, J., McDowell, I., and Hill, G. (1997, Summer). Dementia among seniors. *Canadian Social Trends*, 24–27.

Cadotte, M. (1985). Hotel-Dieu. In J.H. Marsh (ed.), *The Canadian Encyclopedia* (p. 835). Edmonton: Hurtig.

Calman, K.C. (1988). Palliative medicine: On the way to becoming a recognized discipline. *Journal of Palliative Care*, 4(1–2), 12–14.

Cameron, J., and Parkes, C.M. (1983). Terminal care: Evaluation of effects on surviving family of care before and after bereavement. *Postgraduate Medical Journal*, 59, 73–78.

Campion, B. (1994). Is there a place for a good death? *Catholic Health Association of Canada Review*, 22(1), 4–5.

Canadian Council on Social Development. (1999). *Personal Security Index, 1999*. Ottawa: Renouf Publishing.

Canadian Healthcare Association. (1998). *Directory of Hospitals and Long Term Care Facilities in Canada*. Ottawa: Author.

Canadian Nurses Association. (1964). Submission on aging. *Canadian Nurse Journal*, 60(8), 741–744.

Canadian Palliative Care Association. (1997). *The Canadian Directory of Services: Palliative Care and HIV/AIDS*, 1997. Ottawa: Author.

Carter, W.H. (1973). *Medical Practices and Burial Customs of North American Indians*. London, ON: Namind.

Catholic Health Association of Canada. (1991). *Health Care Ethics Guide*. Ottawa: Author.

Chappell, N. (1992). *Social Support and Aging*. Toronto: Butterworths.

Charlton, R., and Dovey, S. (1995). Attitudes to death and dying in the UK, New Zealand, and Japan. *Journal of Palliative Care*, 11(1), 42–47.

Chen, J., Wilkins, R., and Ng, E. (1996). Health expectancy by immigrant status, 1986 and 1991. *Health Reports*, 8(3), 29–38.

Chernomas, R., and Sepehri, A. (1991). Is the Canadian health care system more effective at expenditure control than previously thought? A reply to Peter Coyte. *International Journal of Health Services*, 21(4), 793–804.

Chin, A.E., Hedberg, K., Higginson, G.K., and Fleming, D.W. (1999). Legalized physician-assisted suicide in Oregon: The first year's experience. *New England Journal of Medicine*, 340(7), 577–583.

Chochinov, H.M., Tataryn, D., Clinch, J.J., and Dudgeon, D. (1999). Will to live in the terminally ill. *The Lancet*, 354, 816–819.

Choudhry, N.K., Ma., J., Rasooly, I., and Singer, P.A. (1994). Long-term care facility policies on life-sustaining treatments and advance directives in Canada. *Journal of the American Geriatrics Society*, 42(11), 1150–1153.

Christakis, N.A., and Iwashyna, T.J. (1998). Attitude and self-reported practice regarding prognostication in a national sample of internists. *Archives of Internal Medicine*, 158(21), 2389–2395.

Chui, T. (1996, Autumn). Canada's population: Charting into the 21st century. *Canadian Social Trends*, 3–7.

Clark, G.T. (1993). *Personal Meanings of Grief and Bereavement*. Doctoral Dissertation. Edmonton, University of Alberta.

Clifton, J.A. (1991). Folklore. In R. Lachmann (ed.). *The Encyclopedic Dictionary of Sociology*. (4th ed., p. 115). Guilford, CT: Dushkin.

CMA Policy Summary. (1995). Joint statement on resuscitative interventions (Update 1995). *Canadian Medical Association Journal*, 153(11), 1652A–1652C.

Coleman, V. (1985). *The Story of Medicine*. London: Robert Hale.

Colman, P. (1997). *Corpses, Coffin's, and Crypts: A History of Burial*. New York: Henry Holt and Company.

Comartin, M. (1983). Dealing with the dying patient in hospital. *Canadian Nurse*, 79(2), 45–47.

Cook, D.J., Uyatt, G.H., Jaeschke, R., Reeve, J., Spanier, A., King, D., Molloy, D.W., Willau, A., and Streiner, D.L. (1995). Determinants in Canadian health care workers of the decision to withdraw life support from the critically ill. *Journal of the American Medical Association*, 273(9), 708–799.

Corey, M., and Farewell, V. (1996). Determinants of mortality from cystic fibrosis in Canada, 1970–1989. *American Journal of Epidemiology*, 143(10), 1007–1017.

Corlett, W.T. (1935). *The Medicine-Man of the American Indians and His Cultural Background.* Springfield, IL: Charles C. Thomas.

Counts, D.R., and Counts, D.A. (1991). Conclusions: Coping with the final tragedy. In D.R. Counts and D.A. Counts (eds.), *Coping with the Final Tragedy: Cultural Variation in Dying and Grieving* (pp. 277–291). Amityville, NY: Baywood.

Cox, C. (1981). The choice. *American Journal of Nursing*, 81(9), 1627–28.

Coyte, P.C. (1990). Current trends in Canadian health care: Myths and misconceptions in health economics. *Journal of Public Health Policy*, 11(2), 169–188.

Curran, W.J., and Hyg, S.M. (1984). Quality of life and treatment decisions: The Canadian Law Reform report. *New England Journal of Medicine,* 310(5), 297–298.

Curtin, L.L. (1996). First you suffer, then you die: Findings of a major study of dying in U.S. hospitals. *Nursing Management*, 27(5), 56–60.

Curtis, E.B., Krech, R., and Walsh, T.D. (1991). Common symptoms in patients with advanced cancer. *Journal of Palliative Care*, 7(2), 25–29.

D'Amico, M., Agozzino, E., Biagino, A., Simonetti, A., and Marinelli, P. (1999). Ill-defined and multiple causes of death certificates: A study of misclassification in mortality statistics. *European Journal of Epidemiology*, 15(2), 141–148.

Davies, B. (1996). Assessment of need for children's hospice program. *Death Studies*, 20(8), 247–268.

Davies, B., and Steele, R. (1996). Challenges in identifying children for palliative care. *Journal of Palliative Care*, 12(3), 5–8.

DeCoster, C., Roos., N.P., and Bogdanoci, B. (1995). Utilization of nursing home resources. *Medical Care*, 33(12), DS37–DS82.

Degner, L.F., Henteleff, P.D., and Ringer, C. (1987). The relationship between theory and measurement in evaluations of palliative care services. *Journal of Palliative Care*, 3(2), 8–13.

Dellenbaugh, F.S. (1906). *The North Americans of Yesterday.* New York: G.P. Putnam's Sons.

den Daas, N. (1995). Estimating length of survival in end-stage cancer: A review of the literature. *Journal of Pain and Symptom Management*, 10(7), 548–555.

Des Aulniers, L. (1993). The organization of life before death in two Quebec cultural configurations. *Omega*, 27, 35–50.

Desmeules, M., Huang, J., and Mao, Y. (1993). Projections of deaths and hospitalizations among elderly Canadians. *Chronic Diseases in Canada,* 14(4), 145–150.

DeSpelder, L.A., and Strickland, A.L. (1999). *The Last Dance: Encountering Death and Dying* (5th ed.). Mountain View, CA: Mayfield Publishing.

de Veber, L.L., Henry, F., Nadeau, R., Cassidy, E., Gentles, I., and Bierling, G. (1992). *Public Policy, Private Voices: The Euthanasia Debate.* Toronto: Human Life Research Institute.

Dickason, O.P. (1984). *The Myth of the Savage And the Beginnings of French Colonialism in the Americas.* Edmonton: University of Alberta Press.

DiMarco, M.M., and Storch, J.L. (1995). History of the Canadian health care system. In D. Wilson (ed.), *The Canadian Health Care System* (pp. 5–16). Edmonton: Author.

Diment, M.M., and Evans, B.L. (1995). Implementation of a pharmaceutical care practice model for palliative care. *Canadian Journal of Hospital Pharmacy*, 48(4), 228–237.

Doka, K.J. (1995). Disenfranchised grief. In L.A. DeSpelder and A.L. Strickland (eds.), *The Path Ahead: Readings in Death and Dying* (pp. 271–275). Mountain View, CA: Mayfield.

Dolgoy, R. (Director), and Phillips, D. (Producer). (1991). *Living With Dying*, [Video]. National Film Board of Canada.

Donnelly, S., Walshi, D., and Rybicki, L. (1995). The symptoms of advanced cancer: Identification of clinical and research priorities by assessment of prevalence and severity. *Journal of Palliative Care*, 11(1), 27–32.

Downe-Wamboldt, B. (1985). Hospice program eases fear, pain and loneliness. *Dimensions*, 28–29, 37.

Driedger, S.D. (1997, November 17). Should Latimer go free? *Maclean's*, 110(46), 12–15.

Ducharme, F., and Corin, E. (1997). Le veuvage chez les hommes et les femmes âgés: une étude exploratoire des significations et des stratégies adaptatives. *Canadian Journal on Aging*, 16, 112–141.

Duff, R.S. (1987). "Close up" versus "distant" ethics. *Seminars in Perinatology*, 11(3), 244–253.

Duffy, C.M., Pollock, P., Levy, M., Budd, E., Caulfield, L., and Koren, G. (1990). Home-based palliative care for children, Part 2: The benefits of an established program. *Journal of Palliative Care*, 6(2), 8–12.

Durkheim, E. ([1915] 1965). *The Elementary Forms of Religious Life*. New York: Free Press.

Dush, D.M. (1993). High-tech, aggressive palliative care: In the service of quality of life. *Journal of Palliative Care*, 9(1), 37–41.

Dysart, R. (1964). Abdominoperineal resection. *Canadian Nurse Journal*, 60(10), 961–963.

Eastaugh A.N. (1996). Approaches to palliative care by primary health care teams: A survey. *Journal of Palliative Care*, 12(4), 47–50.

Eisenberg, L. (1984). Barriers to care. *Canadian Journal of Psychiatry*, 29(6), 452–459.

Elash, A. (1997). Legalized MD-assisted suicide needed to improve care, physician tells right to die group. *Canadian Medical Association Journal*, 157(1), 763–764.

Ellershaw, J.E., Sutcliffe, J.M., and Saunders, C.M. (1995). Dehydration and the dying patient. *Journal of Pain and Symptom Management*, 10(3), 192–197.

Ellison, L.F., Morrison, H.I., de Groh, M.J., and Villneuve, P.J. (1999). Health consequences of smoking among Canadian smokers: An update. *Chronic Diseases in Canada*, 21(1), 36–39.

Eng, B., and Davies, B. (1992). Canuck Place: A hospice for children. *Canadian Oncology Nursing Journal*, 2(1), 18–20.

Epp, J. (1986). *Achieving Health for All: A Framework for Health Promotion*. Ottawa: Minister of Supply and Services Canada.

Erichsen-Brown, C. (1979). *Use of Plants for the Past 500 Years*. Aurora, ON: Breezy Creeks Press.

Ericksen, J., Rodney, M.P., and Starzomski, R. (1995). When is it right to die? *Canadian Nurse*, 91(8), 29–34.

Evans, R.G. (1992). Canada: The real issues. *Journal of Health Politics, Policy and Law*, 17(4), 739–762.

Ewart, W.B. (1983). Causes of mortality in a subarctic settlement (York Factory, MB.), 1714–1946. *Canadian Medical Association Journal*, 129(6), 571–574.

Faber-Langendoen, K., and Bartels, D.M. (1992). Process of forgoing life-sustaining treatment in a university hospital: An empirical study. *Critical Care Medicine*, 20(5), 570–577.

Fair, M. (1994). The development of national vital statistics in Canada, Part 1: From 1605 to 1945. *Health Reports*, 6(3), 355–372.

Farncombe, M.L. (1991). Symptom control in a regional cancer centre: An innovative outpatient approach. *Journal of Palliative Care*, 7(4), 21–25.

Federal, Provincial and Territorial Advisory Committee on Population Health. (1996). *Report on the Health of Canadians: Prepared by the Federal, Provincial and Territorial Advisory Committee on Population Health for the Meeting of Ministers of Health*. Toronto, ON: Author.

Feser, L. (1992). An open letter: Hospice for Calgary. *Alberta Association of Registered Nurses*, 48(7), 30.

Finne-Soveri, U.H., and Tilvis, R.S. (1998). How accurate is the terminal prognosis in the minimum data set? *Journal of the American Geriatrics Society*, 46(8), 1023–1024.

Fishbane, S. (1989). Jewish mourning rites: A process of resocialization. *Anthropologica*, 31, 65–84.

Flynn, D. (1993). *The Truth about Funerals. How to Beat the High Cost of Dying (An Insider's Perspective)*. Burlington, ON: Funeral Consultants International.

Foot, R. (1997, December 23). Doctor convicted in aiding suicide: Toronto AIDS physician pleads guilty to two charges of giving potent pills to HIV patients. *Edmonton Journal*, A7.

Fortier, R. (Director), and Grana, S. Fortier, R. and Howells, B. (Producers). (1984). *The Last Right*, [Video]. National Film Board of Canada.

Frager, G. (1996). Pediatric palliative care: Building the model, bridging the gaps. *Journal of Palliative Care*, 12(3), 9–12.

Frank, A.W. (1991). *At the Will of the Body: Reflections on Illness*. Boston: Houghton Mifflin.

Fries, J.F. (1980). Aging, natural death and the compression of mortality. *New England Journal of Medicine*, 303(3), 130–135.

Fry, P.S. (1997). Grandparents' reactions to the death of a grandchild: An exploratory factor analytic study. *Omega*, 35, 119–140.

Fry, R. Sr., and Schuman, J.E. (1986). Providence expands palliative care to meet patients' needs better. *Dimensions*, 63(8), 31–33.

Gardner-Nix, J.S., Brodie, R., Tjan, E., Wilton, M., Zoberman, L. Barnes, F., Friedrich, J., and Wood, J. (1995). Scarborough's palliative "at-home" care team (PACT): A model for a suburban physician palliative care team. *Journal of Palliative Care*, 11(3), 43–49.

Garner, J. (1976). Palliative care: It's the quality of life remaining that matters. *Canadian Medical Association Journal*, 115(2), 179–180.

Gaudette, L.A., Altmayer, C.A., Wysocki, M., and Gao, R. (1998). Cancer incidence and mortality across Canada. *Health Reports*, 10(1), 51–69.

Gee, E.M. (1987). Historical change in the family life course of Canadian men and women. In V.W. Marshall (ed.), *Aging in Canada: Social Perspectives*. (2nd ed., pp. 265–287). Markham, ON: Fitzhenry and Whiteside.

Gee, E.M. and Kimball, M.M.. (1987). *Women and Aging*. Toronto: Butterworths.

Gentles, I. (1988). Funeral customs in historical context. *Journal of Palliative Care*, 4(3), 16–20.

Genuis, S.J., Genuis, S.K., and Change, W. (1994). Public attitudes towards the right to die. *Canadian Medical Association Journal*, 150(5), 701–708.

Gerard, L., Flandre, P., Raguin, G., Le Gall, J., Vilde, J., and Leport, C. (1996). Life expectancy in hospitalized patients with AIDS: Prognostic factors on admission. *Journal of Palliative Care*, 12(1), 26–30.

Gilson, M. (Director), and Daly, T. (Producer). (1980). *The Last Days of Living*, [Video]. National Film Board of Canada.

Glaser, B.G., and Strauss, A.L. (1965). *Awareness of Dying*. Chicago: Aldine.

Glaser, B.G., and Strauss, A.L. (1968). *Time for Dying*. Chicago: Aldine.

Goffman, E. (1963). *Stigma*. Englewood Cliffs, NJ: Prentice-Hall.

Gordon, M., and Cheung, M. (1993). Poor outcomes of on-site CPR in a multi-level geriatric facility. *Journal of the American Geriatrics Society*, 41(2), 163–166.

Gotay, C.C., Crockett, S., and West, C. (1985). Palliative home care nursing: Nurses' perceptions of roles and stress. *Canada's Mental Health*, 33(2), 6–9.

Gow, C., and Williams, J.I. (1977). Nurses' attitudes toward death and dying: A causal interpretation. *Social Science and Medicine*, 11, 191–198.

Grant, J.H.B. (1946). Immunization in children. *Canadian Medical Association Journal*, 55, 493–497.

Gray, C. (1998). Legalize use of marijuana for medical purposes, MDs and patients plead. *Canadian Medical Association Journal*, 158(10), 1265–1266.

Gray, R.E. (1993). Suicide prevention consultation in Canada's Northwest Territories: A personal account. In J.D. Morgan (ed.), *Personal Care in an Impersonal World: A Multidimensional Look at Bereavement*. Amityville, NY: Baywood.

Groft, J. (1992). At home with pain. *Canadian Nurse*, 88(4), 36–37.

Guberman, N., Maheu P., and Maille, C. (1992). Women as family caregivers: Why do they care? *Gerontologist*, 32(5), 607–617.

Guest, D. (1985). *The Emergence of Social Security in Canada* (2nd ed.). Vancouver: University of British Columbia Press.

Guidelines for the diagnosis of brain death. (1987). *Le Journal canadien des sciences neurologiques*, 14(4), 653–655.

Haas, J. (1977). Learning real feelings: A study of high steel ironworkers' reactions to fear and danger. *Sociology of Work and Occupations*, 4, 147–170.

Hafferty, F.W. (1988). Cadaver stories and the emotional socialization of medical students. *Journal of Health and Social Behavior*, 29, 344–356.

Hailstone, P. (1979). The growing role of the hospice. *Health Care in Canada*, 21(4), 44–45.

Hall, E. (1947). Health problems of an aging population. *Canadian Nurse Journal*, 43(8), 591.

Hamilton, G. (1997, July 22). Murder charge revives euthanasia debate: Killing them with kindness? *Edmonton Journal*, A1.

Harding le Riche, W. (1979). Seventy years of public health in Canada. *Canadian Journal of Public Health*, 70(3), 155–163.

Hartling, R.N. (1993). *Nahanni: River of Gold ... River of Dreams*. Hyde Park, ON: The Canadian Recreational Canoeing Association.

Harvey, B. (1997, August 10). Mercy-killing drug called the "perfect poison". *Edmonton Journal*, A2.

Hasselback, D., Schreiner, J., and Kuitenbrouwer, P. (1999, June 2). Loewen files for bankruptcy protection. *Financial Post*, C1.

Hauser, D.J. (1974). Seat belts: Is freedom of choice worth 600 deaths a year? *Canadian Medical Association Journal*, 110(12), 1418–1422.

Hayflick, L. (1980). The cell biology of human aging. *Scientific American*, 242(1), 58–65.

Hayter, J. (1968). Organ transplants: A new type of nursing? *Canadian Nurse Journal*, 64(11), 49–53.

Hazzard, W.R., Blass, J.P., Ettinger, W.H., Halter, J.B., and Ouslander, J.G. (1999). *Principles of Geriatric Medicine and Gerontology*. New York: McGraw-Hill.

Heagerty, J.J. (1928). *Four Centuries of Medical History in Canada*. Toronto: Macmillan.

Heagerty, J.J. (1940). *The Romance of Medicine in Canada*. Toronto: Ryerson Press.

Health Canada. (1996). *National Health Expenditures in Canada, 1975-1994*. Ottawa: Author.

Health Canada Working Group on Continuing Care in Consultation with Provincial and Territorial Officials and Others Involved in Palliative Care Services. (1997). *Overview of Provincial and Territorial Palliative Care Programs*, March 1997. Ottawa: Health Canada Working Group on Continuing Care, Policy and Consultation Branch.

Hebert, M.P. (1998). Perinatal bereavement in its cultural context. *Death Studies*, 22, 61–79.

Heffner, J.E., Fahy, B., Hillings, L., and Barbieri, C. (1996). Attitudes regarding advance directives among patients in pulmonary rehabilitation. *American Journal of Respiratory and Critical Care Medicine*, 154(6/1), 1735–1740.

Hendricks, J., and Hendricks, C.D. (1981). *Aging in Mass Society: Myths and Realities* (2nd ed.). Cambridge, MA: Winthrop.

Hertzman, C., and Hayes, M. (1985). Will the elderly really bankrupt us with increased health care costs? *Canadian Journal of Public Health*, 76(6), 373–377.

Hill, G., Forbes, W., Berthelot, J., Lindsay, J., and McDowell, I. (1996). Dementia among seniors. *Health Reports*, 8(2), 7–10.

Hodge, W.H. (1981). *The First Americans*. New York: Holt, Reinhart and Winston.

Howarth, G., and Willison, K.B. (1995, March). Preventing crises in palliative care in the home. *Canadian Family Physician*, 41, 439–444.

Hughes, R. (1999, October 11). In death's throat. *Time*, 78–79.

Iribarren, C., Crow, R.S., Hannan, P.J., Jacobs, D.R., Jr., and Luepker, R.V. (1998). Validation of death certificate diagnosis of out-of-hospital sudden cardiac death. *American Journal of Cardiology*, 82(1), 50–53.

Jack, D. (1981). *Rogues, Rebels, and Geniuses: The Story of Canadian Medicine*. Toronto: Doubleday.

Johansen, H., Nair, C., and Bond, J. (1994). Who goes to hospital? An investigation of high uses of hospital days. *Health Reports*, 6(2), 253–277.

Johansen, H., Nair, C., and Taylor, G. (1998a). Current and future hospitalization after heart attack. *Health Reports*, 10(2), 21–28.

Johansen, H., Nargundkar, M., Taylor, G., and ElSaadany, S. (1998b). At risk for first or recurring heart attack. *Health Reports*, 9(4), 19–29.

Joint Statement on Terminal Illness. (1984). A protocol for health professionals regarding resuscitation intervention for the terminally ill. *Canadian Nurse*, 80(6), 24.

Joseph, S.E. (1994). *Coast Salish Perceptions of Death and Dying: An Ethnographic Study*. Unpublished masters thesis. University of Victoria, Victoria.

Kane, R.S., and Burns, E.A. (1997). Cardiopulmonary resuscitation policies in long-term care facilities. *Journal of the American Geriatrics Society*, 45(2), 154–157.

Kastenbaum, R.J. (1986). *Death, Society, and Human Experience* (3rd ed.). Columbus, OH: Charles E. Merrill.

Kastenbaum, R.J. (1998). *Death, Society, and Human Experience* (6th ed.) Boston: Allyn and Bacon.

Kaufert, J.M., and O'Neil, J.D. (1991). Cultural mediation of dying and grieving among Native Canadian patients in urban hospitals. In D.R. Counts and D.A. Counts (eds.), *Coping with the Final Tragedy: Cultural Variation in Dying and Grieving*, (pp. 231–251). Amityville, NY: Baywood.

Kendall, D., Murray, J.L., and Linden, R. (2000). *Sociology in Our Times* (2nd Cdn. ed.). Scarborough, ON: Nelson.

Kennedy, P., and Milner, B. (1999, June 2). Family at root of Loewen's fall shows sympathy. *Globe and Mail*, B11.

Kent, G. (1996, June/July). Robson: A climber's baptism. *Explore*, 15th Anniversary Issue, 80–83.

Kerr, J.R. (1991). Early nursing in Canada, 1600-1760: A legacy for the future. In J.R. Kerr and J. MacPhail (eds.), *Canadian Nursing. Issues and Perspectives* (2nd ed., pp. 3–11). St. Louis, MO: Mosby Year Book.

Kerr, M., and Kurtz, J. (1999). *Facing a Death in the Family*. Toronto: John Wiley and Sons.

Kinsella, T.D., and Verhoef, M.J. (1995). Assisted suicide: Opinions of Alberta physicians. *Clinical and Investigative Medicine*, 18(5), 406–412.

Kissane, D.W., Street, A., and Nitschke, P. (1998). Seven deaths in Darwin: Case studies under the Rights of the Terminally Ill Act, Northern Territory, Australia. *Lancet*, 352(9134), 1097–1102.

Kouwenhoven, W.B., Jude, J.R., and Knickerbocker, G.G. (1960). Closed-chest cardiac massage. *Journal of the American Medical Association*, 173, 1064–1067.

Kristjanson, L.J., and Balneaves, L. (1995). Directions for palliative care nursing in Canada: Report of a national survey. *Journal of Palliative Care*, 11(3), 5–8.

Kübler-Ross, E. (1969). *On Death and Dying*. New York: Macmillan.

Kurti, L.G. and O'Dowd, T.C. (1995). Dying of non-malignant diseases in general practice. *Journal of Palliative Care*, 11(3), 25–31.

Lack, S.A. (1978). Hospice helps patients "live until they die." *Hospital Administration Currents*, 22(6), 27–30.

Lalonde, M. (1978). *A New Perspective on the Health of Canadians: A Working Document*. Ottawa: Minister of Supply and Services.

Landry, F.J., Kroenke, K., Lucas, C., and Reeder, J. (1997). Increasing the use of advance directives in medical outpatients. *Journal of General Internal Medicine*, 12(7), 412–415.

Langham, P., and Flagel, D. (1991). Medical intervention and the effectiveness of the health care delivery system: A Canadian perspective. *Holistic Nursing Practice*, 5(3), 77–84.

Latimer, E.J. (1985). The impact of palliative care: Present and future. *Journal of Palliative Care*, 1(1), 35–39.

Laurence, M. (1964). *The Stone Angel*. Toronto: McClelland and Stewart.

Lave, J.R., Jacobs, P., and Markel, F. (1992). Transitional funding: Changing Ontario's globe budgeting system. *Health Care Financing Review*, 13(3), 77–84.

Lavigne-Pley, C., and Levesque, L. (1992). Reactions of the institutionalized elderly upon learning of the death of a peer. *Death Studies*, 16(5), 451–461.

Law Reform Commission of Nova Scotia. (1994). *Living Wills in Nova Scotia: A Discussion Paper*. Halifax: Author.

Leftwich, R.E. (1993). Care and cure as healing processes in nursing. *Nursing Forum*, 28(3), 13–17.

Lena, H.F., and London, B. (1993). The political and economic determinants of health outcomes: A cross-national analysis. *International Journal of Health Services*, 23(3), 585–602.

Lessard, R. (1991). *Health Care in Canada during the Seventeenth and Eighteenth Centuries*. Canada: Canadian Museum of Civilization.

Lévy, J.J., Dupras, A., and Samson, J. (1985). La religion, la mort et la sexualité au Québec. *Cahiers de Recherches en Sciences de la Religion*, 6, 25–34.

Levy, M., Duffy, C.M., Pollock, P., Budd, E., Caulfield, L., and Koren, G. (1990). Home-based palliative care for children, Part 1: The institution of a program. *Journal of Palliative Care*, 6(1), 11–15.

Levy, R. (1981). The decline in cardiovascular disease mortality. *Annual Review of Public Health*, 2(2), 49–70.

Ley, D.C. (1985). Palliative care in Canada: The first decade and beyond. *Journal of Palliative Care*, 1(1), 32–33.

Lindsay, C. (1999, Summer). Seniors: A diverse group aging well. *Canadian Social Trends*, 52, 24–26.

Lindsay, E. (1991). Life at all costs. *Canadian Nurse Journal*, 87(3), 16–18.

Lloyd-Jones, D.M., Martin, D.O., Larson, M.G., and Levy, D. (1998). Accuracy of death certificates for coding coronary heart disease as the cause of death. *Annals of Internal Medicine*, 129(12), 1020–1026.

Lubin, S. (1992). Palliative care: Could your patient have been managed at home? *Journal of Palliative Care*, 8(2), 18–22.

Lucas, R.A. (1968). Social implications of the immediacy of death. *Canadian Review of Sociology and Anthropology*, 5, 1–16.

Lyng, S. (1990). Edgework: A social psychological analysis of voluntary risk taking. *American Journal of Sociology*, 95, 851–886.

MacDougall, H. (1994). Sexually transmitted diseases in Canada, 1800-1992. *Genitourinary Medicine*, 70(1), 56–63.

MacKillop, H.I. (1978). Effects of seat belt legislation and reduction of highway speed limits in Ontario. *Canadian Medical Association Journal*, 119(10), 1154–1158.

Malette v. Schulman. (1992). 72 OR (2d) 417 (Ont CA).

Malkin, S. (1976). Care of the terminally ill at home. *Canadian Medical Association Journal*, 115(2), 129–128.

Manga, P. (1990). Chapter 19. Socio-economic inequalities. In Health and Welfare Canada, *Canada's Health Promotion Survey 1990. Technical Report*. Ottawa: Minister of Supply and Services.

Marie, C. (1965). Intensive care unit. *Canadian Nurse Journal*, 61(2), 112–113.

Marquis, S. (1993). Death of the nursed: Burnout of the provider. *Omega*, 27(1), 17–33.

Marsh, J.H. (1985). Disease. In J.H. March (ed.), *The Canadian Encyclopedia* (pp. 833–834). Edmonton: Hurtig.

Marshall, V.W. (1980). *Last Chapters: A Sociology of Aging and Dying*. Monterey, CA: Brooks/Cole.

Marshall, V.W. (1986). A sociological perspective on aging and dying. In V.W. Marshall (ed.), *Later Life: The Social Psychology of Aging* (pp. 125–146). Beverly Hills, CA: Sage.

Martin, K. (1998). *When a Baby Dies of SIDS: The Parents' Grief and Search for Reason*. Edmonton: Qual Institute Press (International Institute for Qualitative Methodology).

Martin, K., and Elder, S. (1993). Pathways through grief: A model of the process. In J.D. Morgan (ed.). *Personal Care in an Impersonal World: A Multidimensional Look at Bereavement* (pp. 73–86). Amityville, NY: Baywood.

Matthews, A.M. (1987). Widowhood as an expectable life event. In V.W. Marshall (ed.), *Aging in Canada: Social Perspectives*, (2nd ed., pp. 343–366). Markham, ON: Fitzhenry and Whiteside.

Matthews, A.M. (1991). *Widowhood in Later Life*. Toronto: Butterworths.

McCann, B.A. (1988). Hospice care in the United States: The struggle for definition and survival. *Journal of Palliative Care*, 4(1,2), 16–18.

McGinnis, J.D. (1985). Public health. In J.H. Marsh (ed.), *The Canadian Encyclopedia* (pp. 1507–1508). Edmonton: Hurtig.

McGowan, S.A. (Director), and Bowen, C. (Producer). (1990). *When the Day Comes*, [Video]. National Film Board of Canada.

McKie, C. (1993, Summer). Population aging. Baby boomers into the 21st century. *Canadian Social Trends*, 2–6.

McNaught, K. (1970). *The History of Canada*. London: Heinemann.

McPhail, A., Moore, S., O'Connor, J., and Woodward, C. (1981). One hospital's experience with a "do not resuscitate" policy. *Canadian Journal of Cardiovascular Nursing*, 125(8), 830–836.

McPherson, B.D. (1998). *Aging as a Social Process: An Introduction to Individual and Social Aging* (3rd ed.). Toronto: Harcourt Brace.

McPherson, K. (1996). *Bedside Matters: The Transformation of Canadian Nursing, 1900-1990.* Toronto: Oxford University Press.

McWhinney, I.R., Bass, M.J., and Orr, V. (1995). Factors associated with location of death (home or hospital) of patients referred to a palliative care team. *Canadian Medical Association Journal,* 152(3), 361–367.

McWhinney, I.R., and Stewart, M.A. (1994). Home care of dying patients. *Canadian Family Physician,* 40, 240–246.

Merckel, L. (1985). DNR: A code of ethics. *Health Care,* 27(5), 15–17.

Messite, J., and Stellman, S.D. (1996). Accuracy of death certificate completion: The need for formalized physician training. *Journal of the American Medical Association,* 275(10), 794–796.

Miller, L.G. (1960). Geriatric nursing in the home. *Canadian Nurse Journal,* 56(7), 606–609.

Millar, W.J. (1983). Sex differentials in mortality by income level in urban Canada. *Canadian Journal of Public Health,* 74(5), 329–334.

Millar, W.J. (1995). Life expectancy of Canadians. *Health Reports,* 7(3), 23–26.

Millar, W.J., and Hill, G.B. (1995). The elimination of disease: A mixed blessing. *Health Reports,* 7(3), 7–13.

Minkler, M., and Cole, T.R. (1992). The political and moral economy of aging: Not such strange bedfellows. *International Journal of Health Services,* 22(1), 113–124.

Mirowsky, J., and Ross, C.E. (1989). *The Social Causes of Psychological Distress.* New York: Aldine de Gruyter.

Mitchell, W.O. (1947). *Who Has Seen the Wind.* Agincourt, ON: Macmillan.

Mor, V., and Masterson-Allen, S. (1987). *Hospice Care Systems: Structure, Process, Costs, and Outcome.* New York: Springer.

Morton, D. (1997). *A Short History of Canada* (3rd rev. ed.). Toronto: McClelland and Stewart.

Mount, B. (1976). The problem of caring for the dying in a general hospital: The palliative care unit as a possible solution. *Canadian Medical Association Journal,* 115(2), 119–121.

Mount, B., and Flander, E.M. (1996). Morphine drips, terminal sedation, and slow euthanasia: Definitions and facts, not anecdotes. *Journal of Palliative Care,* 12(4), 31–37.

Murrant, G., and Strathdee, S. (1992, Summer). AIDS, hospice and volunteers. The Casey House volunteer program. *Journal of Volunteer Administration,* 11–17.

Murray, M. (1981). Palliative care. *Canadian Nurse,* 77(5), 16–17.

Mustard, C.A., Derksen, S., Berthelot, J., Wolfson, M., and Roos, L.L. (1997). Age-specific education and income gradients in morbidity and mortality in a Canadian province. *Social Science and Medicine,* 45(3), 383–397.

Myers, K.A., and Farquhar, D.R. (1998). Improving accuracy of death certification. *Canadian Medical Association Journal,* 158(10), 1317–1323.

Mykitiuk, R., and Paltiel, J.T. (1994). Terminal care, terminal justice: The Supreme Court of Canada and Sue Rodriguez. *Constititutional Forum,* 5(2), 38–52.

National Forum on Health. (1997). *Final Report.* Ottawa: Author.

National nutrition programme announced by government. (1943, January). *Canadian Hospital,* 26.

Nault, F. (1997). Narrowing mortality gaps, 1978 to 1995. *Health Reports*, 9(1), 35–41.

Nault, F., and Ford, D. (1994). An overview of deaths in Canada in 1992. *Health Reports*, 6(2), 287–294.

Nault F., and Wilkins, K. (1995). Deaths, 1993. *Health Reports,* 7(1), 51–60.

No charges in death of girl, 10. (1999, December 3). *Edmonton Journal*, A19.

No jail time for mother who tried to kill child. (1999, December 1). *Edmonton Journal*, A13.

Norris, J. (1994). Widowhood in later life. In *Late-life Marital Disruptions*. Writings in Gerontology, Number 14. Ottawa: National Advisory Council on Aging.

Northcott, H.C. (1984). Widowhood and remarriage trends in Canada, 1956 to 1981. *Canadian Journal on Aging*, 3, 63–78.

Noseworthy, T.W. (1997). Canada deserves a national health system. *Healthcare Management Forum*, 10(1), 39–46.

Novak, M. (1997). *Aging and Society: A Canadian Perspective*. (3rd ed.). Toronto: ITP Nelson.

Ogden, R. (1994). The right to die: A policy proposal for euthanasia and aid in dying. *Canadian Public Policy*, 20, 1–25.

O'Neill, S. (1978). Palliative care at the Royal Victoria Hospital. *Canadian Nurse*, 74(10), 3–6.

Ontario Coalition of Senior Citizens Organizations. (1995). *Life before Medicare: Canadian Experiences*. Toronto: Author.

Osgood, R. (1994). Palliative care and euthanasia: A continuum of care? *Journal of Palliative Care*, 10(2), 82–85.

Ostbye, T., and Crosse, E. (1994). Net economic costs of dementia in Canada. *Canadian Medical Association Journal*, 151(10), 1457–1464.

Ostry, A. (1994). Public health and the Canadian State: The formative years, 1880-1920. *Canadian Journal of Public Health*, 22(3), 293–294.

Ott, B.B., and Nieswiadomy, R.M. (1991). Support of patient autonomy in the do not resuscitate decision. *Health and Lung*, 29(1), 66–72.

Pannuti, F., and Tanneberger, S. (1992). The Bologna eubiosia project: Hospital-at-home care for advanced cancer patients. *Journal of Palliative Care*, 8(2), 11–17.

Patterson, R.M. (1989 [1954]). *Dangerous River*. Toronto: Stoddart.

Pavelich, M.D. (1992). Palliative care and the art of dying. *Leadership in Health Care Services*, 1(5), 21–23.

Pett, L.B. (1943, February). Nutritional deficiencies. *Canadian Hospital*, 40.

Phillips, J.R. (1992). Choosing and participating in the living-dying process: A research emergent. *Nursing Science Quarterly*, 5(1), 4–5.

Porush, J.G., and Faubert, P.F. (1991). *Renal Disease in the Aged*. Boston: Little, Brown.

Posner, J. (1976). Death as a courtesy stigma. *Essence*, 1, 39–49.

President's Commission for the Study of Ethical Problems in Medicine and Biomedical and Behavioral Research. (1982). *Making Health Care Decisions*. Washington, DC: U.S. Government Printing Office.

President's Commission for the Study of Ethical Problems in Medicine and Biomedical and Behavioral Research. (1983, March). *Deciding to Forego Life-Sustaining Treatment: A Report on the Ethical, Medical, and Legal Issues of Treatment Decisions*. Washington, DC: U.S. Government Printing Office.

Preston, R.J., and Preston, S.C. (1991). Death and grieving among northern forest hunters: An East Cree example. In D.R. Counts and D.A. Counts (eds.). *Coping with the Final Tragedy: Cultural Variation in Dying and Grieving* (pp. 135–155). Amityville, NY: Baywood.

Priest, A. (1987). Care for the dying. *Registered Nurses' Association of British Columbia News*, 19(5), 11–13.

Pringle, D., and Taylor, D. (1984). Palliative care in the home: Does it work? *Canadian Nurse*, 80(6), 26–29.

Ramsden, P.G. (1991). Alice in the afterlife: A glimpse in the mirror. In D.R. Counts and D.A. Counts (eds.). *Coping with the Final Tragedy: Cultural Variation in Dying and Grieving* (pp. 27–41). Amityville, NY: Baywood.

Randhawa, J. (1993). Surgical procedures, 1991–92. *Health Reports*, 5(4), 373–376.

Randhawa, J., and Riley, R. (1995). Trends in hospital utilization, 1982–83 to 1992–93. *Health Reports*, 7(1), 41–49.

Rasooly, I., Lavery, J.V., Urowitz, S., Choudhry, S., Seeman, N., Meslin, E.M., Lowy, F.H., and Singer, P.A. (1994). Hospital policies on life-sustaining treatments and advance directives in Canada. *Canadian Medical Association Journal*, 150(8), 1265–1270.

Reutter, L.I., and Northcott, H.C. (1993). Making risk meaningful: Developing caring relationships with AIDS patients. *Journal of Advanced Nursing*, 18, 1377–1385.

Reutter, L.I., and Northcott, H.C. (1994). Achieving a sense of control in a context of uncertainty: Nurses and AIDS. *Qualitative Health Research*, 4, 51–71.

Reutter, L.I., and Northcott, H.C. (1995). Managing occupational HIV exposures: A Canadian study. *International Journal of Nursing Studies*, 32, 493–505.

Robb, N. (1998). The Morrison ruling: The case may be closed but the issues raised are not. *Canadian Medical Association Journal*, 158(8), 1071–1072.

Robertson, G.B. (1991). Advance directives: A legal view. *Health Law Review*, 1(1), 3–6.

Robillard, D. (1981, May/June). Caring for the terminally ill: Further initiatives in Quebec. *Catholic Health Association of Canada Review*, 17–18.

Rodney, P. (1994). A nursing perspective on life-prolonging treatment. *Journal of Palliative Care*, 10(2), 40–44.

Rodney, P., and Starzomski, R. (1993). Constraints on the moral agency of nurses. *Canadian Nurse*, 89(9), 23–26.

Roland, C. (1985). History of medicine. In J.H. March (ed.), *The Canadian Encyclopedia* (pp. 1112–1114). Edmonton: Hurtig.

Roos, N.P., Brownell, M., Shapiro, E., and Roos, L.L. (1998). Good news about difficult decisions: The Canadian approach to hospital cost control. *Health Affairs*, 17(5), 239–246.

Roos, N.P., Montgomery, P., and Roos, L.L. (1987). Health care utilization in the years prior to death. *Milbank Quarterly*, 65(2), 231–254.

Rosenberg, M.W., and Moore, E.G. (1997). The health of Canada's elderly population: Current status and future implications. *Canadian Medical Association Journal*, 157(8), 1025–1032.

Rubenstein, L.Z., Josephson, K.R., Wieland, G.D., and Kane, R.L. (1986). Differential prognosis and utilization patterns among clinical subgroups of hospitalized geriatric patients. *Health Services Research*, 20(6), 881–895.

Rutman, D. (1992). Palliative care needs of residents, families, and staff in long-term care facilities. *Journal of Palliative Care*, 8(2), 23–29.

Schachter, S. (1992). Quality of life for families in the management of home care patients with advanced cancer. *Journal of Palliative Care*, 8(3), 61–66.

Schmidt, K. (1999). Physiology and pathophysiology of senescence. *International Journal of Vitamin and Nutrition Research*, 69(3), 150–153.

Schriever, S.H. (1990). Comparison of beliefs and practices of ethnic Viet and Lao Hmong concerning illness, healing, death and mourning: Implications for hospice care with refugees in Canada. *Journal of Palliative Care*, 6, 42–49.

Scott, D.H. (1988). Is palliative care a discipline? *Journal of Palliative Care*, 34(1–2), 10–11.

Scott, J.F. (1992a). Palliative care: What's stopping us? *Journal of Palliative Care*, 8, 5–8.

Scott, J.F. (1992b). Palliative care education in Canada: Attacking fear and promoting health. *Journal of Palliative Care*, 8(1), 47–53.

Seamark, D.A., Williams, S., Hall, M., Lawrence, C.J., and Gilbert, J. (1998, June). Dying from cancer in community hospitals or a hospice: Closest lay carers' perceptions. *British Journal of General Practice*, 1317–1321.

Sebag-Lanoe, R., Legrain, S., and Lefevre-Chapiro, S. (1998). Geriatric specifics of palliative care. *Revue de Geriatrie*, 23(2), 147–152.

Senate of Canada. (1995). *Of Life and Death: Report of the Special Senate Committee on Euthanasia and Assisted Suicide. Final report.* Ottawa: Author.

Shapiro, E. (1983). Impending death and the use of hospitals by the elderly. *Journal of American Geriatrics Society*, 31(6), 348–351.

Shepley, E.E. (1936). Cancer: An effective offensive. *Canadian Medical Association Journal*, 34(6), 672–676.

Sheth, T., Nair, C., Nargundkar, M., Anand, S., and Yusuf, S. (1999). Cardiovascular and cancer mortality among Canadians of European, south Asian and Chinese origin from 1979 to 1993: An analysis of 1.2 million deaths. *Canadian Medical Association Journal*, 161(2), 152–153.

Silverman, P.R., Nickman, S., and Worden, J.W. (1995). Detachment revisited: The child's reconstruction of a dead parent. In L.A. DeSpelder and A.L. Strickland (eds.), *The Path Ahead: Readings in Death and Dying.* (pp. 260–270. Mountain View, CA: Mayfield.

Simmons, A. (1996). *Reflections on Life and Death in a Technological Society: Experiences of Doctors and Nurses with Dying Patients in Intensive Care.* Unpublished PhD dissertation, Toronto School of Theology and Emmanuel College of Victoria University, Toronto.

Simmons-Tropea, D., and Osborn, R. (1987). Disease, survival and death: The health status of Canada's elderly. In V.W. Marshall (ed.), *Aging in Canada: Social Perspectives* (2nd ed., pp. 399–423). Richmond Hill, ON: Fitzhenry and Whiteside.

Singer, P.A. (1994). Advance directives in palliative care. *Journal of Palliative Care*, 10(3), 111–116.

Singleton, R. (1992). Palliative home care program for terminally ill children. *Leadership in Health Care Services*, 1(1), 21–27.

Smith, G.P. (1995). Restructuring the principle of medical futility. *Journal of Palliative Care*, 11(3), 9–16.

Smith, S.P., and Varoglu, G. (1985, September). Hospice: A supportive working environment for nurses. *Journal of Palliative Care*, 1(1), 16–23.

Sneiderman, B. (1993). The case of Nancy B: A criminal law and social policy perspective. *Health Law Journal*, 1, 25–38.

Sneiderman, B. (1994). The Rodriguez case: Where do we go from here. *Health Law Journal*, 2, 1–38.

Somerville, M.A. (1995). "Should the grandparents die?" Allocation of medical resources with an aging population. *Law, Medicine and Health Care*, 14(3–4), 158–163.

Stanley, P.H. (1964). Open heart surgery. *Canadian Nurse Journal*, 60(3), 259–268.

Stark, A.J., and Gutman, G.M. (1986). Client transfers in long-term care: Five years' experience. *American Journal of Public Health*, 76(11), 1312–1316.

Statistics Canada. (1991). *Canada Yearbook, 1992*. Ottawa: Author.

Statistics Canada. (1997). *National Population Health Survey Overview, 1996–97*. Ottawa: Minister of Industry.

Statistics Canada. (1998). *1999 Canada Yearbook*. Ottawa: Minister of Supply and Services.

Statistics Canada. (1999). CANSIM matrices. Path: *http://www. statcan.ca/english/ Pgdb/People/Population/demo31c.html*

Stephenson, P.H. (1992). "He died too quick!" The process of dying in a Hutterian colony. In L.A. Platt and V. R. Persico, Jr. (eds.), *Grief in Cross-Cultural Perspective: A Casebook*, (pp. 293–303). NY: Garland Publishing.

Stephenson-Cino, P., Roe, D.J., Latimer, E., Walton, L., and Thomson, N. (1987). An examination of palliative shift care funding. *Journal of Palliative Care*, 2(2), 13–17.

Stern, M.P. (1979). The recent decline in ischemic health disease mortality. *Annals of Internal Medicine*, 91, 630–640.

Stokes, J., and Lindsay, J. (1996). Major causes of death and hospitalization in Canadian seniors. *Chronic Diseases in Canada*, 17(2), 63–73.

Stone, E. (1962). *Medicine Among the American Indians*. New York: Hafner.

Storch, J.L., and Dossetor, J. (1994). Public attitudes towards end-of-life treatment decisions: Implications for nurse clinicians and nursing administrators. *Canadian Journal of Nursing Administration*, 7(3), 65–89.

Stroebe, M., Gergen, M.M., Gergen, K.G. and Stroebe, W. (1995). Broken hearts or broken bonds: Love and death in historical perspective. In L.A. DeSpelder and A.L. Strickland (eds.), *The Path Ahead: Readings in Death and Dying* (pp. 231–241). Mountain View, CA: Mayfield.

Suarez-Almazor, M.E., Belzile, M., and Bruera, E. (1997). Euthanasia and physician-assisted suicide: A comparative survey of physicians, terminally ill cancer patients, and the general population. *Journal of Clinical Oncology*, 15(2), 418–427.

Sudnow, D. (1967). *Passing On: The Social Organization of Dying.* Englewood Cliffs, NJ: Prentice-Hall.

Symons, D. (1992). Palliative response team. *Canadian Nurse,* 88(9), 36–37.

Taylor, M.G. (1987). *Health Insurance and Canadian Public Policy: The Seven Decisions that Created the Canadian Health Insurance System* (2nd ed.). Montreal: McGill-Queens's University Press.

Teno, J.M., Branco, K.J., Mor, V., Phillips, C.D., Hawes, C., Morris, J., and Fries, B.E. (1997). Changes in advance care planning in nursing homes before and after the patient Self-Determination Act: Report of a 10-state survey. *Journal of the American Geriatrics Society,* 45(8), 939–944.

Terris, M. (1984, September). Newer perspectives on the health of Canadians: Beyond the Lalonde report. *Journal of Public Health Policy,* 327–337.

Trudeau, R. (1997). Monthly and daily patterns of death. *Health Reports,* 9(1), 43–50.

Truman, C., and Trueman, G. (1995). The determinants of health. In D. Wilson (ed.), *The Canadian Health Care System.* Edmonton, AB: Author.

Tully, P., and Mohl, C. (1995). Older residents of health care institutions. *Health Reports,* 7(3), 27–30.

Tully, P., and Saint-Pierre, E. (1997). Downsizing Canada's hospitals, 1986/87 to 1994/95. *Health Reports,* 8(4), 33–39.

Turner, K., Chye, R., Aggarwal, G., Philip, J., Skeels, A., and Lickiss, J.N. (1996). Dignity in dying: A preliminary study of patients in the last three days of life. *Journal of Palliative Care,* 12(2), 7–13.

Valente, S.M., and Trainor, D. (1998). Rational suicide among patients who are terminally ill. *AORN Journal,* 68(2), 252–264.

Valentine, P.E.B. (1994). A female profession: A feminist management perspective. In J.M. Hibberd and M.E. Kyle (eds.), *Nursing Managment in Canada* (pp. 372–390). Toronto: W. B. Saunders.

van den Hoonaard, D.K. (1997). Identity foreclosure: Women's experiences of widowhood as expressed in autobiographical accounts. *Ageing and Society,* 17, 533–551.

Van der Maas, P., van der Wal, G., Haverkate, I., Graff, C., Kester, J., Onwuteaka-Philipsen, B., van der Heide, A., Bosma, J., and Willems, D.L. (1996). Euthanasia, physician-assisted suicide, and other medical practices involving the end of life in the Netherlands, 1990–1995. *New England Journal of Medicine,* 335(22), 1699–1705.

Van Weel, H. (1995). Euthanasia: Mercy, morals and medicine. *Canadian Nurse,* 91(8), 35–36.

Veatch, R.M. (1989). *Death, Dying, and the Biological Revolution. Our Last Quest for Responsibility* (rev. ed.). New Haven, CT: Yale University Press.

Ventafridda, V., Ripamonti, C., Conno, F.D., Tamburini, M., and Cassileth, B.R. (1990). Symptom prevalence and control during cancer patients' last days of life. *Journal of Palliative Care,* 6(3), 7–11.

Vezina, J., Bourque, P., and Belanger, Y. (1988). Spousal loss: Depression, anxiety and well-being after grief periods of varying lengths. *Canadian Journal on Aging,* 7, 388–396.

Vigano, A., Dorgan, M., Bruera, E., and Suarez-Almazor, M.E. (1999). The relative accuracy of the clinical estimation of the duration of life for patients with end of life cancer. *Cancer*, 86(1), 170–176.

Viszmeg, J. (Director, Writer, and Editor), and Krepakevich, J. (Producer). (1998). *My Healing Journey: Seven Years with Cancer*, [Video]. National Film Board of Canada.

Waldie, P., and Kennedy, P. (1999, June 2). Loewen files for court protection. *Globe and Mail*, B1.

Webb, M. (1997). *The Good Death: The New American Search to Reshape the End of Life*. New York: Bantam Books.

Weisman, A., and Hackett, T. (1961). Predilections to death. *Psychosomatic Medicine*, 23(3), 14–19.

Wells, L.M. (1990). Responsiveness and accountability in long-term care: Strategies for policy development and empowerment. *Canadian Journal of Public Health*, 81(5), 382–385.

Wilinsky, C.F. (1943, January). Hospitals have place in public health programme. *Canadian Hospital*, 36, 12.

Wilkins, K. (1996, Summer). Causes of death. *Canadian Social Trends*, 11–17.

Wilkins, K., and Park, E. (1996). Chronic conditions, physical limitations and dependency among seniors living in the community. *Health Reports*, 8(3), 7–15.

Wilkins, K., and Park, E. (1997). Characteristics of hospital users. *Health Reports*, 9(3), 28–36.

Wilkins, K., and Park, E. (1998). Home care in Canada. *Health Reports*, 10(1), 29–37.

Williamson, J.B., Evans, L., and Munley, A. (1980). *Aging and Society*. New York: Holt, Rinehart and Winston.

Wilson, D.M. (1991). Long-term tube feeding practices and involvement of nurses in tube feeding decisions. *Canadian Journal on Aging*, 10(4), 333–344.

Wilson, D.M. (1993). Supporting life through tube feeding: Factors influencing surrogate decision-making. *Canadian Journal on Aging*, 12(3), 298–310.

Wilson, D.M. (1996). Highlighting the role of policy in nursing practice through a comparison of "DNR" policy influences and "no CPR" decision influences. *Nursing Outlook*, 44(6), 272–279.

Wilson, D.M. (1997). A report of an investigation of end-of-life patient care practices in health care facilities,and the influences for those practices. *Journal of Palliative Care*, 13 (4), 34-40.

Wilson, D.M., Anderson, M.C., Fainsinger, R.L., Northcott, H.C., Smith, S.L., and Stingl, M.J. (1998). *Social and Health Care Trends Influencing Palliative Care and the Location of Death in Twentieth-Century Canada. NHRDP Final Report*. Edmonton: Author.

Wilson, D.M., Truman, C., and Northcott, H.C. (1999, May). *Hospital Utilization by Terminally Ill Albertans, 1992/93 to 1996/97. Preliminary Report*. Edmonton, AB: Author.

Wilson, K. (1983). *The Fur Trade in Canada*. Toronto: Grolier.

Wilson, S.A. (1989). *The Ethnography of Death, Dying and Hospice Care*. Unpublished PhD dissertation, The University of Wisconsin, Milwaukee.

Winterfeldt, E. (1991). Historical perspective, Part 1: Dietary management of diabetes mellitus, 1675–1950. *Topics in Clinical Nutrition*, 7(1), 1–8.

Wolfe, S., and Badgley, R.F. (1974). How much is enough? The payment of doctors: Implications for health policy in Canada. *International Journal of Health Services*, 4(2), 245–264.

Wolfson, M.C. (1996). Health-adjusted life expectancy. *Health Reports*, 8(1), 41–46.

Woman doctor arrested in murder probe. (1997, May 7). *Edmonton Journal*, A3.

Wood, C. (February 28, 1994). The legacy of Sue Rodriguez. *Maclean's*, 21–25.

Wood, G.C., and Martin, E. (1995). Withholding and withdrawing life-sustaining therapy in a Canadian intensive care unit. *Canadian Journal of Anaesthesia*, 42(3), 186–191.

World Health Organization. (1989). *Health of the Elderly: Report of a WHO Expert Committee*. Geneva: World Health Organization.

Wuest, J. (1993). Institutionalizing women's oppression: The inherent risk in health policy that fosters community participation. *Health Care for Women International*, 14(5), 407–417.

Zilm, G., and Warbinek, E. (1995). Early tuberculosis nursing in British Columbia. *Canadian Journal of Nursing Research*, 27(3), 65–81.

Index

Garamond Press Titles in Print

Following is a select listing of recent publications. Please contact us at the address below for more information, and for a complete list of our publications.

Pat Armstrong et al

Heal Thyself: Managing Health Care Reform
1-55193-024-2

David Coburn et al

Medicine, Nursing and the State
1-55193-022-6

Robert Hackett and Richard Gruneau

The Missing News: Filters and Blindspots in Canada's Press
1-55193-027-7

Steven Langdon

Global Poverty, Democracy and North South Change
1-55193-016-1

D.W. Livingstone

The Education-Jobs Gap: Underemployment or Economic Democracy
1-55193-017-X

John McMurtry

Unequal Freedoms: The Global Market as an Ethical System
1-55193-003-X • 1-55193-005-6 hc

Albert Mills and Tony Simmons

Reading Organization Theory: A Critical Approach to the Study of Organizational Behaviour, 2nd edt.
1-55193-015-3

James P. Mulvale

Reimagining Social Welfare: Beyond the Keynesian Welfare State
1-55193-030-7

Janice Newton et al

Voices From the Classroom: Reflections on Teaching and Learning in Higher Education
1-55193-031-5

H. C. Northcott and Donna M. Wilson

Dying and Death in Canada
1-55193-023-4

Christopher Schenk and John Anderson

Re-Shaping Work II: Union Responses to Technological Change
1-55193-029-3

Wallace Seccombe
and D.W. Livingstone

Down to Earth People: Beyond Class Reductionism and Postmodernism
1-55193-019-6

Gary Teeple

Globalization and the Decline of Social Reform: Into the 21st Century
1-55193-026-9

Garamond Press Ltd., 63 Mahogany Court, Aurora, Ontario L4G 6M8
Tel (905) 841-1460 • Fax (905) 841-3031 • garamond@web.ca • www.garamond.ca

AGMV Marquis

MEMBER OF SCABRINI MEDIA

Quebec, Canada
2001